What Government Do

"If DU enters the body, it has the potential to generate significant medical consequences. The risks associated with DU in the body are both chemical and radiological."

"Personnel inside or near vehicles struck by DU penetrators could receive significant internal exposures."
> From the Army Environmental Policy Institute (AEPI), *Health and Environmental Consequences of Depleted Uranium Use in the U.S. Army*, June 1995

"Short-term effects of high doses can result in death, while long-term effects of low doses have been implicated in cancer."

"Aerosol DU exposures to soldiers on the battlefield could be significant with potential radiological and toxicological effects."
> From the Science Applications International Corporation (SAIC) report, included as Appendix D of AMMCOM's *Kinetic Energy Penetrator Long Term Strategy Study*, Danesi, July 1990.
> This report was completed six months before Desert Storm.

"Inhaled insoluble oxides stay in the lungs longer and pose a potential cancer risk due to radiation. Ingested DU dust can also pose both a radioactive and a toxicity risk."
> *Operation Desert Storm: Army Not Adequately Prepared to Deal With Depleted Uranium Contamination*, United States General Accounting Office (GAO/NSIAD-93-90), January 1993, pp. 17-18.

What the Government Is Telling Us

"The Committee concludes that it is unlikely that health effects reports by Gulf War Veterans today are the result of exposure to depleted uranium during the Gulf war."
> *From the Final Report: Presidential Advisory Committee of Gulf War Veterans Illnesses, December 1996.*

Metal of Dishonor
Depleted Uranium

How the Pentagon Radiates Soldiers and
Civilians with DU Weapons

Selections compiled and edited by
John Catalinotto and Sara Flounders of the
Depleted Uranium Education Project

International Action Center
New York City

Metal of Dishonor
Depleted Uranium
How the Pentagon Radiates Soldiers and Civilians
with DU Weapons

©Copyright 1997
©Revised edition 1999
Depleted Uranium Education Project
International Action Center

39 West 14th St., #206, New York, NY, 10011
Tel: 212-633-6646, Fax: 212-633-2889
email: iacenter@iacenter.org

Suggested Cataloging Data

Depleted Uranium Education Project
METAL OF DISHONOR
Depleted Uranium
How the Pentagon Radiates Soldiers and Civilians with DU Weapons
296 pp.; 15 x 22.5 cm. Includes index.
ISBN: 0-9656916-0-8: $12.95
1. Radioactive Substances -- Toxicology -- Depleted Uranium. 2. Persian Gulf War-1991- . 3. Veterans -- United States -- Diseases. 4. Atomic Weapons -- Testing -- Physiological Effects. 5. Indians of North America -- Mines and Mining. I. Depleted Uranium Education Project. II. Title.
Printed in the United States of America
Library of Congress Catalog Card Number: 97-70773

We dedicate this book to the victims of depleted-uranium weapons, and we dedicate ourselves to the struggle to stop these weapons from being used again.

Contents

Section VII: Can a Legal Battle Be Waged To Ban DU?

Appendices

Preface

Metal of Dishonor grew out of the work of the Depleted Uranium Education Project and the other organizations that contributed to building a meeting at the United Nations Church Center in New York on September 12, 1996. Hundreds of individuals have made *Metal of Dishonor* and the entire Depleted Uranium Education Project possible. Their contributions document the hazardous, radioactive nature of depleted uranium weapons.

Scientific papers, scholarly briefs, and forceful arguments—some based on talks given at the September 12 meeting—make up the articles in this book. Scientists, medical and legal experts, political analysts and community activists wrote them.

This heterogeneous collection of articles, most published here for the first time, makes a strong case that depleted-uranium weapons are not only lethal to their intended targets, they are dangerous for the humans who handle them and for the present and future environment of the planet. They also show there is potential for building a movement to end this danger.

On February 27, 1997, the Pentagon admitted that eight days of logs documenting chemical exposure have "disappeared." These logs were stored on disc and hard copy in different places. This monumental slip raises these questions: How much other information has also disappeared or been suppressed? Is an even larger coverup taking place? Is something vital about DU also being covered up?

We have not yet found data that enumerate how many women, poor people, how many African American, Latino and other people of color suffer from Gulf War Syndrome. But we know that youth in Black, Latino and other communities that face racism are disproportionately pushed into the military by lack of economic opportunity in U.S. society. Almost half the troops in the Gulf were Black and Latino. The largest number of women in military history served in the Gulf War. It is routine for both the military and the government to ignore these sectors of society regarding benefits and care. It is also that part of the population most likely to need government benefits to get any health care.

We have gathered material to explain the impact of uranium mining and waste on Native American lands, the impact on peoples of the South Pacific and U.S. veterans exposed to nuclear blast sites, the impact on peoples living near nuclear reactors and the impact on peoples in the Middle East. Further research in all of these areas is

needed along with research on the health and environmental consequences in areas surrounding military test sites and production
facilities.

Although some of the articles in *Metal of Dishonor* cover more
than one subject, we've grouped them all in specific sections based on
a major subject covered. For the convenience of the reader, we've
published the more important quotes from government sources in
Appendix I. And we have included a section on organizations and
resources in Appendix VII that should make it easy for anyone
motivated by reading this book to connect with the groups that are
carrying out the struggle against DU.

Some questions of style. We've presented the writers' references all
as notes at the end of each article. For articles that require careful
calculation or comparison of numbers, we have expressed these
numbers with numerals, which is a different style from the rest of the
book.

We hope *Metal of Dishonor* will serve as an organizing tool that
will contribute to the fight for an independent inquiry into the causes
of Gulf War Syndrome and an eventual ban on the use of depleted-
uranium weapons.

The Depleted Uranium Education Project
of the International Action Center
March 1, 1997

Preface to the Second Edition

As we prepare the second edition of Metal of Dishonor, we in the Depleted Uranium Project of the International Action Center are confronted with a grave new danger: the Pentagon is spreading the radioactive residue of depleted-uranium weapons through another world region. The NATO countries' brutal and massive bombing attack on Yugoslavia and their imminent use of A-10 Warthog jet tank-killers make this poisoning certain. Meanwhile in Iraq the living conditions of the people have grown worse and the environment's degradation from DU has borne bitter fruit.

This new assault on the Balkans is bringing the same kind of calamity to the peoples of that peninsula as the 1991 Gulf War did to the Iraqis. Reports from the Yugoslav army March 27, 1999, that DU weapons had been used add another dimension to this calamity. A prolonged war will certainly mean more destruction of the environment of the Balkans and its poisoning with DU weapons. DU shells are now standard Pentagon issue and used in most NATO countries. Pentagon analysts are using the A-10 "Warthog" jet plane as the workhorse of the campaign targeting Yugoslav tanks and ground troops. The A-10 can fire 4,000 rounds of DU-fortified 30-caliber shells per minute. It did fire 940,000 30-millimeter DU shells against Iraq.

Metal of Dishonor's first edition has proved an invaluable tool for people all over the world protesting nuclear and radioactive weapons and defending the environment. It has sparked further struggle, studies and symposia, and provided both the political and scientific background for them. It has also been translated and published in full into two Arabic and one Japanese edition, and in parts in many other languages. As its editors intended, it has built international solidarity against this deadly weapon.

We are adding three articles to help our readers keep up with these new developments. In the first, the editors summarize a report from Yugoslavia showing how DU weapons were used against

Serbian targets in Bosnia while NATO planes dropped bombs and fired rockets and other shells in that republic in 1995.

The second is World Food Program executive Ashraf El-Bayoumi's report from a conference held in Baghdad in December 1998 to discuss the use of DU weapons in the Gulf War. It especially focuses on the consequences of DU use on cancer rates in the southern part of Iraq, illnesses among Iraqi Gulf War veterans and birth deformities among their children.

The third is an article by eminent scientist Dr. Asaf Durakovic. Dr. Durakovic was employed by the Veterans Affairs Department to do tests on Gulf War veterans exposed to DU from shrapnel. But the study that found that 14 of the 24 GIs had been contaminated was buried after the government "lost" all records of these examinations. Dr. Durakovic's article succinctly presents the scientific basis for his assertion that while uranium is safe in the ground, it is dangerous when it finds a way into the human body.

To expedite printing this edition, these new articles will be placed in the front of the book before the first edition's Section 1. The authors' biographies are printed with the articles instead of in the biography section.

In addition to introducing these three reports, we want to note that this book has contributed to veterans' groups in the United States and in Britain recognizing depleted uranium as a probable contributing factor to Gulf War Syndrome. This ailment continues to plague close to one hundred thousand veterans of that conflict—not counting the Iraqi veterans.

Preparing this in the midst of a world crisis, we remain hopeful that the intervention of the mass of the world's people can stop the Pentagon's war machine from again spewing its poison throughout the world. We see this book as a contribution to bringing about that intervention.

Sara Flounders & John Catalinotto, editors
April 1999

SECOND EDITION

Special Section:

Baghdad DU symposium
U.S. used DU in Bosnia
Internal danger of DU

Depleted Uranium Symposium held in Baghdad, Iraq, in December 1998

Cancer and Gulf War Syndrome patients of different nationalities— British, American and Iraqi—shared their dreadful plight and experiences as both Gulf War participants and victims.

ASHRAF EL-BAYOUMI

The December 2-3, 1998, Baghdad Symposium was attended by several Iraqi and International researchers who presented eleven studies dealing with the effects of the use of the radioactive weapon depleted uranium on human beings and their environment—soil, water, plants, and animals. Most of the studies focused on the investigation of the frequency and the pattern of cancer primarily in southern Iraq, and on the health implications for future generations in view of the high incidence of congenital deformities. Data on the relationship between the high incidence of cancer and DU explosions was presented.

As a scientist specializing in Physical Chemistry and Molecular Biophysics I was quite impressed by the thoroughness of the studies presented and the strict adherence to scientific methodology, and by the extensive discussions that followed the presentation of most papers. It is indeed remarkable that this research was conducted under extremely adverse conditions, and with minimal equipment and limited facilities because of the severe effects of over eight years of sanctions. Needless to say, the complete isolation of Iraqi scientists from their counterparts outside Iraq, and the absence of recent periodicals, made their investigations more difficult. In spite of all this, Iraqi scientists were able to provide valid evidence of the cause-effect relationship between the use of DU during the Gulf War and the high incidence of cancer and congenital deformations, particularly in southern Iraq.

During the symposium it was very moving to see cancer and Gulf War Syndrome patients of different nationalities—British, American and Iraqi—share their dreadful plight and experiences as both Gulf War participants and victims.

The following are summaries of three important studies given at the symposium:

Impact on Environment

In a paper by M.M. Saleh and A.J. Meqwer the long-term effects of DU on the Iraqi environment in six selected regions in the south were examined. Plant and animal tissues, soil, and water samples were collected and analyzed. The presence of isotopes of uranium-238 series in over a third of the collected plant samples was confirmed using gamma spectrometric analysis. Some wild plant samples had high concentrations of radioactive elements, with levels reaching up to three times the natural background.

Average radioactive doses delivered to the population in the study area via inhalation, ingestion of meat and milk, and external exposure were measured for the period of 1991-96. The dose delivered to infants and children under fifteen years of age represented 70% of the total dose delivered to the general populations. Calculations showed that in areas covered by the study an estimated 845,000 tons of edible wild plant were contaminated with radioactive materials and 31% of the animal resources in the area were exposed to radioactive contaminants.

Incidence of Cancer

In a paper by M.M. Al-Jebouri of the College of Medicine, University of Tekrit, I.A. Al-Ani of the College of Science, University of Al-Anbar and S.A. Al-Jumaili of the College of Medicine, University of Mosul, the frequency of incidence of cancer diseases as well as the distribution of different types of cancer were examined among male and female patients in four hospitals in Mosul, the capital of Ninevah governorate, before and after the 1991 Gulf War. Cancer diseases were recorded in these four hospitals from August 1989 to March 1990 and later from August 1997 to March 1998. The frequency of cancer cases increased five-fold, with lung, leukemia, breast, skin, lymphoma, and liver cancer diseases being prevalent. The study revealed that solid tumors were more frequent.

The distribution of the cancer diseases among males and females before and after the war was different, pointing to a new factor, namely the impact of the war, and probably the use of DU weapons. In 1996 one of the authors (Al-Jumaili) reported a remarkable increase in Uranium concentration, especially in Al-Muthana and Thee-Qar, southern governorates where the Republican Guards were concentrated. It is important to note that before the war the prevalence of cancer diseases was, in decreasing order of frequency: lung, lymphoma, larynx, leukemia, and breast. After the war in 1997-98 the order became: lung, lymphoma, breast, larynx, skin, and leukemia. A sharp increase is reported in the incidence of most of these types of cancer diseases: lung (five-fold), lymphoma (four-fold), breast (six-fold) larynx (four-fold) and skin (eleven-fold).

Among less prevalent cancer diseases, the increase is even sharper: uterus (nearly ten-fold), colon (six-fold), hyper-nephroma (seven-fold), malignant myeloma (sixteen-fold), liver (eleven-fold), ovaries (sixteen-fold), peri-anal tumor (twenty-fold). These values were calculated from data obtained from the paper. The percentage of patients that were exposed to DU explosions is not clear from the paper.

Iraqi war veterans
The results of an extensive epidemiological and clinical investigation by Al-Ani of Baghdad Medical College covering military personnel (all males) who were exposed to DU show clearly the radiological and chemically toxic effects of uranium. The 1425-case sample involved Iraqi military personnel who participated in the war in the southern region of Iraq. The study covered the period 1991-97, and the age group 19-50 years.

Results clearly show a change in the pattern of different types of cancer as well as an overall increase in cancer, especially lymphomas, leukemia, lung, bone, brain, gesture-intestinal and liver cancers. The increase reached a maximum in 1996 and the majority of the cases—averaging 84% for the period 1993-97 as calculated from the paper's data—are among military personnel exposed to DU explosions, as ascertained by personnel interviews. One of the most important findings reported in this study is the difference in the pattern of cancer diseases between those exposed to DU explosions compared to those who were not.

The pattern among those exposed is: lymphoma (30%), leukemia (23%), lung (15%), brain (11%), gastrointestinal (5%), testicular and bone (4% each), pancreatic (3%), liver and salivary gland (2% each). Among those not exposed the pattern is: lung (25%), gastrointestinal (20%), leukemia (15%), lymphoma (14%), liver (10%), bone (9%)

and brain (7%). The order of prevalence has dramatically changed as a result of DU exposure. While lymphoma, leukemia, lung, and brain cancers are prevalent among the exposed, with frequency decreasing in the order indicated, lung, gastrointestinal, leukemia, and lymphoma are prevalent among those not exposed. The higher odds ratio signifies the close association between DU and cancer cases. This is particularly true for lymphomas (odd ratio 5.6), leukemia (4.8), and brain (4.5), which indicate DU as the causative agent for these types of cancers. There is a lesser degree of association for lung, gastrointestinal, bone, and liver cancers. [The "odds ratio" indicates— assuming all other things to be equal, that these conditions were that many times more likely to have occurred to the group under study— Editor.]

The percentage of still births, congenital anomalies, and secondary infertility in families of military participants exposed to DU are 1.9, 5.2, and 5.7, respectively. The paper quotes a 1995 U.S. Army Environmental Institute report and a 1997 Department of Veterans Affairs report that "DU has an effect on the shape of chromosomes in terms of increase in sister chromated exchange." That was proven through lymphocyte culture of two groups of people working in uranium manufacturing in the U.S.

The probability is that DU has a chemically toxic and radiological effect resulting in infertility, congenital anomalies and low birth weight of babies of mothers and fathers exposed to DU.

The study concludes that the extensive use of DU weapons, estimated as 630 tons, and the resulting dust and aerosol of uranium oxide caused extensive pollution of regions in south Iraq and neighboring areas of Kuwait and Saudi Arabia. Direct transmission to the human body of uranium dust or aerosol occurs through the respiratory or gastro-intestinal system, wounds, or contaminated shrapnel. Transmission occurs indirectly through pollution of the environment: soil, plant, food, animal, surface and ground water.

Symposium proposals
Several proposals were put forward including further exhaustive studies of health problems related to the use of DU during the Gulf War, training doctors and enhancing needed equipment and training advanced technologists for cancer screening and treatment, allowing collaboration with scientists from countries that were exposed to

radiation from DU or other sources, and giving immediate clinical epidemiological screening of all Iraqi citizens.

ASHRAF EL-BAYOUMI attended the "International Scientific Symposium on the Use of Depleted Uranium and Its Impact on Man and Environment in Iraq" held on December 2-3, 1998, in Baghdad, while in Baghdad as an independent, self-financed scholar to gather additional information on the impact of sanctions on Iraq. He headed the Observation Unit of the World Food Program (WFP) between March 1997 and May 1998. WFP is the UN agency responsible for food distribution and observation as part of the Oil For Food Program in Iraq.

NATO used DU Shells in Bosnia in 1995

During the NATO bombing raids in late August and early September of 1995 against the Republic of Srpska—the Serbian-led side of the civil war in Bosnia—technicians from the army of that republic found that shells of a new kind had been fired against them in various parts of the country. They set up an "experts group" to examine these shells and determine just what they were. Further study also showed that shells of this type had been fired by "airplanes bearing markings of foreign states" at targets on Mount Romanija, in Srbinje, Kalinovik, as well as in the western part of the Republic of Srpska.

D. Ristic, R. Benderac and Z. Vejnovic of the Institute of Security, and M. Orlic and S. Pavlovic of the Institute of Nuclear Sciences "Vinca" in Belgrade performed the study. Their examination of the rounds of ammunition with a spectrometer— Philips model PW 1480— established that 30-caliber depleted-uranium shells produced in the United States were involved. Following these findings the team made the following conclusions:

1. During the air raids and bombing of populated areas in the territory of the municipality of Hadzici, repair and maintenance service buildings and installations in Hadzici, and nearby agglomerations and civilian establishments in the Republic of Srpska, the airplanes with markings of foreign states used special 30-millimeter ammunition launched from guns mounted on these airplanes.

2. The projectile cores characterized by great density, hardness and penetrability are made of uranium-238.

3. Under optimum conditions the above-described projectiles can pierce a homogeneous, approximately 57.70 mm-thick steel slab.

4. The projectile cores are radioactive. Radioactivity derives from the products of decay of uranium238 and uranium-235, as well as from their daughters.

5. Radioactivity of uranium-238 is 3.4 Mbq. Total intensity of the emission of the alpha rays from the surface of the core is 1,198 alpha rays, while total intensity of the emission of the beta rays is 35,914 beta rays.

6. This type of ammunition is made of nuclear waste. Due to the presence of radioactivity it can be classified as a radiological

weapon, therefore its use for warfare purposes is completely unjustified from both military and political aspects.

7. The effects of its use against enemy personnel or the civilian population are fatal. In case of wounding, tissues are destroyed, which also involves radiological contamination.

8. In contact with the projectiles, due to the presence of radioactivity, skin changes (necrosis and ulceration) can become manifest in less than 80 hours.

9. The use of this type of ammunition is inhuman both from the aspect of poisoning and radiation of people and that of pollution of the environment.

10. Under the Yugoslav regulations in force and international standards uranium falls within the category of toxic elements and is classified in the second group of radionuclides of very high toxicity.

11. This type of ammunition has been used massively both for military and civilian targets in a broad area of the Republic of Srpska.

12. The attention of the local population whose territory was exposed to air raids with markings of foreign states should be dren to the consequences that may be caused in contact with the projectile.

13. It is necessary as a matter of urgency to organize the gathering of these projectiles in affected areas, as well as their stocking in radioactive waste dumps.

14. The use of this kind of ammunition is inhuman and represents a crime against humanity and is incompatible with international law.

15. The experts group is of the opinion that a protest should be lodged with the United Nations, OSCE, the European Union, the International Atomic Energy agency in Vienna, the World Health Organization and with other relevant international political and humanitarian organizations.

For the Experts Group
Prof. Dr. Dragoljub Ristic

According to a report to the International War Crimes Tribunal for the Former Yugoslavia in the Hague [Netherlands], "Expert conclusions have been confirmed by the aftereffects of this inhuman use of this toxic weapon. In a number of places in the Republica Srpska which were exposed to bombing raids (Milici,

Vlasenica, Han Pijesak, Sokolac, Pale, Vogosca, Rogatica, etc.), an increasing number of miscarriages, embryonic degradation, premature hemorrhages in initial stages of pregnancy, premature births, still births, etc., has been established. Cases of deaths of livestock and defects in their offspring are also on the increase."

Medical Consequences of Internal Contamination with Depleted Uranium

The present controversy regarding DU's role in Gulf War Syndrome should be resolved by well-planned objective research— which is still lacking. It is a moral and ethical requirement to control exposure to depleted uranium below the levels of adverse consequences for the environment and human health.

DR. ASAF DURAKOVIC

Depleted uranium (DU) is a byproduct of the uranium enrichment process with uranium-235 depleted to one third of its original content in natural uranium. The high density of depleted uranium—19g/cm3—makes it a superior armor-penetrating material.[1] It oxidizes at room temperature as well as in water vapor, which makes it necessary to use an aluminum protective coating. In the U.S. Air Force, DU is alloyed with 0.75% of titanium; the U.S. Navy has used the alloy of 2% of molybdenum, while the U.S. Army uses an alloy called QUAD, containing 0.5% titanium, 0.75% molybdenum, 0.75% zirconium and 0.75% niobium.

The chemical and metallic properties of DU are largely identical with natural uranium, with similar hazards in chemical and radiation toxicity. The United States Nuclear Regulatory Commission classifies DU as a resource material governed by general and specific licensing requirements. General licensing governs the use and transfer of DU in the amount of 15 pounds at a given time and a maximum of 150 pounds in a calendar year. Specific license requires written documentation of the intended use of DU with specific reference to the equipment, compliance with health and safety regulations and personnel training.[2]

The isotopic content of DU (U-238 = 99.75%, U-235 = 0.25%, U-234 = 0.005%) has a specific activity of 3.6×10^{-7} A/g, compared with natural uranium (U-238 = 99.25%, U-235 = 0.75, U-234 = 0.006%) which has a specific activity of 6.77×10^{-7} A/g. Uranium isotopes have different metabolic behavior in the human body, depending on their physical and chemical properties. Three isotopes of uranium of medical concern: U-238 (half-life = 4.5×10^{9} years), U-235 (half-life = 7.1×10^{8} years), and U-234 (half-life = 2.5×10^{5}

years) are alpha, beta and gamma emitters with spontaneous fission below the level of criticality.

The physiological behavior of uranium compounds depends mainly on their solubility. The soluble (uranyl U-VI) compounds in internal contamination cause chemical damage in the proximal convoluted tubules of the kidney, with resulting hematuria, albuminuria, hyaline and granular casts, azotemia and tubular necrosis. Less soluble (uranous U-IV) compounds are primarily retained in the lung when inhaled[3] or in the bone mineral phase. They also assert metabolic toxic effects by inhibiting the metabolism of carbohydrates in the ATP-uranyl-hexokinaise complex, blocking the transfer of phosphate to glucose and inhibiting its first step of metabolic utilization.

High organospecificity of uranium isotopes, combined with a long half life and corpuscular radiation, results in chemical and radiation damage to the target organs, namely the bronchoalveolar tree,[4] the kidneys and the bone, causing somatic and genetic alterations. Uranium compounds retained in the bone may cause malignant changes in the cells of the skeletal tissue and in the stem cells, while DU retained in the respiratory tree may result in the induction of lung cancer.

While alpha radiation from uranium isotopes in DU is not a significant external hazard, beta radiation of a DU penetrator of 2.29 MeV (234Pa) has a range of 0.5 cm in aluminum and several centimeters in human tissue, producing beta exposure of 217 ± 20.4 mR/hr. Gamma rays are the main type of radiation in a DU round with photon energies of 700 keV to 1MeV. The surface of a 120mm DU penetrator produces gamma exposure of 26 ± 2.7mR/hr. This is similar to the exposure rates of natural uranium. Internal contamination with depleted uranium presents both a chemical and a radiation hazard after entry into the internal environment of the organism through dermal, oral or pulmonary portal of entry or through wounds or burns. Gastrointestinal absorption of uranium isotopes is relatively low in the adult human organism, influenced by morphological and functional integrity of intestinal mucosa, age and dietary regimens. The intestinal pathway is the least adverse portal of entry in uranium contamination. Internal contamination with DU through wounds has been encountered in the Persian Gulf War veterans with DU-contaminated shrapnel. While the information about these patient studies is unavailable, contamination with DU by simulated shrapnel wounds has been studied and reported in experimental animal models.[5] Embedded DU particles produced a significant increase of uranium isotopes in the body fluids six months after DU pellet implantation, with elevated oncogene levels indicating that DU may be a critical factor in the induction of malignant changes in the contaminated organism. These results of DU induced transformation to the tumorigenic cell phenotype at a low radiation dose of 0.13 Gy indicate the role of DU in the oncogenic expression in experimental animals.[6]

Depleted uranium can also be absorbed through the intact skin. Dermal exposure to soluble uranium compounds causes severe poisoning and death with well documented experimental evidence of uranium trioxide, fluoride, nitrate, pentachloride and ammonium diuranate in the internal environment of the organism after absorption through the skin.[7] Repeated application of soluble uranium compounds was observed to be better tolerated as a cumulative dose than in a single application.

The inhalational pathway of internal contamination with depleted uranium is the most important route of entry in the extracellular fluids via the bronchoalveolar tree if soluble inhaled DU particles gain access to systemic circulation. Bronchoalveolar deposition of radioactive particles has been studied for decades in both animal models and occupational contamination in humans with a special emphasis on uranium and actinites.

The International Commission on Radiation Protection (ICRP) introduced a general model of the parameters for the studies of respiratory pathways in uranium contamination.[8] According to this model, about 25% of uranium particles are immediately exhaled, 50% are translocated to the nasopharynx where they can be expectorated or swallowed, while 25% of the particles are deposited in the bronchoalveolar tree, with about 10% reaching systemic circulation and 15% ascending to the nasopharynx by expectoration and upward motion of the ciliary epithelium. Soluble components of uranium are absorbed to the systemic circulation while less soluble components are retained in the respiratory system.[9]

The respirability of the DU particles is determined by the aerodynamic equivalent diameter (AED), which renders particles non-respirable if they are over ten microns in AED, those of five microns being 25%, 3.5 microns 50%, 2.5 microns 75% and 2 microns 100% respirable. The particles in the respirable range may be retained in the lung, producing local radiation injury, or absorbed into the blood stream and deposited in the target organs. Pulmonary retention is determined by the particle size, concentration, density and shape, and the exposed person's breathing pattern.

The airborne fraction of DU ranges from 0.9% to 70%, depending on penetrator size, velocity and target material. The impact of a 150mm DU penetrator releases 2.4kg of airborne depleted uranium. Half of the airborne DU particles sampled during the testing of 105mm DU projectiles were in respirable range, reaching the nonciliated bronchial tree.[10] In other studies over 70% of the airborne DU particles were less than 7 microns in size upon impact, thus within respirable range. Particles larger than ten microns and very small particles of less than 1 micron AED are not respirable.

Soluble DU compounds have a rapid access to the blood stream and consequent toxic effects in the target organs. Insoluble DU particles are retained in the lung tissue for years. One study reported over 60% of insoluble uranium retention in the lungs for over 500 days,[11] while another report indicated pulmonary retention of 1,470 days.[12] One recent report of hazard evaluations confirmed the relationship between the respiratory pathway of uranium contamination and lung cancer[13] and suggested reconsideration of the ratio between genetic and environmental cancer induction. Although the pulmonary pathway is the single most important point of entry of DU into the internal environment of the human organism, there have been very few controlled studies of human exposure to the uranium compounds by inhalation.

Urinary excretion after a single inhalation of uranium particles shows both rapid and slower components of the curve, with half times of 7 and 100 hours respectively. Over 60% of uranium mobilized from the lung into systemic circulation is retained in the kidney and bone, while 40% is excreted in urine. Uranium oxide retained in the lungs may result in a neoplastic disease such as squamous-cell carcinoma. Radiation toxicity of depleted uranium has been recently examined in the epidemiological studies of human exposure and in animal models.

The industrial and environmental impact of DU exposure has recently been suggested to be a factor in increased cancer mortality. The Monte Carlo (MCMC) method of analysis applied to twenty years of records indicates that several counties in Ohio in the vicinity of the depleted-uranium fuel processing facility had increased incidence of lung cancer.[14] Most recent experimental evidence clearly indicates the role of depleted uranium in the induction of the tumorigenic phenotype in cell culture study. Human osteoblasts exposed to DU underwent a fourfold increase in tumor transformation frequency. The implication from these studies is that depleted uranium is a carcinogenic risk comparable to other biologically reactive cancer-inducing compounds.[15]

It has been recently reported that uranium exposure in German miners was associated with the alpha particle intrachromosomal alterations with the tumor suppressor gene being the target of uranium alpha particles.[16] The analysis of lymphocytes from uranium mine workers in Namibia has recently determined that uranium exposure is associated with increased malignant transformation.[17] These results are in agreement with reports of the relationship between uranium exposure and lung cancer in the mines of South Africa[18], and with reports of a significant increase of mortality in the Bohemian uranium mines the Czech Republic.[19]

The Canadian reports confirm increased lung cancer mortality in Ontario uranium miners.[20] It is also in agreement with the French reports of excessive lung cancer mortality in the underground uranium miners in France,[21] Russian reports of cancer mortality in nuclear power plants in the nuclear industry[22], as well as numerous reports from the United States confirming uranium exposure risks.

These results are critically evaluated in the analysis of cancer rates and genetic malformations in the population of Iraq exposed to depleted uranium in the 1991 Persian Gulf War,[23] as well as in Gulf War Veterans of the United States, Canada and Great Britain.[24] The legacy of depleted uranium continues to be an area of concern in the unresolved issues surrounding previously unknown illnesses such as Al Eskan disease and Persian Gulf syndrome.[25] Recent studies have reported a relationship between the Persian Gulf Illnesses and depleted uranium, with a conclusion that DU is a contributing factor in the diseases encountered in the Persian Gulf War,[26] where it was used for the first time in the history of warfare.[27]

Current research conducted by independent scientists in the United States and Canada has produced preliminary studies indicating that Gulf War Veterans have increased concentrations of uranium isotopes in their urine eight years after the Gulf War. The uranium has the isotopic ratio of depleted uranium.[28] The present controversy regarding the role of DU in the Gulf War Syndrome should be resolved only by well-planned objective research—which is still lacking. It is not only a matter of specific concern for tens of thousands of veterans with incapacitating illnesses, but a moral and ethical requirement to control exposure to depleted uranium below the levels of adverse consequences for the environment and human health.

ASAF DURAKOVIC, MD, DVM. MSC, PHD, FACP, is a clinical professor of Radiology and Nuclear Medicine, and a world leading specialist in all aspects of nuclear and radiation medicine for over 25 years. His extensive experience includes research into nuclear disaster medicine in the U.S., Canada, Europe and Asia. He served as the United States Medical Team leader in the American-Soviet Joint Nuclear Verification Experiment in Soviet Central Asia. He is currently involved in issues concerning internal contamination with Uranium isotopes. He is listed in Marquis Who's Who, the International Biographical Institute of Contemporary Men of Achievement, Cambridge, England.

References

1. Code of Federal Regulations (CFR-10): Chapter 1. Nuclear Regulatory Commission (NRC) Washington, D.C. 1990.

2. Luessentrop A.J, Gallimore J.C, Sweet W.H., Struxness E.G., Robinson J.: The toxicity in man of hexavalent uranium following intravenous administration, Am. J. Roentgenol. Radiate. Ther. Nucl. Med. 79, 83, 1958.

3. Chambers D.R., Markland R., Clary M.K., Bowman R.L.: Aerosolization characteristics of hard impact testing of deplete uranium penetrators, Aberdeen Proving Grounds, U.S. Army Armament Research and Development Command, Ballistic Research Lab, publication ARBRL-TR-02435, 1982.

4. Durakovic A.: Internal contamination with medically significant radionuclides, in: Conclin J.J. Walker R.I.: Military Radiobiology, Academic Press, 243-264,1987.

5. Miller A.C., Whittaker T., McBride S., Hogan J., Benson K, Sin H.: Biomarkers for carcinogenesis: Oncogenic activation by depleted uranium vivo, Pros. Amer. Assoc. for Cancer Research, 38,462, 1997.

6. Ribera D, Labrot F., Tisnerat G., Narbonne J.F.: Uranium in the Environment: Occurrence, transfer and biological effects, Review of Environmental. Contam. & Toxicology, 146, 53-89, 1996.

7. Scott K.L, Axelrod D.J., Crowley J., Hammilton J.G.: Deposition and rate of plutonium, uranium, and their fission products inhaled as aerosols in rats and man, Archives of Pathology, 48, 31-54, 1949.

8. Recommendations of International Commission on Radiological Protection, Brit, J. Radiol. Suppl. 6, 1955.

9. West C.M., Scott L.M.: Uranium cases showing long chest burden retention, Health Phys. 17, 781-791, 1969.

10. Mercer T.T.: Definitions of respirable activity, In: McCormick W., editor, Aerosol Technology and evaluation, Academic Press, 1973.

11. Ensminger D.A., Bucci S.A. Procedures to calculate radiological and toxicological exposures from airborne releases of Depleted Uranium, The Analytical Science Corporation, Publication TR-3135, Washington, D.C. 1980.

12. Sullivan M.F.: Actinide absorption from the gastrointestinal tract. In: Wrenn M.E.: Actinides in Man and animals, University of Utah Press, Salt Lake City, Utah, p232-236, 1981.

13. Crowell R.E., Gilliard F.D., Temes R.T., Harmes H.J., Neft R.E., Heaphy E.: Detection of Trosomy 7 in non-malignant individuals at risk from lung cancer, Cancer Epidemiol. Biomarkers Prev. 5, 631-636, 1996.

14. Xia H.,Carlin B.P.,: Spatio-Temporal models with errors in covariates: Maping Ohio lung cancer mortality, Statistics in Medicine, 17, 2025-2043, 1998.

15. Hsu H.: Transformation of human osteoblast cells to the tumorigenic phenotype by depleted uranium, Environm.Health Perspectives, 106,8, 465-471, 1998.

16. Muller K.M.: P53 gene mutation analysis in tumors of patients exposed to alpha particles, Carcinogenesis, 18, 511-516, 1997.

17. Zaire R., Griffin C.S., Simpson P.J., Papworth D.G., Savage J.R., Armstrong S., Hulten M.A.: Analysis of lymphocytes from uranium workers in Namibia, Mutation Res., 57, 1-2, 109-113, 1996.

18. Huizdo E., Murray J., Klempman S.: Lung cancer in relation to exposure to silica dust, silicosis and uranium production in South Africa gold miners, Thorax, 52, 271-275,1997.

19. Thomadek L., Swerdlow A.J., Darby S.C., Placek V., Kunz E.: Mortality in uranium miners in west Bohemia: a long-term cohort study, Occupational & Environmental Medicine. 51(5): 308-15, May 1994.

20. Kusiak RA., Ritchie AC., Muller J., Springer J.: Mortality from lung cancer in Ontario uranium miners, British Journal of Industrial Medicine. 50(10): 920-928, 1993.

21. Tirmarche M., Raphalen A., Chameaude J.: Epidemiological study of French uranium miners, Cancer Detection & Prevention. 16(3): 169-172, 1992.

22. Baisogolov G.D., Bolotnikova M.G., Galstian I.A.,Guskova A.K., Koshurnikova N.A., Lyzlov A.F., Nikipelov B.V.`Pesternikova, V.S., Shilnikova N.S.: Malignant neoformations of the hematopoietic and lymphoid tissues in the personnel of the first plant of atomic industry, Voprosy onkologii 37 (5) 553-559, 1991.

23. Matthews, J.: Radioactive bullets raise cancer fears, Journal of the National Cancer Institute, 85 (13) 1029-1030, 1993.

24. Birchard K.: Does Iraq's depleted uranium pose a health risk, Lancet, 35, 9103, 657, 1998.

25. Jamal G.A.: Gulf War Syndrome – A model for complexity of biological and environmental interaction with human health, Adverse drug reactions and toxicological reviews, 17, (1) 1-17, 1998.

26. Korenyi-Both A.L., Juncer D.J.: Al Eskan disease: Persian Gulf Syndrome, Military Medicine. 162(1): 1-13, 1997.

27. Doucet I.:Desert Storm Syndrome: sick soldiers and dead children, Medicine & War. 10(3): 183-94, 1994.

28. Durakovic A., Sharma H.: Urinary excretion of uranium isotopes in the Gulf War Veterans after inhalational exposure to depleted uranium, Third International congress of the Croatian Society of Nuclear Medicine, Opatija, Croatia, May 1999.

Authors' Biographies

GLENN ALCALAY is an anthropologist from New York and a member of the National Committee for Radiation Victims. He has worked on nuclear issues for more than twenty years. His main research and work has been in radioactive contamination of the Marshall Islands.

FRANK ALEXANDER, who prepared the photo exhibit and helped coordinate the material for this book, has been active in the environmental and anti-war movements.

BARBARA NIMRI AZIZ is an anthropologist and journalist specializing on Middle East issues. She travels extensively throughout the Middle East and visited Iraq often both before and since the Gulf War to follow in detail social and economic developments. She specializes in analyzing the impact of the war and sanctions on Iraqi agriculture. Dr. Aziz produces a Saturday afternoon radio program on Pacifica-WBAI in New York.

ROSALIE BERTELL, GNSH, is a founding member and current president of the International Institute of Concern for Public Health and Editor in Chief of *International Perspectives in Public Health*. Dr. Bertell directed the International Medical Commission–Bhopal, which investigated the aftermath of the Union Carbide disaster in Bhopal, and the International Medical Commission–Chernobyl. She wrote *Handbook for Estimating the Health Effects of Ionizing Radiation* and the ground-breaking *No Immediate Danger: Prognosis for a Radioactive Earth*.

PAT BROUDY is legislative director of both the National Association of Atomic Veterans and the National Association of Atomic Survivors. Broudy helped found radiation exposure victims' organizations after her husband—exposed to radiation three times by the military—died from lymphoma in 1977. Since then she has testified twenty times before Congressional committees, including the recent Presidential Advisory Committee on Gulf War Illnesses and Human Radiation Exposure.

HELEN CALDICOTT, Australian physician and anti-nuclear activist, was one of the most influential leaders of the worldwide nuclear freeze movement in the 1980s. She founded Physicians for Social Responsibility and Women's Action for Nuclear Disarmament. Dr. Caldicott was nominated for the Nobel Prize in 1985. She is the author of *Nuclear Madness*, *If You Love This Planet* and *Missile Envy*.

JOHN CATALINOTTO, a mathematics lecturer at the City University of New York, was a national organizer of the American Servicemen's Union from 1967 to 1971. In 1992 he helped organize the International War Crimes Tribunal on U.S. crimes in the Gulf War. Since 1982 he has been a managing editor of *Workers World* weekly newspaper.

RAMSEY CLARK, former U.S. attorney general during the Johnson administration, is an internationally known lawyer and human-rights activist. Clark was instrumental in building worldwide opposition to the Gulf War as well as the sanctions against Iraq. Clark founded the International Action Center in 1992 to establish a permanent response network for global crises. He has been an opponent of U.S. military interventions in Vietnam, Grenada, Panama, Nicaragua, Libya and Somalia.

LEONARD A. DIETZ, physicist, worked from 1955-1983 at the Knolls Atomic Power Laboratory, which General Electric operated for the Atomic Energy Commission. He devised new techniques for high-precision isotopic analysis of uranium, plutonium and other elements. Dietz has published in numerous scientific journals and is a charter member of the American Society for Mass Spectrometry.

TOD ENSIGN, a lawyer, is director of Citizen Soldier, a non-profit GI/veterans rights advocacy organization. He is author of two books on the military and has contributed chapters to several others, including a chapter on "U.S. War Crimes in Vietnam and America's Veterans" for an anthology on the Vietnam war to be published by Syracuse University Press in 1997.

DAN FAHEY, a Gulf War Syndrome activist, is researching DU use in the Gulf region. Dan is a case manager at Swords to Plowshares, a veterans' rights organization, and is on the Board of Directors of the National Gulf War Resource Center, Inc. He is a member of the Military Toxics Project's Depleted Uranium Citizen's Network, Veterans for Peace, and commander of Veterans of Foreign Wars' Post 5888 in Santa Cruz, California.

SARA FLOUNDERS is a co-coordinator of the International Action Center. She initiated the Anti-Sanctions Project of the IAC, which produced the 1996 book, *The Children Are Dying*, to expose and end the use of economic sanctions as a weapon of mass destruction. She coordinated the International War Crimes Tribunal which held hearings on U.S. war crimes in the Gulf in thirty U.S. cities and over twenty countries. She has organized opposition to U.S. military intervention in Bosnia, Panama and Somalia.

LENORA FOERSTEL has been the North American Coordinator of Women for Mutual Security since 1990. She is also on the board of Women's Strike for Peace. A cultural historian whose research on the South Pacific included extended field work with Margaret Mead, Foerstel has written numerous articles, produced films and recently edited the book, *Creating Surplus Population: The Effect of Military and Corporate Policies on Indigenous Peoples.*

JAY M. GOULD is a former member of the EPA Science Advisory Board, which has researched and exposed the dangers of low-level radiation. He is the author of *Deadly Deceit: Low Level Radiation, High Level Cover-Up; The Quality of Life in Residential Neighborhoods* and his most recent, *The Enemy Within—The High Cost of Living Near Nuclear Reactors.*

SIEGWART-HORST GUENTHER, founder and president of the Austrian Yellow Cross International, carried out several relief actions for the sick and starving Iraqi people. He was professor of Infectious Diseases and Epidemiology at Baghdad University. A Berlin court fined him in 1993 for violating the "Atomic Energy Law" when he attempted to bring a spent DU bullet into Germany.

ERIC HOSKINS is a medical doctor specializing in public health and epidemiology. Since 1990, he has provided humanitarian assistance and documented the Gulf crisis's impact on Iraqi children and women. As medical coordinator of the Harvard Study Team's surveys of health and welfare in postwar Iraq, Hoskins prepared the 1993 report for UNICEF, *Children, War and Sanctions*. In 1991, he was awarded Canada's most prestigious humanitarian award, the Lester B. Pearson Peace Medal.

MICHIO KAKU is a well-known nuclear physicist, author and commentator. Since 1977 he has been a professor of nuclear physics at the Graduate Center of City University of New York. He has written more than seventy articles and nine books, including his latest bestseller, *Hyperspace*. His Wednesday evening national Pacifica radio program has a wide audience.

SUZY T. KANE is a member of Women's International League for Peace and Freedom and past co-chair of the North East Westchester (N.Y.) SANE/Freeze. Her chapter is from her forthcoming book, *The Hidden History of the Persian Gulf War*.

DOLORES LYMBURNER is a national organizer for the Military Toxics Project and the national coordinator of the Depleted Uranium Citizens' Network. This organization was the first to organize attention on DU, highlighting its many manufacturing and testing facilities in the U.S. She has been an environmental activist since 1986.

CAROL H. PICOU, Sergeant First Class, Army (retired), served with the 41st Combat Support Hospital in the Gulf War which drove past and worked among miles of incinerated Iraqi vehicles on the "Highway of Death." Picou has testified at Congressional hearings on Gulf War Syndrome. Because she demanded to know what happened to her and others' health, her career in the military ended. She co-founded MISSION Project–Military Issues Surfacing In Our Nation.

MANUEL PINO, an environmental activist from the Acoma Pueblo in New Mexico, has worked since 1979 on uranium-mining issues. He is currently an instructor at Scottsdale Community College in Arizona. Pino continues to work with American Indian Nations throughout the United States that have been impacted by the nuclear fuel cycle and military testing.

ANNA RONDON is a member of and community planner for the Dineh Nation (Navajo) in New Mexico and an organizer for the Southwest Indigenous Uranium Forum. She participated in the September 1996 Indigenous Anti-Nuclear Summit and testified at the World Uranium Hearing in Salzburg, Austria, in 1992. She has been active in nuclear issues since she was sixteen. Her activism began with the AIM Freedom Survival School.

VICTOR SIDEL helped found Physicians for Social Responsibility. Since 1993, he has been co-president of the International Physicians for the Prevention of Nuclear War. An outspoken opponent of the arms race, he is on the Board of the Physicians for a National Health Program, which advocates a Canadian-style single-payer system for the United States. He is also co-editor of *War and Public Health*, recently published by Oxford University Press.

ALICE SLATER is the president of Global Resource Action Center for the Environment, which provides technical support and economic analysis of employment alternatives to communities with nuclear facilities. GRACE aims to connect individuals and organizations engaged in research, policy and grassroots community work to preserve the future of the planet. Slater is on the board of the Lawyers Committee on Nuclear Policy and is a founding mother of the Abolition 2000 Network for the Elimination of Nuclear Weapons.

ALYN WARE is the executive director of the Lawyers' Committee on Nuclear Policy and the Pacific representative for the International Peace Bureau in Aotearoa—New Zealand—his home country. He established the Mobile Peace Van, a peace education service for schools nationwide. He has worked as a UN researcher for the World Federalist Movement and was the UN Representative for the Gulf Peace Team.

PHILIPPA WINKLER is a researcher and activist in the U.S. and the UK. She was project director of the book *Hidden Casualties: The Environmental, Health and Political Consequences of the Persian Gulf War*. Winkler; Karen Parker, an attorney specializing in humanitarian law; and Dr. Beatrice Boctor were the main actors in bringing the issue of sanctions against Iraq and depleted uranium to the UN Commission on Human Rights in March 1996.

Section I:

Introduction and Call to Action Against DU

1 | The Struggle for an Independent Inquiry

We need a commission of those with real interest in finding the cause of Gulf War Syndrome: suffering U.S. vets, independent scientists, Iraqis, and past victims—atomic veterans and their families, veterans exposed to Agent Orange, and Native miners and community organizations.

SARA FLOUNDERS

Today in discussing the possible causes of the Gulf War Syndrome that affects over 90,000 U.S. veterans, there is an elephant in the room. The entire debate is taking place with everyone pretending the elephant doesn't exist.

This book is about the elephant—radioactive conventional weapons.

A new generation of weapons is in place around the world. These weapons contain a dense material—depleted uranium. DU weapons make all others so much scrap metal, giving the U.S. military machine and military contractors a huge advantage.

It matters little to the Pentagon in its race for unrestrained military dominance in every type of warfare that this new weapon not only kills those it targets, it poisons soldiers who handle it, civilians for hundreds of miles surrounding the battlefields who breathe the air and drink the water, and unborn generations.

DU is a delayed response weapon. It will take decades and generations before we know the true casualties as more veterans and their children cope with rare and unknown conditions, cancers, deformities and congenital diseases.

In the U.S. racism impacts on every social issue. Black, Latino and other Third World troops have been disproportionately at risk on the front lines. During the Vietnam War this meant more deaths, injuries and long term delayed combat stress syndrome. According to Department of Defense personnel data (September 30, 1992), during the Gulf War almost half the troops stationed in the Gulf region were Black or Latino, although they make up only twenty percent of the population. This means that Gulf War Syndrome had the greatest impact in communities already oppressed and impoverished.

Gulf War Syndrome's symptoms—chronic fatigue, chronic headache and joint pain, gastrointestinal distress, insomnia and memory loss—make holding a job, stabilizing a family and obtaining medical help much more difficult. Many thousands of seriously ill and demoralized, disoriented or homeless veterans are not part of the count of those suffering from Gulf War Syndrome. That one third of the homeless in the U.S. today are veterans speaks to the hidden costs of the Gulf and Vietnam wars.

Is DU the sole cause of Gulf War Syndrome? Or does DU's low-level radiation suppress people's immune system and make them more susceptible to disease? To answer either question deserves more than the passing mention and out-of-hand dismissal the Presidential Commission and the Department of Defense's public statements on Gulf War Syndrome give DU. However, even the Defense Department's own internal studies show how well it knows the dangers. We quote these studies extensively here to prove the government has too much at stake to judge DU objectively.

Those who really want to know what has happened to the health of tens of thousands of young women and men who just a few years ago were in the prime of health must raise their voices and organize to demand a genuinely independent commission to investigate this issue.

I first became aware of the dangerous radioactive impact of depleted-uranium weapons in 1991 when I was researching for Ramsey Clark's book on the Gulf War, *The Fire This Time*. His book predicted that "the people of the Gulf region will have to face the effects of radiation poisoning for years to come."

What raised our concern was a secret report by the United Kingdom Atomic Energy Authority (UKAEA) prepared in April 1991, a month after the end of the war. Leaked to the London *Independent* and published that November, this early report described the potential problems of radioactive dust spreading over the battlefields and getting into the food chain and the water. At that time it warned that forty tons of radioactive debris left from DU weapons could cause over five hundred thousand deaths. Now we find the amount of radioactive debris left behind is over three hundred tons.

Iraqi Children with Cancers
In 1994 I traveled to Iraq to see the consequences of the Gulf War and the continuing sanctions. I saw infants with obvious genetic deformities who wouldn't live long and wards of children wasting away from cancers such as leukemia, lymphomas and Hodgkin's disease. Because of the sanctions, Iraqi doctors lacked even basic medicines and were helpless to intervene. They could only note the escalating numbers.

And the Iraqis are not the only ones who need to know the truth about DU and want to see that truth published. Gulf War veterans and their families are desperate to understand what has happened to their health since they returned from the Gulf.

This book attempts to explain the uses of depleted uranium in weapons and to present what is already known about exposure to low-level radiation and its threat to the environment and to all of humanity. Most important, this collection of articles is a resource for those ready to challenge the long history of government coverups and denials regarding military toxics and poisons.

For two generations the Pentagon and the entire scientific community have studied the dangers of radiation while Congress allocated a trillion dollars to build the world's largest nuclear arsenal.

Thousands of studies and hundreds of books explain the dangers of radioactivity. Millions of people worldwide have marched and organized to oppose the danger nuclear weapons pose to the future of the planet.

Billions of dollars have been put into federal funds to clean up nuclear waste sites. Now we learn that the Environmental Restoration Branch of the Department of Energy has used these funds to ship nuclear waste to countries all over the world to be recycled into weapons production.

The U.S. Department of Defense has more than a billion pounds of nuclear waste in storage from fifty years of nuclear weapons production. Part of its clean-up program is to give the depleted uranium away free to munitions manufacturers. Knowing the dangers, the military-industrial complex has moved straight ahead designing, testing and manufacturing a new generation of weapons using radioactive waste material.

Metal of Dishonor Exposes the Deception

As the contributors to *Metal of Dishonor* expose the dangers of low-level radiation, they demonstrate that even "depleted" uranium weapons are radioactive and highly toxic. They trace a history of government lies and coverups regarding the dangers of radioactivity, with policies that have denied compensation to veterans and to Native populations hurt most by these dangers. They show the Pentagon's motives for using DU weapons, the military industry's drive to manufacture them, and the passion of both to cover up the truth.

The chapters by **Helen Caldicott, Michio Kaku, Leonard A. Dietz, Rosalie Bertell** and **Jay M. Gould** scientifically delineate the perils of low-level radiation and meticulously document the extensive knowledge the military possessed about DU's long-term consequences long before the Gulf War.

Dietz explains with mathematical detail how uranium metal burns rapidly on impact and forms tiny airborne particles that can travel tens of miles to be inhaled or ingested into the body where they lodge in vital organs. **Caldicott** makes the necessary but daring leap to correctly characterize the Gulf War as a nuclear war.

Kaku writes, "Our troops were used as human guinea pigs for the Pentagon. Thousands must have walked through almost invisible clouds of uranium dioxide mist, not realizing that micro-sized particles were entering into their lungs."

Gould links increases in cancers and auto-immune diseases to the impact of low-level radiation on the population surrounding nuclear weapons complexes, test sites and nuclear reactors. **Bertell** lists the major scientific studies that have defined the danger for many years.

A look at the experiences of earlier victims of U.S. war preparations helps expose how cover-ups, stonewalling, and fraudulent promises of compensation for unfortunate mistakes are standard operating procedures.

Pat Broudy's husband was one of the approximately eight hundred thousand GIs purposely exposed to nuclear radiation during atomic tests in the Southwest or in the Pacific. Her article exposes the Defense Department's criminal coverup.

Anna Rondon, a Navajo activist from the South West Indigenous Uranium Forum, and **Manuel Pino**, from the Acoma Pueblo, explain the bitter experiences of the Native nations with uranium mining and testing.

Despite Congressional hearings, media coverage and special legislation, only 455 Atomic Veterans and fifty Native miners' widows received compensation. And only seventeen families have been compensated of the twenty-three thousand Americans, mainly prisoners, poor people or disabled people, who were directly injected without their knowledge or consent with highly radioactive materials since 1945.

To these we can add the thousands of Marshall Islanders consciously used as human guinea pigs, moved back to the "most contaminated places in the world," the islands hit by fallout from sixty-seven atomic and hydrogen bombs. **Glenn Alcalay** describes this catastrophe in his article.

Every piece of information in this whole criminal history had to be leaked or pried out by independent efforts. The government has never willingly provided any relevant information. It is hidden under "top secret" classifications.

How can we expect anything different from government studies of Gulf War Syndrome or DU?

Dolores Lymburner exposes a leaked Army Environmental Policy Institute report that acknowledges "if DU enters the body it has the potential to generate significant medical consequences. The risks associated with DU in the body are both chemical and radiological." The Army first denied this report's existence.

With thorough documentation, **Dan Fahey** explains how the density, speed and impact of DU weapons greatly increased the kill range of U.S. tanks. He also shows just how well the military planners understood DU's dangers.

Former Army Nurse **Carol Picou**, who volunteered for front-line duty, describes her horror at passing the thousands of burning Iraqi vehicles—many destroyed by DU projectiles—on the "highway of death." Then she describes the devastating deterioration and ruin of her own health and of the others in her unit from contact with the toxins in the region, as well as the government's stonewalling and denial of responsibility.

In the Gulf War, Iraqi casualties were enormous. Over one hundred thousand troops were killed and eighty-five thousand captured. In January 1992 a Greenpeace investigation estimated that ninety thousand of the three hundred thousand injured Iraqi troops had died.

In contrast, the U.S. military suffered 147 combat deaths, more than half due to friendly fire. The low casualties were the selling point of these new, high-tech weapons. U.S. troops had become seemingly invincible. That is the lie. The ninety thousand chronically ill U.S. soldiers make up the real casualty figures. Tens of thousands of British, French, Saudi, Egyptian, Australian, Canadian and other soldiers who served in the Gulf in early 1991 are also sick.

As **John Catalinotto** explains, 147 combat deaths is a very important figure to the military planners and to the major corporations who profit from military production. Lower casualty figures may mean less domestic resistance to future conflicts. If the real casualty figures become a topic of debate, if long-term illness, genetic deformities to future generations and environmental damage become issues, opposition to new military adventures will surely grow.

All the government hearings, commissions and reports outdo each other talking about concern for the health of all the military personnel, protecting our soldiers, finding the cause, etc. The real casualty figures expose what the generals and military corporations think of the rank-and-file GI—an expendable item. DU's victims need to organize themselves independently of those who have the biggest stake in arranging a cover-up.

No easy task. **Lenore Foerstel** examines the corporate connections between the media and the military industries. The Pentagon orchestrates the news through press pools and staged events. Even after the war, the media has continued to cover up the dangers from DU and its role in Gulf War Syndrome.

High-intensity Conflict

The forty-three-day war against Iraq in 1991 was the highest intensity conflict in military history, fought for control of the richest mineral reserves in the world. The U.S.-led coalition poured unprecedented volumes of firepower, money and technology—including seven billion tons of military materiel—into the Gulf area. They fought the war with an electronic battlefield of stealth bombers, satellites and cruise missiles.

Despite all the propaganda attacking so-called Iraqi weapons of mass destruction, most analysts agree that Iraq has not one weapon in its entire arsenal that is capable of destroying a U.S. bomber, aircraft carrier or even a U.S. tank. **Ramsey Clark, Eric Hoskins, Siegwart-Horst Guenther, Barbara Nimri Aziz and Suzy Kane** discuss the impact of a war that was actually an attack on a country that was defenseless against the new weapons of mass destruction. We also publish a report on the impact of allied radioactive weapons that the **Iraqi UN Mission** presented to the United Nations Center for Human Rights in Geneva.

The Gulf War showed that those countries that already held nuclear monopolies also dominated in so-called conventional warfare. Furthermore, it showed that nuclear weapons have become obsolete as a distinct category. Now weapons composed of radioactive material are classified as conventional weapons and are deployed around the world by U.S. and NATO forces in Bosnia, Somalia and Haiti. These weapons are flooding the world arms market. U.S. industry provides seventy-five percent of all weapons sold worldwide. Desert Storm was a great advertisement for the DU weapons it sells.

A Field of Wheat

Dr. Barbara Nimri Aziz describes the war's impact on a field of wheat, a flock of chickens, on the children. The sanctions keep information on the scope of the catastrophe from reaching the world. **Dr. Siegwart Guenther** boldly brought a spent DU bullet from Iraq to Germany, where he was arrested for transporting radioactive material. But what about the tons of NATO weapons containing DU that are stored, tested and transported throughout Europe? Or the radioactive NATO shells and land mines exploded in Bosnia?

The Pentagon has issued a fumbling series of denials, cover-ups and finally partial admissions that Gulf War Syndrome exists. Yet it has omitted any mention of radioactive weapons. This omission is no accident. The Pentagon has never come forward to admit the human consequences of its actions, unless a mighty struggle forced out the truth.

Some scientists have proposed alternatives to depleted uranium weapons, claiming that fast, hard missiles could be made at greater expense by using other, perhaps less toxic heavy metals, such as tungsten or a tungsten alloy. Has this not occurred to military contractors? Is this just an oversight, a mistake in the heat of battle?

The military industry is built on super profits. How can they resist, no matter how dangerous, a raw material that is available free of charge? The Department of Defense and the major military contractors control most of the supply. The largest corporations in the U.S. today are corporations whose very existence depends on military contracts, an issue that goes to the very heart of the U.S. economy.

The Pentagon and the military corporations clearly consider contamination of their own soldiers, of the environment and of millions of civilians as an acceptable cost. As we learn from the experience of past veterans, this has always been true.

Lockheed Martin, Boeing (now merged with McDonnell Douglas), General Electric, Raytheon and AT&T have been involved for decades in the production of weapons that threaten the health of millions. How can these corporations resist a super weapon, made out of cheap material, that creates a demand for a whole new round of weapons?

Military contracts are a source of growing demand on the federal budget. The billions of dollars that they consume come at the cost of cutbacks in every social program from jobs programs to education, health care, infant immunization programs, subsidized housing, rebuilding infrastructure or environmental cleanup. People's needs are never part of the calculation.

Weapons are U.S. industry's most profitable export items. These military industries are truly merchants of death.

The U.S. military machine is larger than all of its potential competitors put together—and it is not shrinking. President Clinton has pledged a forty-percent increase in funds for new weapons development. Congress has voted to extend the Strategic Defense Initiative, or Star Wars. Nuclear weapons testing has been banned in the air, under sea and under ground, but it persists in the Pentagon's sophisticated laboratories.

The military acts like it has license to threaten the health and livelihood of millions globally and then hide it under national security. Can we challenge the military's behavior?

Today, the Pentagon fears no military weapon. The Pentagon fears only one thing: people in motion—informed, mobilized and angry. Mass protest stopped nuclear testing, stopped the use of Agent Orange, helped end the Vietnam War.

It has become impossible for generals, in the interests of corporate profit, to send tens of thousands of youth directly into machine gun fire as they did in earlier wars. But it is essential to expose that DU is a delayed response bullet that shoots both ways.

Part of changing what happens is to change the way millions of people perceive an issue. Do they have information? Do they see a way to intervene? With bold ideas, a few individuals and small groups can lay the groundwork and push the struggle forward.

We hope this book will provide the evidence and demonstrate the urgent need for an independent inquiry.

Demand an Independent Inquiry

Because of their involvement in the development of these poisonous weapons, the Department of Defense and the major military contractors cannot be trusted to give an honest review of the possible causes of Gulf War Syndrome.

The Presidential Advisory Commission whitewashes the truth, **Tod Ensign** shows, when it concludes: "It is unlikely that health effects reported by Gulf War veterans today are the result of exposure to depleted uranium during the Gulf War." The commission was supposedly an independent blue-ribbon panel of scientists and others who are above self-interest in their conclusion. Hardly the case.

An honest, aboveboard and exhaustive inquiry is urgently needed. The commission must be made up of those with a real interest in finding the cause of Gulf War Syndrome. And the inquiry must prominently include veterans suffering from Gulf War Syndrome. They have the most compelling incentive in truly finding the cause.

An independent commission should also include the veterans of past wars and nuclear testing who have suffered mysterious illnesses and government coverups. Atomic veterans and their families, veterans suffering from Agent Orange poisoning would help get to the bottom of what is going on. Organizations of Native peoples whose land has been poisoned should be part of the inquiry. Community organizations surrounding uranium mines, weapons-production sites, and proving and testing grounds could lend their expertise.

Since African American and Latino troops make up such a large proportion of those in the field of combat—and thus suffer disproportionately from Gulf War Syndrome—groups from these communities must also be represented in the commission.

Scientists who are independent of the nuclear industry and the military should be called on to testify, along with medical doctors, epidemiologists and geneticists, and trade unionists who work in atomic and especially DU weapons production.

To understand the full dimensions of Gulf War Syndrome, it is essential to bring into the light of day what was done to Iraq's population. Medical teams must be able to visit Iraq, and Iraqi doctors should be able to testify on the medical catastrophe they face.

Such an inquiry could give enormous impetus to an international campaign to ban DU.

Grassroots campaigns can have enormous creative dynamism if the local organizers have information. No matter how dangerous DU weapons are shown to be, the military will not of its own accord stop their production. In the past, every step in preventing use of deadly materials came about because an aroused, organized population made it unfeasible for the military to use the weapon.

An International Ban on DU

The many groups worldwide that understand the enormous dangers of radiation must begin to organize and demand a ban on the use of depleted uranium, its containment and a cleanup of all radioactive waste. We have included a proposed ban that former U.S. Attorney General and well known human rights activist **Ramsey Clark** drafted.

This ban proposal can be used in many ways. It can be utilized in international forums and tested in international law. With the articles by **Victor Sidel, Philippa Winkler** and **Alyn Ware**, we have also included experiences of other groups that have opposed the threat from nuclear weapons or shown how to use international law to combat specific weapons.

Most developments in technology sneak up on us. Change spreads rapidly, making earlier methods obsolete overnight. The implications can reshape our lives before we are even aware of them. But the same is true of ideas.

Former slave and great abolitionist organizer Frederick Douglass explained, "Power concedes nothing without a struggle." Every step forward in human rights seemed in the beginning like an impossible task. Whether the struggle was against slavery, for civil rights, for the right of workers to unionize, for women's suffrage, for the eight-hour day, to oppose bigotry against lesbian and gay people, or the movement against nuclear war and testing—in the beginning it always seems that all law, culture and tradition defend life the way it was at that very moment. But in the face of new ideas and a bold challenge, even entrenched power can lose its undisputed position.

Information is power. When mobilized it can undergo a transformation and become outrage. Then it has explosive potential. It has the potential to force great sweeping changes. That is our secret weapon against the Pentagon.

2 | Ban Depleted Uranium Weapons

Is it acceptable by any human standard that we would permit one shell of depleted uranium to be manufactured, to be stored, to be used? No! Stop it now!

RAMSEY CLARK

On December 4, 1990, the General Assembly of the United Nations, meeting just a few hundred yards from here and apparently having decided that the United States was determined to attack Iraq and that it was powerless to prevent the attack, resolved that no attack should be made on any nuclear reactor—an inherently dangerous facility. The vote on this resolution was 144 to 1; only the U.S. voted against.

The resolution should not have been necessary—such attacks have been war crimes since Protocol 1 Additional to the Geneva Conventions of 1977. Article 56 of the Protocol prohibits what would obviously be catastrophic to life, any "attack (that) may cause the release of dangerous forces... and consequent severe losses among the civilian population." The article protects works and installations from an attack which can endanger thousands and thousands of people in the immediate vicinity and beyond and perhaps in ways we don't know.

On January 23 of 1991—the end of the first week of the assault on Iraq—General Colin Powell announced—and the international media were all there—that Iraq's "two operating reactors... are both gone. They're down. They're finished." (*New York Times*, January 24, 1991, p. A11.) He said it proudly and no member nation of the UN, no member of the U.S. Congress, no international leader, none of the media said a mumbling word in protest.

A week later on January 30, 1991—and many of us in this room saw it when it happened—General Schwarzkopf on worldwide television proudly announced that "allied forces," meaning U.S. forces, had attacked eighteen major chemical plants in Iraq, ten major biological, and three nuclear plants. Apparently one more nuclear plant was attacked than existed. The Geneva Conventions which prohibit making "Works or installations containing dangerous forces ... the object of attack, even where their objectives are military objectives" were not mentioned. (*New York Times*, January 31, 1991, p. A1.)

No one asked about the effects of such criminal attacks on the people of Iraq. No one asked how it is that the Pentagon can defy with impunity the resolution of the General Assembly and the Geneva

Conventions forged from the horrible experiences of the two great world wars of this century, this most violent century in human history.

These proud boasts of senior military officers expose a central problem of militarism: There is no respect for law, or life, there is no restraint on violence, there is no accountability for crimes, there is glorification of superior violence. Worse, there is general applause from the American people. It sounds like a good day's work to have destroyed all those facilities, but there is little concern over what it means for humanity, or, at least, "their" humanity.

After the assault on Iraq, the world slowly learned that there was a new weapon employed against Iraq. There may be others we haven't learned about yet. Those who studied the assault on Iraq saw some evidence of it because this new weapon seemed to be able to penetrate solid steel plates destroying tanks and armored vehicles.

As we began to hear more and more about it from the military, the message was what a wondrous weapon it was. The silver bullet, the Army called it. It's the one that always hits the target in the cause of justice.

After a lot of research and effort while we were working on *The Fire This Time*—our book about the Gulf War—we were able to count from all sources then available between five thousand and six thousand depleted uranium shells fired by the U.S. Army. This was compiled from all sources, including replies by the Pentagon to direct questions. It was the number we could verify by the time we went to press in 1992, after an exhaustive search. The Army now concedes there were at least fourteen thousand depleted-uranium shells fired into Iraq.

All our efforts in research for *The Fire This Time* led us to believe that there were about fifty thousand depleted-uranium missiles and rockets fired from U.S. aircraft in more than 110,000 aerial sorties over Iraq. U.S. aircraft dropped over eighty-eight thousand tons of bombs on that country, the equivalent of seven-and-one-half bombs of the size of the atomic bomb that incinerated Hiroshima. We believed then and reported that there were about fifty thousand DU rockets and missiles fired. Only now are we learning there were probably more than nine hundred thousand rounds of depleted-uranium ammunition fired on Iraq.

The Pentagon does not seem to care about the consequences of its use of depleted uranium, even for its own soldiers, and certainly not for people living in southern Iraq and the other areas in Iraq where there was a concentrated presence of depleted uranium from this kind of firing. The Pentagon doesn't care about future generations, or what widespread release of depleted uranium might mean to survival of life on the planet. The Pentagon has a new weapon and it intends to deploy and use it and sell it to other governments regardless of the consequences of its use. It will go right on. It will deploy, even sell depleted uranium missiles worldwide. It will cover up its deployment, use and sales; it will lie about its use and distribution of this extremely dangerous substance. And it will flout the law.

Pentagon scientists and contractors in the laboratories are working to find more efficient means of killing people on the quick. We have to stop it, or it will stop us. And if we don't have the will to do it, then perhaps it is justice that we suffer the consequences. This is because we are responsible for the acts of our agents and, like it or not, they are our agents.

How many years did it take to find out about Agent Orange? How long will the struggle go on to find the real consequences of DU? How many soldiers will die from exposure to DU weapons and debris from their use? What are the causes of "Gulf War Syndrome"?

If you want to see professionals suffer, look at the doctors in Iraq. It's wonderful to read about the doctors of Japan working with all the resources, facilities, medicines and therapies to help surviving victims of the atomic attacks on Hiroshima and Nagasaki. Nobel laureate Kinzaburo Oe's book *Hiroshima Notes* tells of the doctors who treated those victims, what courageous professionals they were, some devoting their whole careers and lives to the even more courageous Japanese who bore the living death scars of those blasts. But the doctors in Iraq work with nothing except their wits and their training, for they have no medicines, no medical supplies, no sanitation, not even pain killers, nothing to help the thousands still dying monthly in Iraq from the combined effects of aerial assaults and the sanctions.

In the south of Iraq, with all the horror they had seen during the bombing, medical doctors had rarely heard of diseases caused by severe malnutrition such as kwashiorkor and marasmus. Soon tens of thousands of people were dying from them. Bad water, spoiled food, dehydration, uncontrolled preventable diseases were killing thousands and thousands of people each year.

Then in 1993, when we went back to Iraq, doctors told us that suddenly they were seeing things that were very difficult to understand, that they hadn't seen before. They were diagnosing many more people with leukemia, particularly children. There were increases in leukemia, tumors, cancers, birth defects, unlike anything they had seen before, or heard of.

When we went to Iraq in 1994 the cause of these radical increases in leukemia, tumors, cancers, birth defects and other problems had become the preeminent concern for the Ministry of Health in Iraq. They didn't know where the tumors were coming from: what was causing these tragic, death-dealing unprecedented increases in this range of abnormalities. They just knew the numbers of new cases were leaping out at them. They still don't know when it will stop or how far such cases will spread. But they are convinced that the many tons of depleted uranium left in their soil, ground water and air is the major, perhaps sole contributing cause of this human tragedy.

Iraq is a country that has lost a million people to sanctions. This is a crime against humanity. Sanctions are a weapon of mass destruction like a neutron bomb. Sanctions kill life and preserve property. However, DU is even more dangerous. We know about hunger and we know about sickness and what happens when we don't have food and medicines for the sick and hungry. We know food and medicines can prevent hunger and heal the sick.   But we really don't know the full consequences from what the Pentagon has done and is doing with depleted uranium, only that nothing has stopped the Pentagon from doing what it wants to do and that depleted uranium can kill, cause cancer, mutations and will continue to do its work at more than half its present force for two hundred fifty thousand years.

If the U.S. military wants to bomb Iraq tomorrow [September 13, 1996] as it has done often since September 1991, it will do it. If it chooses to use depleted-uranium shells, when will we know?

This government defies world opinion. Consider the blockade against Cuba. The United Nations General Assembly voted again last year to condemn the United States for its blockade against Cuba. This time the margin was 107 for condemnation, two [the U.S. and Israel] against. Washington couldn't care less. Even if the whole nation is hungry and every living human being in Cuba or in Iraq suffers, the U.S. government intends to continue this policy.

It is a vital moment in the struggle to prevent the use of depleted uranium and sanctions that punish an entire population. DU is a symbol of the challenge to people who want to stop such mindless violence. Sanctions are the symbol of the challenge to people who want to end poverty, hunger, sickness and their uses to control poor nations.

If we in the United States can come to grips with the absolute need to stop DU and sanctions, it is conceivable that we can meet the challenge to stop all uses of technology against life, even those grimmest reapers—militarism and forced impoverishment as a means of control.

Is it acceptable by any human standard that we would permit for one moment one weapon using depleted uranium to be manufactured, to be stored, to be used, or one child to die of sanctions?

No! We must stop both now. End them now. Abolish DU weapons, criminalize sanctions, prohibit them forever. Deal with the manufacture and use of DU weapons as the war crime it is. Deal with sanctions as a crime against humanity. Prosecute those who violate the law. And realize that this is only the beginning of the challenge.

Technology was supposed to be able to liberate all of humanity from want. Instead it exposes humanity to unprecedented suffering and death. Technology is used both to create weapons of mass destruction and to isolate whole populations to enforce death dealing sanctions. If we don't come to grips with the effects of technology used against life, that same technology, that liberator, will destroy us. Weapons technology is not the liberation we should seek. The question is, who is to be the master of technology—the people, or the plutocracy?

We need your help. We must accept this challenge and persevere for the duration in this struggle. We must stop DU now, and sanctions and militarism and nuclear weapons and plutocracy which wrings its wealth from the suffering of the poor.

(Developed from a talk given September 12, 1996 at the UN Church Center in New York.)

3 | A New Kind of Nuclear War

Never in my wildest dreams did I think that the United States would be detonating nuclear shells to poison its own soldiers and the surrounding civilian populations with radioactive isotopes.

DR. HELEN CALDICOTT

The United States has conducted two nuclear wars. The first against Japan in 1945, the second in Kuwait and Iraq in 1991.

The first nuclear war fissioned a plutonium bomb and one made of uranium. The second nuclear war utilized depleted-uranium weapons, but nuclear fission was not involved.

For many years the United States has been using depleted uranium, a by-product from the production of enriched fuel for nuclear reactors and weapons, to manufacture shells, bullets and protective armour of tanks. This excess uranium, composed mainly of the uranium isotope U-238 is called "depleted" because it has a lower than normal content of the isotope U-235, the fissionable material. But it has one very "excellent" property—it is extremely dense and capable of penetrating heavily armored vehicles. This capability was ably demonstrated in the Gulf massacre of 1991. "Massacre" describes what happened better than "war."

But another physical property, which is not so desirable, is that depleted uranium spontaneously burns on impact, creating tiny aerosolized particles less than five microns in diameter, small enough to be inhaled. At least seventy percent of the uranium in these weapons is released in this form on impact, and these tiny particles travel long distances when airborne.

Another undesirable physical property is the U-238 decays to thorium 234, which has a half life of 24.10 days. This then decays to protactinium, or a stable concentration some twenty-five weeks after the relatively pure U-238 has been manufactured and thereafter becomes an integral component of the uranium.

Uranium 238 emits both alpha and gamma radiation, while the two "daughter" elements mentioned in the above paragraph are both beta and gamma emitters. Gamma radiation is non-particulate radioactive energy, which can induce genetic mutations the instant it traverses a cell. Alpha and beta radiation are particulate forms which, when they pass through a living cell, are likely also to induce either cellular death or a genetic mutation. Alpha is very carcinogenic while beta, because it is a smaller particle, is less so. Mutations in a regulatory gene of a normal body cell can induce cancer years later. Mutation in the germ cells—ova and sperm—can cause genetic abnormalities in future generations.

Now let's talk about the Gulf massacre, which lasted six weeks. During that time, 940,000 small DU shells were fired from U.S. planes, 14,000 larger DU shells from tanks, and many of these shells spontaneously ignited when they hit their targets. Further, on two separate occasions vehicles loaded with uranium shells accidentally exploded, showering friends and foes alike with tiny respirable particles of deadly uranium.

Uranium can remain in the lung for many years, irradiating a small volume of cells, several of which may become a cancer years later. It also concentrates in the kidney. A large quantity of uranium in the kidney can impair renal function, and any amount can induce renal cancer. After inhalation or ingestion, uranium can be transported around the body in the blood stream, thus exposing other organs and blood cells to its carcinogenic effects.

Because of the long incubation time for cancer—five to sixty years, we will not necessarily expect malignancies to be occurring yet. Still, according to an article in the October 21, 1996, issue of *The Nation* by Bill Mesler, "The Pentagon's Radioactive Bullet," Iraq presented a study to the United Nations in August 1995 demonstrating a sharp increase in leukemia and cancer incidence in the Basra region, and a secret British Atomic Energy Authority report estimated that there was enough depleted uranium in the form of empty shells in the area to account for five hundred thousand potential deaths. But their calculations were unrealistically based upon forty tons, not the three hundred tons of uranium left behind after the United States military vacated the region.

I am shocked to discover that the United States is also involved in exporting these immoral radiological weapons to other countries such as Taiwan, Thailand, Korea, Bahrain, Israel, Saudi Arabia, Greece, Turkey, Kuwait and others.

In few discussions in the mainstream media have I seen mention of the nuclear component of the Gulf War Syndrome—chemical, biological and oil-fire damage, but not nuclear. And what about the children in the area, many of whom are still playing with empty uranium shells?

The United States still retains a stockpile of five hundred thousand additional tons of depleted uranium, to continue the manufacture and export of these hideous weapons.

At the time in 1991, I believed the Gulf massacre was highly immoral, what with a huge barrage of cruise missiles, smart bombs and the like—weapons that were originally designed to deliver nuclear bombs—a near nuclear war I called it. But never in my wildest dreams did I think that the United States would be detonating nuclear shells to poison its own soldiers and the surrounding civilian populations with radioactive isotopes and to pollute the land on which the military activities took place for virtually the rest of time—the half life of depleted uranium being 4.5 billion years.

An International Appeal to
Ban the Use of Depleted Uranium Weapons

Drafted by Ramsey Clark

Depleted-uranium weapons are an unacceptable threat to life, a violation of international law and an assault on human dignity. To safeguard the future of humanity, we call for an unconditional international ban forbidding research, manufacture, testing, transportation, possession and use of DU for military purposes. In addition, we call for the immediate isolation and containment of all DU weapons and waste, the reclassification of DU as a radioactive and hazardous substance, the cleanup of existing DU-contaminated areas, comprehensive efforts to prevent human exposure and medical care for those who have been exposed.

During the Gulf War, munitions and armor made with depleted uranium were used for the first time in a military action. Iraq and northern Kuwait were a virtual testing range for depleted-uranium weapons. Over 940,000 30-millimeter uranium tipped bullets and "more than 14,000 large caliber DU rounds were consumed during Operation Desert Storm/Desert Shield." *(U.S. Army Environmental Policy Institute)*

These weapons were used throughout Iraq with no concern for the health and environmental consequences of their use. Between 300 and 800 tons of DU particles and dust have been scattered over the ground and the water in Kuwait, Saudi Arabia and Iraq. As a result, hundreds of thousands of people, both civilians and soldiers, have suffered the effects of exposure to these radioactive weapons.

Of the 697,000 U.S. troops who served in the Gulf, over 90,000 have reported medical problems. Symptoms include respiratory, liver and kidney dysfunction, memory loss, headaches, fever, low blood pressure. There are birth defects among their newborn children. DU is a leading suspect for a portion of these ailments. The effects on the population living in Iraq are far greater. Under pressure, the Pentagon has been forced to acknowledge Gulf War Syndrome, but they are still stonewalling any connection to DU.

Communities near DU weapons plants, testing facilities, bases and arsenals have also been exposed to this radioactive material which has a half-life of 4.4 billion years. DU-weapons are deployed with U.S. troops in Bosnia. The spreading toxicity of depleted uranium threatens life everywhere.

DU weapons are not conventional weapons. They are highly toxic, radioactive weapons. All international law on warfare has attempted to limit violence to combatants and to prevent the use of cruel and unfocused weapons. International agreements and conventions have tried to protect civilians and non-combatants from the scourge of war and to outlaw the destruction of the environment and the food supply in order to safeguard life on earth.

Consequently, DU weapons violate international law because of their inherent cruelty and unconfined death-dealing effect. They threaten civilian populations now and for generations to come. These are precisely the weapons and uses prohibited by international law for more than a century including the Geneva Conventions and their Protocols Additional of 1977.

Section II:

How DU Weapons Harmed Gulf War Veterans

5 | Collateral Damage: How U.S. Troops Were Exposed To Depleted Uranium During the Persian Gulf War

"When DU is indicted as a causative agent for Desert Storm illness, the Army must have sufficient data to separate fiction from reality. Without forethought and data, the financial implications of long-term disability payments and health-care costs would be excessive."
—U.S. Army Environmental Policy Institute[1]

DAN FAHEY

Introduction

One of the legacies of the 20th Century will undoubtedly be the frightening evolution of weapons capable of killing or injuring large numbers of people both during and after their intended wartime use. With the passage of time, the variety of these weapons only grows: chemical and biological agents, land mines, nuclear weapons, and poisonous herbicides. In the wake of the Persian Gulf War, we must add to this list weapons made of a nuclear waste product called depleted uranium.

Tank armor and armor-piercing rounds made of depleted uranium proved highly effective in their first wartime use, but because depleted uranium weapons were so effective, dozens of countries now have or are developing depleted uranium weapons for their arsenals. The rapid proliferation of depleted uranium weapons will, in the near future, level the playing field and eliminate any battlefield advantage they currently provide.

Unfortunately, spreading depleted uranium in an uncontrolled fashion across battlefields can have severe health consequences for friend and foe alike. During the Persian Gulf War, most U.S. troops were unaware of the presence and dangers of depleted uranium on the battlefield. As a result, thousands of servicemen and women came in contact with contaminated vehicles which had been hit by depleted uranium rounds. The Pentagon is reluctant to discuss the dangers of depleted uranium weapons because of their effectiveness in combat and the prospect of costly health care and disability compensation for U.S. veterans who have been and are being exposed.

However, the impact of depleted uranium weapons is felt far beyond the veterans of the Persian Gulf War. Workers in the domestic uranium industry who mine and process uranium and manufacture depleted uranium weapons, in addition to civilians who live near processing plants, manufacturing plants, testing ranges and contaminated battlefields, are also affected. This paper focuses on the use of depleted uranium weapons in the Persian Gulf War, and the ways in which U.S. troops were exposed to them.

What is Depleted Uranium?

Depleted uranium (DU) is the highly toxic and radioactive byproduct of the uranium enrichment process. "Depleted" uranium is so called because the content of the fissionable U-235 isotope is reduced from 0.7% to 0.2% during the enrichment process. The isotope U-238 makes up over 99% of the content of both natural uranium and depleted uranium. Depleted uranium is roughly 60% as radioactive as naturally occurring uranium, and has a half life of 4.5 billion years.[2] As a result of 50 years of enriching uranium for use in nuclear weapons and reactors, the U.S. has in excess of 1.1 billion pounds of DU waste material.[3]

In the early 1970s, the government began exploring ways to dispose of DU which would relieve it of the burden of having to store it in low-level radioactive waste repositories. DU has several characteristics which make it attractive for use in munitions: it is extremely dense, available in large quantities, and given for free to arms manufacturers.

During the 1970s and 1980s, testing at more than a dozen domestic sites including Aberdeen Proving Ground in Maryland, Jefferson Proving Ground in Indiana, and Yuma Proving Ground in Arizona demonstrated that large and small caliber rounds made of depleted uranium were highly effective in piercing armor. At the same time, the Army found that incorporating depleted uranium metal into tank armor made tanks less vulnerable to penetration from conventional rounds. But while the Army conducted many tests to evaluate the effectiveness of DU bullets and armor, they failed to "closely coordinate the planning and performance of experiments for DU health and environmental assessments."[4] After years of research, development and testing, Operation Desert Storm provided the first opportunity for the Pentagon to test DU munitions in combat.

Depleted Uranium Weapons in the Persian Gulf War

The Tomahawk Cruise Missiles launched on the first day of Operation Desert Storm, and used during the September 3, 1996, attack on Iraq during Operation Desert Strike, contain DU in their tips to provide weight and stability. When they impact a target or other hard surface, the resultant area can become contaminated by the DU. A U.S. Navy instruction manual notes that teams involved in the recovery of Tomahawk missiles which crash during testing must have radiological protection clothing, gloves, respirators, and dosimeters.[5]

The Navy also uses DU in ammunition for its Phalanx Close-In Weapons System gun. While this gun is primarily designed for missile defense, it is also effective against other targets, as was shown in June 1996 when a Japanese ship firing a U.S.-made Phalanx gun accidentally shot down an American jet during training exercises in the Pacific. The Navy's use of weapons containing depleted uranium during Desert Storm was small, however, when compared to their use by the Army, Air Force, and Marines.

The Army and Marine Corps employed more than 1,900 M1A1 Abrams main battle tanks, plus several hundred M1 and M60 model tanks, in combat during Desert Storm.[6] U.S. tanks typically carry a mixed load of high explosive and depleted uranium sabot rounds. The M1A1 tanks fire 120mm rounds, while the M1 and M60 tanks fire 105mm rounds. The weight of the DU penetrator dart in a 120mm tank round is 10.7 pounds; in a 105mm round it is 8.5 pounds.[7] The Army reports that a total of 14,000 DU tank rounds were expended during the war. 7,000 rounds were fired during training before the war into sand berms in Saudi Arabia; 4,000 rounds were fired during combat; and 3,000 were lost due to fires or other accidents.[8] In addition, British Challenger tanks fired at least 100 DU tank rounds in combat.

The extended range of DU penetrators combined with the highly accurate fire control system and gun of the M1A1 provided American tankers with a considerable advantage over their Iraqi counterparts. While Iraqi T-72 tanks had an effective firing range of under 2,000 meters, U.S. tanks had an effective firing range of approximately 3,000 meters. In one case, the frontal armor of a T-72 was penetrated by a 3,500 meter shot (over 2 miles) from an M1A1.[9] But the longest confirmed kill of the war was by a British Challenger tank, which destroyed an Iraqi tank with a DU round over a distance of 5,100 meters (over 3 miles).[10] Even over these extended ranges, the DU rounds proved highly effective in penetrating Iraqi tank armor. In one case, a DU round "hit the turret of a Russian-made Iraqi T-72 tank, passed completely through the turret, and hit (and destroyed) a second T-72."[11]

Though the Army and Marine Corps fired thousands of DU rounds in battle, the Air Force by far fired the majority of DU rounds used during the war. The Air Force's A-10 "tank-killer" aircraft were used extensively against Iraqi armored vehicles and artillery. The A-10 fired approximately 940,000 30mm DU rounds in combat.[12] The weight of the DU penetrator in a 30mm round is 272 grams, so roughly 564,000 pounds of depleted uranium were fired from A-10s during the war.[13]

DU penetrator rounds fired by American aircraft and American and British tanks destroyed approximately one-third of the 3,700 Iraqi tanks lost in battle.[14] In addition, artillery pieces, armored personnel carriers and other equipment destroyed by DU rounds number in the thousands. By war's end, roughly 300 tons of uranium from spent rounds lay scattered in various sizes and states of decay across the battlefields of Iraq and Kuwait.

When a depleted uranium projectile strikes a hard surface, up to 70% of the penetrator is oxidized and scattered as small particles in, on and around the target.[15] A fact sheet issued by the U.S. Army Armament, Munitions, and Chemical Command (AMCCOM) states:

> When a DU penetrator impacts a target surface, a large portion of the kinetic energy is dissipated as heat. The heat of the impact causes the DU to oxidize or burn momentarily. This results in smoke which contains a high concentration of DU particles. These uranium particles can be ingested or inhaled and are toxic.[16]

Of the aerosolized particles produced, 60% are particles less than five microns in diameter (less than 10 microns being considered as respirable size).[17] Army field tests have shown that when a vehicle is struck by a DU penetrator, the heaviest contamination occurs within 5 to 7 meters of the vehicle.[18] However, DU particles thrown into the air by the round's impact, or by resultant fires and explosion, can be carried downwind for 25 miles or more.[19]

The DU armor on the M1A1 tanks proved effective in protecting tank crews from enemy fire, although the tank crews were continually irradiated by their own armor and DU rounds for the months many of them lived with their tanks. For example, a tank driver receives a radiation dose of 0.13 mrem/hr to his head from overhead DU armor.[20] After just 32 continuous days, or 64 twelve-hour days, the amount of radiation a tank driver receives to his head will exceed the Nuclear Regulatory Commission's annual standard for public whole-body exposure to man-made sources of radiation.[21] Unfortunately, U.S. tank crews were not monitored for radiation exposure during the Persian Gulf War.

During the ground war, only seven M1A1's were hit by rounds fired from the Iraqi's T-72 tanks, with none being seriously damaged. The Army reported that the Iraqi armed forces "destroyed no Abrams tanks during the Persian Gulf War."[22] Nine Abrams tanks were destroyed during the war: seven due to friendly fire and two were intentionally destroyed to prevent capture after they became disabled.[23] One incident in particular demonstrates the effectiveness of armor-piercing rounds and tank armor made of depleted uranium. As allied forces pushed into southern Iraq at the start of the ground war, an M1A1 tank became stuck in the mud.

> The unit (part of the 24th Infantry Division) had gone on, leaving this tank to wait for a recovery vehicle. Three T-72's appeared and attacked. The first fired from under 1,000 meters, scoring a hit with a shaped-charge (high explosive) round on the M1A1's frontal armor. The hit did no damage. The M1A1 fired a 120mm armor-piercing (DU) round that penetrated the T-72 turret, causing an explosion that blew the turret into the air. The second T-72 fired another shaped-charge round, hit the frontal armor, and did no damage. The T-72 turned to run, and took a 120mm round in the engine compartment (which) blew the engine into the air. The last T-72 fired a solid shot (sabot) round from 400 meters. This left a groove in the M1A1's frontal armor and bounced off. The T-72 then backed up behind a sand berm and was completely concealed from view. The M1A1 depressed its gun and put a (DU) sabot round through the berm, into the T-72, causing an explosion.[24]

U.S. forces came in contact with DU on the battlefield in a variety of ways. Some were exposed during combat. Some were exposed during the recovery of contaminated U.S. vehicles which had been hit by friendly fire incidents. Some were exposed during a massive fire in July, 1991, at the U.S. base in Doha, Kuwait. And some who continue to work with DU weapons, or deploy to contaminated areas in Kuwait, are being exposed today. In most of these scenarios, exposure to DU could have been prevented or minimized if our troops had been warned ahead of time about the use of DU weapons and effective safety measures, and if they had been issued protective clothing including respirators and gloves. No warnings or protective gear were issued before the war, however, because "Army officials believe that DU protective methods can be ignored during battle or other life-threatening situations because DU-related health risks are greatly outweighed by the risks of combat."[25]

Friendly Fire Incidents
During Operations Desert Shield and Desert Storm, 29 U.S. vehicles were contaminated with DU on the battlefield. Twenty-one of these vehicles (six Abrams tanks and 15 Bradley fighting vehicles) were penetrated by DU rounds during friendly fire incidents. A total of 13 soldiers were killed and 50 wounded in friendly fire incidents involving DU rounds.[26] Twenty-two of the wounded soldiers retained uranium shrapnel in their bodies.[27] Thirty of the soldiers wounded in the friendly fire incidents, including most of those with DU shrapnel, are being monitored by the Depleted Uranium Program at the Baltimore, Maryland, VA Medical Center.

Five years after they were exposed to DU on the battlefield, 15 of the 30 still have elevated levels of uranium in their urine.[28] Leonard Dietz, a retired atomic scientist, has noted that "if you've got any indication of it [DU] at this late date, even at low levels, it would indicate you'd had a pretty heavy dose five years ago."[29]

Because the Army failed to conduct even one study about the long term health effects of imbedded DU fragments during its twenty years of DU weapon development, these veterans have unwittingly become the subjects the Army needed for such a study.[30] As part of the study, the Army has recommended periodic examinations of the veterans who retain DU shrapnel "to watch for and catalogue signs of chronic kidney toxicity, granuloma induction, and cancer."[31]

Recovery Personnel
The 144th Army National Guard Service and Supply Company, based in Hammonton, New Jersey, was assigned to recover all damaged and destroyed U.S. combat vehicles, including the 29 contaminated with DU. In 1993, the U.S. General Accounting Office (GAO) disclosed that approximately 27 soldiers from the 144th worked on the

contaminated Bradleys and Abrams vehicles "without prior knowledge of the existence of DU contamination or radiation hazards and without any protective gear."[32] These people worked on and in the contaminated vehicles for three weeks before the Army Armament, Munitions, and Chemical Command informed them that the vehicles were contaminated.

At the time of the GAO investigation, the Army Surgeon General's Office reported that 12 of these soldiers had been tested for DU, with none showing elevated levels of internalized uranium.[33] But a comprehensive June 1995 report by the Army Environmental Policy Institute (AEPI), entitled *Health and Environmental Consequences of Depleted Uranium Use in the U.S. Army*, stated that as of May 1994, only 9 soldiers of the 144th had been tested for DU by means of urinalysis, with none showing elevated levels of DU in their bodies.[34]

However, the value of testing these soldiers by means of urinalysis three years after their exposure must by questioned. Urinalysis is effective for testing for DU shortly after exposure, while the body purges some of the heavy metal. However, for the uranium which remains trapped in the lungs, kidneys, bones, or other organs, more sensitive testing methods are needed to accurately determine the amount of uranium which may be retained in the body three years after exposure. If the Army continues to test these and other veterans for DU solely by means of urinalysis, it is unlikely to provide the veterans, or the public, with an accurate assessment of the potential for internalization of DU, or the extent of the current problem.

Contact with Contaminated Vehicles on the Battlefield

It is difficult to say how many troops, or civilians, have come in contact with DU on the battlefields of Desert Storm. Although the U.S. recovered its own vehicles contaminated in friendly fire incidents, virtually none of the thousands of contaminated Iraqi vehicles littering the battlefields have been cleaned up. In addition, thousands of DU penetrators which missed their mark remain on the battlefields in various states of decay.

The Army Surgeon General has stated that troops who breathed smoke from or had incidental contact with vehicles struck by DU penetrators were unlikely to have internalized DU and do not warrant medical follow-up.[35] Despite the Army Surgeon General's assertion, the AEPI report acknowledged that for troops on the battlefield, "the potential for internalization is high enough that the Army should further investigate and analyze the risks."[36]

Experimental data from testing, and field experience from Desert Storm, indicate that "the potential for DU internal exposure during combat is directly related to the location of the soldiers exposed."[37] Army studies have found that "personnel inside or near vehicles struck by DU penetrators could receive significant internal exposures."[38] In addition, "recovery and maintenance soldiers working in and around DU contaminated vehicles can inhale or ingest resuspended DU particles."[39] In effect, the Army has found that anyone who breathes smoke from, climbs on, or enters vehicles which were hit by DU rounds is at a high risk of inhaling or ingesting DU particles.

In one survey of over 10,000 Gulf vets, 82% indicated that they entered Iraqi vehicles after the war.[40] Some of these soldiers entered the shattered hulks to salvage any usable equipment. Others climbed on and entered the vehicles to look for souvenirs or pose for pictures during informal "battlefield tours." While not all the vehicles on the battlefield had been hit by DU rounds, several thousand of them were in the Army's own word, "contaminated."

It was not until March 7, 1991, after most of the fighting had subsided, that the Army Armament, Munitions, and Chemical Command sent a message to commanders in the Gulf warning that "any system struck by a DU penetrator can be assumed to be contaminated with DU."[41] The same message also warned that "personnel exposed to DU contamination should wash exposed areas and discard clothing."

In June 1991, several months after the end of Desert Storm, the Army Armament, Munitions and Chemical Command sent a fact sheet to Army training centers for use in educating troops about DU. The fact sheet noted:

> If a burned out vehicle must be entered, precautions must be taken to avoid inhaling or ingesting DU particles. Respirator or protective mask should be worn at minimum along with gloves. Ideally protective clothing should be worn as well. After exiting the vehicle, hands should be washed thoroughly. All dust should be brushed off of clothing or protective clothing should be discarded.[42]

The Army has so far offered no explanation as to why these warnings were not issued to troops before they went into battle. Even since the

Persian Gulf War, the Army has done a poor job educating its own troops about the use and dangers of depleted uranium weaponry.[43] Although the Departments of Defense (DoD) and Veterans Affairs (VA) have provided medical exams to more than 85,000 Gulf War veterans who have confirmed health problems, only a handful of these veterans have been tested for DU exposure. Some persistent veterans who breathed smoke from or entered contaminated vehicles have forced the VA to test them for DU, and have shown elevated levels of DU in their urine several years after the war.

Clearly, more widespread testing of Gulf War veterans needs to take place to determine the extent to which veterans were exposed. At this point in time, testing for DU should involve *in vivo* monitoring, in addition to urinalysis, to provide an accurate assessment of the amount of internalized DU. However, the DoD and VA are reluctant to conduct such testing because of the large cost involved and potentially damaging attention which would be brought to a prized weapon.

Doha, Kuwait Fire

On July 11, 1991, a Field Artillery Ammunition Support Vehicle (FAASV) loaded with ammunition caught fire in the motor pool and ammunition storage area of the U.S. Army base in Doha, Kuwait. The fire quickly spread to surrounding vehicles and artillery, which were combat loaded with live ammunition. Severe explosions ensued for six hours and residual fires burned well into the following day. Roughly $15 million in ammunition and $23 million in vehicles were destroyed, along with more than $2 million in damage to property.[44]

At the time of the fire, approximately 3,500 soldiers from the 11th Armored Cavalry Regiment (ACR) were at Doha, along with a contingent of British soldiers. Fifty-two American and six British soldiers, along with two civilian workers, were injured during the fire. Most of the injuries were the result of people being struck by falling debris or injuring themselves while fleeing the explosions.[45]

During the fire four M1A1 Abrams tanks with DU armor were destroyed, along with 660 tank rounds and 9,720 small caliber 25mm DU rounds. These destroyed rounds represent over 9,000 pounds of depleted uranium which potentially burned up in the fire.[46]

A February 1985 report, *Potential Behavior of Depleted Uranium Penetrators Under Shipping and Bulk Storage Accident Conditions*, notes that "under severe fire conditions, the (DU tank) penetrators remained in the fire and were oxidized to powder rather than being ejected undamaged from the fire."[47] Thus we can expect that a sizable amount of the 9,000 pounds of DU was oxidized to powder and spread around the compound during the hours of violent explosions. In addition, a steady wind of approximately eight knots blowing from the northwest likely carried airborne DU particles many miles from the site of the fire.[48]

The long distances that DU particles can be carried by the wind was discovered following the 1979 release of airborne DU particles by the National Lead factory in Colonie, New York. National Lead was manufacturing 30mm DU rounds for the Air Force at the time of the releases. DU particles of respirable size released by the plant were discovered in air filters at Knolls Atomic Power Laboratory facilities located 11 and 26 miles from the National Lead plant. Unrelated to the discovery of the DU particles in the laboratory's air filters, the State of New York later shut down the National Lead plant because each month they were releasing into the air around Albany, New York, a quantity of DU roughly equal to that contained in one 30mm round.[49] Note that the Air Force fired almost one million of these rounds during Desert Storm.

Most of the troops at Doha were unaware of the risks posed by burning DU rounds, even though an Explosive Ordnance Disposal (EOD) team en route to Doha while the fire was raging warned its commanders of the danger. A Central Command log for July 11, 1991, notes:

> EOD POC (point of contact) states that burning depleted uranium puts off alpha radiation. Uranium particles when breathed can be hazardous. 11ACR has been notified to treat the area as though it were a chemical hazard area; i.e. stay upwind and wear protective mask in the vicinity.[50]

A Radiological Contamination (RADCON) team sent to Doha after the fire confirmed that the fire caused oxidization and dispersal of DU:

> The radiological contamination seemed to be confined to specific locations of the concrete pad surfaces and specific vehicles. ... Elevated levels of localized DU contamination, above normal background levels, were detected. In some

instances, verification could not be made that these levels were associated with the DU munitions or from DU armor.[51]

Soldiers involved in cleanup operations several days after the fire were not warned of the presence of DU contamination, and wore no protective gear during or after the fire, despite the warning from the Explosive Ordnance Disposal team. In one incident, several soldiers were sent in to clean the compound with no protective clothing or masks. During the hot summer day, these soldiers repeatedly drew water from a jug which they had placed on some 55 gallon drums. Near the end of the day, several officers appeared and ordered the soldiers to move the water jug. The officers then placed radioactive contamination warning markers on the drums, which contained DU penetrator fragments.[52]

U.S. troops were exposed to DU at Doha during both the fire and subsequent cleanup operations. Although a warning was issued about the dangers presented by burning DU, this word was apparently never passed on to the troops. The Army does not know, or will not release the data, about how much DU was carried downwind, and what threat from unremediated DU exists today for troops deployed to the U.S. base at Doha.[53]

Other Exposures
In addition to the thousands of troops who passed through areas contaminated with DU, many others were more than likely exposed to DU as a result of the war. Soldiers and civilians downwind of burning vehicles on the battlefields could have been exposed to airborne DU. A-10 and M1A1 maintenance crews may have come in contact with DU in the course of their work. Medical personnel may have been exposed to DU when they treated wounded soldiers and civilians. In fact, recent testimony at a meeting of the Presidential Advisory Committee on Gulf War Veterans' Illnesses suggested that some medical personnel were afraid to work on people who had been wounded by uranium shrapnel.[54]

Though the routes of exposure are numerous, the largest numbers of people exposed to DU during and after the Persian Gulf War are those who came in contact with some of the more than 300 tons of DU scattered among the wreckage on the battlefield. The United States has denied any responsibility for the cleanup of DU on battlefields in Kuwait and Iraq, and as a result, virtually no battlefield cleanup of DU has taken place.[55]

Local populations, and U.S. troops who continue to deploy to Kuwait and train in battlefield areas, are being exposed to DU on an ongoing basis. In addition, because DU particles can be transported by wind or water, the contamination may be migrating to other areas and possibly into the food and water supplies of local populations.

Health Effects

The long term effects of internalized depleted uranium are not fully known, but the Army has admitted that "if DU enters the body, it has the potential to generate significant medical consequences."[56] Inhaled DU particles of respirable size may become permanently trapped in the lungs. Inhaled DU particles larger than respirable size may be expelled from the lungs and ingested.

DU may also be ingested via hand-to-mouth transfer or contamination of water or food supplies. DU which is ingested, or enters the body through wound contamination, will enter the bloodstream and migrate throughout the body, with most of it eventually concentrating in the kidney, bone, or liver. The kidney is the organ most sensitive to DU toxicity.[57]

Much of the ingested DU will be excreted by the body shortly after the exposure, but the DU that remains acts as a chemical and radiological toxin in organs and bones for the remainder of a person's lifetime. Because many of the soldiers exposed to DU during the war were in their twenties, they have many years in which to develop the cancers, kidney problems, and other health problems. Veterans who have shown elevated levels of DU in their urine several years after the war may have received significant internal DU exposures on the battlefield. For those who have not yet been tested, urinalysis may no longer be effective for determining levels of internalized DU.

Reports from Iraq indicate that large numbers of children who lived in or near contaminated areas have developed leukemias and other health problems which may be associated with exposure to DU.[58] In addition, many children of American veterans exposed to DU have been born with birth defects and serious health problems. The relationship between exposure to DU and the health problems affecting American and Iraqi children needs to be further investigated.

The Army admits that it has not fully assessed the risks to troops who are exposed to DU on the battlefield.[59] However, they now have a large soldier and civilian control group in which they will study the long term health effects of internalized DU.

Research

In its rush to field DU weapons for battlefield use, the Army failed to exercise enough vision to consider the health and environmental consequences of DU use. Only since the Persian Gulf War has the Army begun to assess the extent to which even its own troops may be exposed on the battlefield. The 1995 AEPI report noted that "previous studies of the health and environmental consequences of the use of DU have indicated that the Army needs to conduct several additional investigations to more fully understand its consequences."[60]

Additional studies are needed, but we cannot trust the Army to do them. Even the Army's own AEPI report recommended that:

> Reports should be reviewed inside and outside DoD to increase the number of expert reviewers and to enhance the credibility of reports. Independent peer review is crucial because too often studies are performed by or for an organization that has a vested interest in the results.[61]

Unfortunately, most of the current research on DU is being conducted by the military, industrial, and federal organizations which have a "vested interest" in the continued use of DU weapons. In addition to removing all research from the hands of these vested interests, previous studies which are invoked by the Army to deny that troops were exposed to DU should be reviewed for their accuracy.

Though several studies are underway to further investigate the health and environmental consequences of depleted uranium weapons, the motivation behind these investigations is unclear. The following section from the introduction of the AEPI report, which was leaked to the Depleted Uranium Citizens' Network of the Military Toxics Project in late 1995, is particularly enlightening in this respect:

> The potential for health effects from DU exposure is real; however, it must be viewed in perspective. It is unlikely that any of the DU exposure scenarios described in this report will significantly affect the health of most personnel. In several areas, neither the scientific community nor the Army have adequate medical or exposure information to defend this assertion. ... When DU is indicted as a causative agent for

Desert Storm illness, the Army must have sufficient data to separate fiction from reality. Without forethought and data, the financial implications of long-term disability payments and health-care costs would be excessive.[62]

The Army admits that it lacks the data needed to justify its assertions that few troops were exposed to DU on the battlefield, and that the health effects from battlefield DU exposure will not be significant. In addition, the Army appears to state that the primary motivating force driving their research and positions on DU weapons is a desire to avoid the "excessive" cost of disability compensation and health care for veterans exposed to depleted uranium.

In response to a congressional inquiry, Dr. Stephen Joseph, the Assistant Secretary of Defense for Health Affairs, clearly stated the Pentagon's position on DU:

> The Department of Defense fully recognizes the problems associated with DU in combat. However, the use of this material in shielding designs for combat vehicles substantially increases personnel survivability on the battlefield. In addition, the significant increase in the range of DU munitions provides the kind of tactical advantage that is important in reducing the casualty rate for our forces.[63]

The Pentagon, and the American public, are concerned about reducing battlefield casualties. However, in the process of increasing battlefield survivability, the Pentagon has found it acceptable to sacrifice the long-term health of its own troops by exposing them to depleted uranium. If we allow the Pentagon or other federal agencies to conduct further research about DU, we can expect their "forethought and data" to be driven by a desire to deny and minimize the health and environmental consequences of depleted-uranium weapons.

Conclusion

The Persian Gulf War was the first war in which DU weapons were used, but it will not be the last. DU rounds are being developed for use in an increasing array of U.S. weapons systems, including the Bradley Fighting Vehicle, the Vulcan air defense gun, and a variety of combat helicopters. The AEPI report ominously notes:

> Since DU weapons are openly available on the world arms
> market, DU weapons will be used in future conflicts. ... The
> number of DU patients on future battlefields probably will be
> significantly higher because other countries will use systems
> containing DU.[64]

Though the U.S. was the first country to use DU weapons in war, the
United Kingdom, France, Russia, Sweden, Greece, Turkey, Israel,
Saudi Arabia, Jordan, Bahrain, Egypt, Kuwait, Pakistan, Japan,
Thailand, Taiwan, South Korea, and other countries are now
developing or have already developed DU weapons in their arsenals.[65]
The rapid proliferation of depleted uranium weapons will eventually
level the playing field and eliminate any battlefield advantage U.S.
armed forces currently enjoy. In addition, if past wars give us any
insight into the future, American troops may be killed or poisoned on
the battlefield by "enemy" forces using DU weapons made in the
U.S.A.

DU weapons are a symptom of a larger problem. That problem is
war. The causes of war—greed, profit, racism, religion, injustice, and
ethnocentrism—have not changed much throughout history. But the
tools used to wage wars have changed to such an extent that, in just
the last century, the weapons of war now threaten the "survivability"
of life on our planet.

Starting today, we must clean up contaminated sites in the U.S., the
Middle East, and wherever else DU weapons are being developed,
tested and used. We must provide medical care and disability
compensation for those who have already been poisoned by DU. And
the Pentagon must begin periodic testing of servicemen and women
who work with or are otherwise exposed to depleted uranium
weapons.

As soon as possible, we must ban the development and use of
weapons containing depleted uranium. Like land mines, nuclear
weapons, herbicides such as Agent Orange, and chemical and
biological weapons, depleted uranium weapons can kill friend and foe
indiscriminately, for an extended time after their intended battlefield
use. A ban of depleted uranium weapons, and all other weapons of
mass destruction, is in the best interests of all Americans, and in the
best interests of all the earth's peoples.

References

1. U.S. Army Environmental Policy Institute (AEPI), *Health and Environmental Consequences of Depleted Uranium Use in the U.S. Army: Technical Report*, June 1995, p. 4.

2. *Ibid.*, pp. 10, 24

3. Bureau of National Affairs, Inc.: Daily Report for Executives, "Public Input Sought on Depleted Uranium/DOE to Assess Disposition of 505,000 Tons," February 7, 1996.

4. AEPI, *op. cit.*, p. 94.

5. U.S. Navy, Pacific Missile Test Center Cruise Missile Recovery instruction, COMPMTCINST 8800.1, May 14, 1984, quoted in Bukowski, et. al., *Uranium Battlefields Home and Abroad*, March 1993, p. 54.

6. U.S. General Accounting Office (GAO), *Operation Desert Storm: Early Performance Assessment of Bradleys and Abrams*, GAO/NSIAD-92-94, January 1992, p. 3.

7. AEPI, *op. cit.*, p. 39.

8. AEPI, *op. cit.*, p. A-10.

9. Dunnigan, J., and Bay, A., *From Shield to Storm*, 1992, p. 294.

10. *Ibid.*, p. 295.

11. *Ibid.*, pp. 295-296.

12. Lopez, D., *Friendly Fire: The Link Between Depleted Uranium Munitions and Human Health Risks*, March, 1995, p. 3.

13. Lowenstein, p. , "Industrial Uses of Depleted Uranium," photocopy in Bukowski, et.al., *Uranium Battlefields Home and Abroad*, March 1993, p. 136.

14. Dunnigan, *op. cit.*, pp. 285-286.

15. AEPI, *op. cit.*, p. 78.

16. U.S. Army Armament, Munitions, and Chemical Command, "Depleted Uranium Facts," photocopy in Bukowski, et. al., *Uranium Battlefields Home and Abroad*, March 1993, p. 97.

17. Bukowski, G., Lopez, D., and McGehee, F., *Uranium Battlefields Home and Abroad*, March 1993, p. 44.

18. AEPI, *op. cit.*, p. 125.

19. Dietz, L., "Contamination of Persian Gulf War Veterans and Others by Depleted Uranium," July 19, 1996, p. 6.

20. AEPI, *op. cit.*, p. 123.

21. AEPI, *op. cit.*, p. 102.

22. GAO, *Early Performance Assessment of Bradleys and Abrams, op. cit.*, p. 24.

23. *Ibid.*

24. Dunnigan, *op.cit.*, p. 294-295.

25. U.S. General Accounting Office, *Operation Desert Storm: Army Not Adequately*

Prepared to Deal with Depleted Uranium Contamination, GAO/NSIAD-93-90, January 1993, p. 4.

26. AEPI, *op. cit.*, pp. 78-79.

27. GAO, *Army Not Prepared to Deal with Depleted Uranium Contamination, op. cit.*, p. 3.

28. Brewer, N., and Hanchette, J., "Veterans still carry uranium shrapnel from gulf war," Gannett News Service, March 12, 1996.

29. Brewer, N., and Hanchette, J., "Some vets say they have not been monitored for radiation exposure," Gannett News Service, March 12, 1996.

30. Daxon, E. and Musk, J.H., "Assessment of the Risks from Imbedded Depleted Uranium Fragments," U.S. Armed Forces Radiobiology Research Institute (AFRRI), March 25, 1992, p. 1.

31. *Ibid.*, p. 7.

32. GAO, *Army Not Adequately Prepared to Deal with Depleted Uranium Contamination, op. cit.*, p. 17.

33. GAO, *Army Not Adequately Prepared to Deal with Depleted Uranium Contamination, op. cit.*, p. 23.

34. AEPI, *op. cit.*, p. 128.

35. AEPI, *op. cit.*, p. 102.

36. AEPI, *op. cit.*, p. 134.

37. AEPI, *op. cit.*, p. 101.

38. AEPI, *op. cit.*, p. 119.

39. AEPI, *op. cit.*, p. 101.

40. Judd, D., "Current Findings: A Health Survey of 10,051 Ill Gulf War Veterans," presented to Presidential Advisory Committee on Gulf War Veterans' Illnesses, November 7, 1995, San Francisco, CA.

41. Headquarters U.S. Army Armament, Munitions and Chemical Command, message 072130Z MAR 91 on "Depleted Uranium Contamination," photocopy in Bukowski, et. al., Uranium Battlefields Home and Abroad, *op. cit.*, p. 93.

42. U.S. Army Armament, Munitions and Chemical Command, "Depleted Uranium Facts," *op. cit.*

43. Testimony of Dr. Stephen P. Shelton to Presidential Advisory Committee on Gulf War Veterans' Illnesses, August 6, 1996, Denver, Colorado, p. 239.

44. U.S. Army Safety Center, Army Accident Report 910711001, September 20, 1991, "Estimated Cost of Damage."

45. *Ibid.*, "Injury Analysis."

46. *Ibid.*, "Injury Analysis."

47. Mishima, J., Parkhurst, M.A., Scherpelz, R.I., and Hadlock, D.E., *Potential Behavior of Depleted Uranium Penetrators Under Shipping and Bulk Storage Accident Conditions*, Battelle Pacific Northwest Labs, PNL-5415, February 1985, p. v.

48. U.S. Army Safety Center, *op. cit.*: "Weather Data."

49. Dietz, L., *op. cit.*, p. 6.

50. United States Central Command log, "11ACR Fire in Doha: Updates from CENTCOM Forward," July 12, 1991, entry 10.

51. U.S. Army Communications-Electronics Command, letter from Safety Office Chief to Freedom of Information Act Officer, June 21, 1996, pp. 2-3.

52. Triplett, W., "Passing Gulf War Syndrome to the Next Generation," *VVA Veteran*, June 1996, p. 17.

53. U.S. Army Communications-Electronics Command, *op. cit.*, pp. 2, 3.

54. Testimony of Dr. Stephen P. Shelton to Presidential Advisory Committee on Gulf War Veterans' Illnesses, *op. cit.*, p. 239-240.

55. AEPI, *op. cit.*, p. 154.

56. AEPI, *op. cit.*, p. 101.

57. AEPI, *op. cit.*, p. 110.

58. Casa, K., "Iraq Embargo Toll Now Surpasses War's Horrors," *Washington Report on Middle East Affairs*, July/August, 1995, p. 105.

59. AEPI, *op. cit.*, p. 126.

60. AEPI, *op. cit.*, p. 91.

61. AEPI, *op. cit.*, p. 96.

62. AEPI, *op. cit.*, p. 4.

63. Letter from Dr. Stephen Joseph, Assistant Secretary of Defense for Health Affairs, to Senator Diane Feinstein, June 5, 1996.

64. AEPI, *op. cit.*, pp. 119-120.

65. AEPI, *op. cit.*, p. A-2.

6 | Living with Gulf War Syndrome

From our medical unit of 150 who went to the front, forty are sick, six have died from homicides, suicides, heart attacks and cancer. Washington told me I couldn't get tested for depleted uranium because I hadn't been hit by friendly fire.

CAROL H. PICOU

It has been six years now that we Gulf War veterans have been fighting for our health. The Vietnam Veterans took 22 years to bring out the issue of Agent Orange. This is an Agent Orange of the nineties for the Persian Gulf veterans. We need your help.

Before I get started, I would also like to thank my husband who is still with me after everything we've been through. I have a nine-year old boy who has been going through a lot since we came home from the Persian Gulf War.

I served my country willingly. I volunteered for patriotic reasons. I wanted to help, and joined the military. I became a drug and alcohol medical health counselor. I counseled Vietnam veterans.

I then changed my career to become a nurse. Because I had a little pull, I became a licensed practical nurse and was getting ready to get my commission. I spent five years in Germany, I went to Africa, I had many opportunities to travel, including to Korea. I spent seven years in foreign lands.

I was back in the United States after returning from Germany. I signed in on the first of August [1990] and I was alerted for the war on the second of August. I was deployed to the Persian Gulf War.

I went willingly. Unfortunately, during the Persian Gulf War the women weren't widely accepted over there and so the command decided the women would stay in the rear and the men would go forward. Our unit split. We had 300; 150 were going to the front and 150 were staying in the rear.

We were the foremost hospital going into Iraq, going into Basra, going into Kuwait. We had to make a jump. Everywhere there was a battle zone we would jump, take care of the wounded, the sick, and move on. Surprisingly when that war started, when the coalition ground forces started moving out, the Iraqi troops surrendered.

A lot of the Iraqis surrendered to us; we gave them every opportunity to surrender. Coalition planes dropped leaflets, troops raised chants to surrender, and the Iraqis surrendered willingly.

In Iraq though, as we drove on the back desert, into the desert, not even a highway, there was just a road that was created for us.

There was ammunition lying everywhere, there were rounds lying everywhere, there were bunkers that were blown up, and we passed through this unprotected, our medical unit of 150. I was included as I was the next highest ranking female. Because seven men refused to go to the front, I had to take seven other women. We who went to the front are all sick. The men who stayed in the rear are perfectly healthy and they got awards. We got nothing.

So what happened in the front? Out of 150 who went to the front, forty are sick, six have died from homicides, suicides, and heart attacks and cancer. Once we hit the highway we saw vehicles there and in the desert that weren't just burning, they were charred beyond recognition. They weren't destroyed, they were just burned. The bodies were charred as black as this microphone. I had never seen anything like that before, though I have seen other burns from the Flugtag disaster at the Ramstein Air Force Base in Germany—I served there for eight hours body-bagging. I had never seen this.

I took photos. I stopped my vehicle and I took photos along the highway. There were things I had never seen before. I was concerned. Driving down the highway—we called it the "highway to hell"—you know it as the "highway of death"—we thought for sure we were going to die on that road. There were bodies everywhere, burning vehicles, and we were not warned of anything. No one warned us of contaminants.

We were stuck in that convoy for over two hours. There were hundreds of tanks rolling out in front of us. We had to pull off and let the tanks pass us. As we headed into Basra, we had to pull our hospital off the road. We pulled in a half a mile off the road and set up our hospital and started treating casualties. We saw over 150 people—Iraqi civilians, babies, nomads who had stepped on land mines as they were out walking with their sheep, POWs who came in malnourished, people suffering from urine retention. It was just unbelievable what we saw. We treated them, we stayed there for fifteen days, unprotected, with all types of artillery around us.

As the division was leaving, the command decided they were going to blow up the bunkers, so we had to remain and help the Explosive Ordnance Division in case there were any accidents. So our hospital had to stay and support the Explosive Ordnance Division. We did that.

When I was in Iraq I started noticing these black specks all over my skin, so I reported it. My health started changing. I was getting sick, I couldn't control my bowels and my bladder anymore. After we pulled out of Iraq and started cleaning our equipment to return to the United States, I went on sick call.

They said it had to be something mechanical, you need to have it checked once you return back to the United States. I did that my first night home. I said to my husband, something is wrong with me, I don't feel the same, my brain doesn't feel the same, my body doesn't feel the same. Something happened over there, and I knew it wasn't combat stress because that war was so quick and so rapid. I have been in worse situations than that war.

So I started seeking answers, and as I started seeking answers, I was threatened with losing my military career—and that happened. I went public to find out what is going on with the Desert Storm soldiers, why the people in our unit are sick. An atomic veteran called me and said, "You have depleted uranium poisoning."

Well, what's depleted uranium? I had no idea what that was. We knew we took anthrax as a vaccine against the disease anthrax. We took the experimental drug for Botulinum Pentavalent. The pyridostigmine—the experimental pills our government gave us—I knew of, but what was depleted uranium? So a member from the Military World Alliance of Accountability called and she said, "You have depleted uranium poisoning."

Okay, what is that? I can research that.

I started to look at what depleted uranium is and how I could get tested for this. I called Washington. They told me I couldn't get tested because I wasn't hit with friendly fire. Okay ... but if you can ingest these particles and breathe these particles, then I should be able to be tested. These particles can travel up to sixty miles.

When the wind blows, those particles blow. We had storms, wind storms every day in Iraq. They were blowing everywhere. So I said okay, let me figure this out. How can I get tested? So I went to a civilian doctor. They said since two years have passed, they would need two weeks of my urine to find these contaminants, and it is very expensive. Then I would have to find a laboratory outside the United States that would test it.

I called my congressman and I asked him if I could be tested for uranium. I finally got tested February of 1994. My results came back positive for uranium. The doctor read it to me on September 10, 1994, and said, "This is nothing to be worried about, it's just indicative of living in San Antonio."

I said, "Excuse me." I didn't want to argue because now I was educated about depleted uranium. I came to Washington, we did a press release. The book came out on battlefields home and abroad. I just accepted it. I said I want my copies. [Bukowski, G., Lopez, D. and McGehee, F., *Uranium Battlefields Home and Abroad*]

So I tested positive, I said. I've been living in San Antonio, but I was only there one day and two months, and then got sent to the war for five months. Then I came back, and now I have depleted-uranium poisoning. There are no uranium mines in San Antonio, there are no tanks, there are no aircraft. How did I get exposed to DU living in San Antonio?

This weapon is scary. To look at me you would think there is nothing wrong with me. But it's a false impression. My husband writes my speeches for me because I can't follow them, so most of the time he writes them. But I don't read them because I get lost. I have long-term/short-term memory deficit. I have toxic encephalopathy—a disease of the brain. I have developed thyroid deterioration.

We Gulf War veterans have our babies born without thyroids. Our atomic veterans suffered from thyroid cancer. I am on synthroid for the rest of my life now. I have developed suspicious squamous cancerous cells of the uterus. I have tested twelve times for the military and they want to keep repeating my tests. My muscles have deteriorated.

I have no control over my bowels or my bladder at all any more. The army issued me diapers and said that I could catheterize myself for the rest of my life. I've been catheterizing myself since January of 1992. I've been wearing diapers for the same time.

Our babies are born with birth defects. When I came home I used all the drugs that they gave us. I had my tubes tied. I was afraid I would have a child born with birth defects. These babies here on the front of *Life* magazine [begins showing enlarged photographs to audience] are born with birth defects. This baby is one of the babies from my support group in San Antonio, made up of 125 families affected by the illness. He is missing his ear and his eye, and his heart is on the wrong side.

This baby was born in Iraq. This photo was sent to me from Iraq. The baby has the same birth defects [points to a picture]. This baby looks just like CJ, our American baby. What happened over there? They claim that these are from rounds that are left in the sand in Iraq. These are babies who were born with these club feet, same as our

American babies. There are babies with these blood vessels, Iraqi babies and American babies, same thing. What happened over there?

These are our compounds, how we set up our hospitals over there, in the sand. So were we exposed? I keep asking. I keep getting told that I don't fall into that category. Yet, on March 8 of 1991, during the war, this report came out written by Major Woodworth and I'm going to read it to you. It is about depleted uranium.

"Any systems containing DU ammunition and involved in a fire can be assumed to be contaminated with DU. Previous experience indicates that the only significant contamination is from inside the system. Any system struck by a DU penetrator can be assumed to be contaminated. Personnel should avoid entering contaminated systems unless life or property is impacted. The DU contamination hazard is not significant enough to preclude entry in these cases. Personnel should wear gloves when handling suspected DU rounds. Mop gear should be worn."

We weren't warned of any of that. I have photos of me sitting there in Iraq with other soldiers, not in uniform, no gloves, we handled these patients, we climbed in and out of the tanks, we retrieved bodies. Here I am in this picture with all these soldiers, no mop gear on, no gloves on.

Were we warned? No. These were their vehicles, you can't see them. These were the Iraqi vehicles still burning as we're passing by, hit with DU rounds. This is the highway where they were destroyed. That's where we left the contaminants. Here they are blowing up the bunkers around us.

Were we exposed to this? I'll never have the answer. The Department of Defense refused to test me, to see me, to answer my questions. I have developed skin burns that used to be a rash and this is what I look like this week. From here down I'm filled with blisters [Points to her abdomen].

I saw the doctor in February of this year. My scheduled appointment is September 18, 1996—next week. Will they lie to me then? Most likely that will be what happens. My next appointment will be six months from then.

Today we are asking you to stand with these people organizing to ban DU. I was in the military for seventeen years. I served my country for seventeen years. If you ask any Vietnam veteran, any Desert Storm veteran, would we serve again? We serve the people. We serve for our country. We serve and protect. We stand by our fallen soldiers. We hold their hands as they are dying. We would do it again.

Do we trust our Department of Defense, who has denied us medical care and treatment? We can't get answers. We have formed groups and come together to try to get our own answers. We started a MISSION Project—that stands for "military issue service in our nation" and it will continue research into the causes of the illness.

My goal is to bring twenty other Desert Storm soldiers and go through the same extensive testing that I've had through a civilian doctor. However, since then I've lost my military career and my husband has lost his career. I've also lost my private health insurance and life insurance because the insurance companies say my illness is combat-related. Yet when the Department of Defense discharged me last March, it called my illness non-combat-related.

I received this document September 1994 anonymously. This is a secret document. The same week I received my positive results on depleted uranium. In 1992 I was diagnosed by a civilian as suffering from toxic exposure chronic encephalopathy of the brain, an abnormal active immune system, a suppressed auto-immune system and antibody development and chemical poisoning. The army would not accept this as "mainstream medicine" for my medical board and I was discharged with "Bowel and Bladder Incontinence—Etiology Unknown."

This report, in this list done in 1994, says that the soldiers will have been exposed to—as a result of the transportation tank foreman who ordered the use of a petroleum tank for hauling bathwaters—in addition to the above exposures, petroleum products, medications, parasites, chemicals, radiation, including depleted uranium, asbestos and paint. Also included is radioactive dust from armored vehicles struck by depleted uranium munitions and down-low chemical fallout.

They admitted it for the first time in this report. They know exactly, and do you know what they said after this, all the exposures? Typically the assorted symptoms take on the following sequential steps: toxic exposures, chemical poisoning, development of abnormal immune systems, and development of abnormal antibodies.

Two years prior to this report I was diagnosed with this and they wouldn't accept it because it wasn't "military medicine." Now we find that in a secret report dated June 1994 they apparently don't know the effects of this uranium. Yet they had all the information.

I stand with you today to fight for your sons and your daughters, the mothers and fathers, whoever went and whoever is over there now, and also for the people of Iraq who are suffering from the contaminants left behind in their land. I hope that you will join us in our fight now. Thank you.

(From a talk given September 12, 1996 at the UN Church Center in New York.)

7 | Another Human Experiment

Despite the army's own admission of health and environmental concerns, depleted-uranium arms are being proliferated largely by U.S. arms sales. The Military Toxics Project and the Depleted Uranium Citizens' Network are exposing DU dangers.

DOLORES LYMBURNER

The Military Toxics Project works to unite activists, organizations, and communities in the struggle to clean up military pollution, to safeguard the transportation of hazardous materials, and to advance the development and implementation of preventive solutions to the toxic and radioactive pollution caused by military activities.

MTP believes that the United States government should assume responsibility for the pollution it has created by funding remediation to the highest standards of protection for health and the environment. It is our position that the military should be the nation's leader in pollution prevention, containment, cleanup, energy conservation and materials recycling.

MTP's membership is composed of individuals, organizations, regional campaigns and networks working on military toxics issues. When a specific issue concerns a number of our members and has the support of our Board, a Network is established. MTP's Networks have included, for example: Rocket Toxics, Chemical Weapons, Base Closure, Conventional Munitions, Electromagnetics and Depleted Uranium.

The Depleted Uranium Citizens' Network began its work in 1992 and introduced itself to the public in March of 1993 with the release of a report entitled *Uranium Battlefields Home and Abroad*. This report was written by DU Network members, the Rural Alliance for Military Accountability, the Progressive Alliance for Community Empowerment, and Citizen Alert. The DU Network's membership consists of people living near uranium enrichment plants, near facilities where DU munitions are made; former workers at those facilities, people living near where DU weapons are tested; and both Persian Gulf Veterans and Atomic Veterans.

In the 1940s and 1950s thousands of American citizens and soldiers were exposed to nuclear fallout from bomb tests. High numbers of these exposed populations have suffered from cancers and genetic effects as a result of those tests. Our country has a poor record on how it has treated military service men and women and private citizens who are exposed to toxic and radioactive poisoning, most of the time without their knowledge or consent.

Atomic Veterans have expressed their concern for the new generation of radiation-exposed veterans. In the Persian Gulf War depleted uranium was used for the first time as tank armor and armor piercing bullets. It was effective on the battlefield, melting through and destroying Iraqi armored vehicles. Iraqi victims of DU were charred in their tanks. DU also accounted for most of our "friendly fire" deaths. Thirty-three of our United States veterans carry DU fragments and many many more were exposed to DU dust particles.

We also left behind us in the Persian Gulf a radioactive battlefield of about 350 tons of DU particles and fragments. The DU particles can travel anywhere that dust can. Of Iraq the Washington Report on Middle East Affairs states, "Health officials have reported alarmingly high increases in rare and unknown diseases, primarily in children." These health officials have reported an increase in leukemia and aplastic anemia.

Birth defects have risen from eight percent before the war to twenty-eight percent. In children over the age of five, liver and kidney disease are the fourth and fifth causes of death. Given that the conditions in Iraq—the lack of proper nutrition and adequate health care—may be a contributory factor, the statistics are still alarming. Dr. Siegwart Guenther of Austria's Yellow Cross attributes much of this increase in childhood disease to depleted uranium. [See Chapter 23.]

The U.S. Senate instructed the Army to commission a report on the health and environmental effects of DU. The Army Environmental Policy Institute, hired to do the report, completed its study in June of 1995 but would not release it. The DU Network had a copy of the report leaked to us and we released it on the fifth anniversary of the Gulf War, January 16, 1996. We also at that time released our response to the Army's report.

The Army's report *Health and Environmental Consequences of Depleted Uranium Use in the U.S. Army* contradicts itself because its conclusions are inconsistent with its scientific findings. The report documents the enormous problems that exist and the radioactive toxic nature of DU. The report acknowledges that "If DU enters the body, it has the potential to generate significant medical consequences. The risks associated with DU in the body are both chemical and radiological. ..." Although the AEPI admits that there is no technology to mitigate DU's deadly radioactive and chemical effects or to clean up contaminated sites, it approved the continued use of DU munitions.

There are more than fifty current and former sites in the U.S. which have been involved in production, manufacture, development, testing and storage of DU. Firing ranges in Madison, Indiana; Yuma, Arizona; and Aberdeen, Maryland have not and may never be able to be cleaned up. Citizens living around the munitions production plant in Concord, Massachusetts, Nuclear Metals Inc., found DU-contaminated soil almost a mile away from the plant. NMI has four hundred thousand pounds of uranium wastes in an unlined pit. Ground water and bedrock and a nearby cranberry bog are contaminated.

Workers at the production plant in Jonesboro, Tennessee went out on strike because of health problems. All of these fifty-plus sites have just begun to face their health and environmental consequences.

Despite the concern of citizens and veterans and despite the Army's own admission of health and environmental concerns, DU arms are being proliferated largely by U.S. arms sales. Sales of DU or DU arms to Britain, France, Canada, Saudi Arabia and Kuwait have been approved. Other countries are in the process or have developed this technology. Without concerted international action this proliferation will continue. Radioactive and chemical weapons are internationally regarded as unacceptable because their effects cannot be directed or contained and because they cause slow, cruel suffering and death.

Civilians, descendants, passersby, and allies are all likely to be victims. DU is an avoidable and unnecessary disaster, one that can and should be stopped now. The Depleted Uranium Citizens' Network has as its mission the pursuit of an international ban on all weapons containing DU.

Section III:

The Politics of War and the Pentagon's Coverup

8 | A Tale of Two Syndromes: Vietnam and Gulf War

The generals plan their high-tech battles so that no one at home sees U.S. troops killed. If GIs die years after the battle—as they would from DU poisoning—the generals hope to limit protest.

JOHN CATALINOTTO

The Pentagon's use of depleted-uranium weapons brings an important contradiction to the fore: the vast goals of the U.S. military on one hand and its need to minimize casualties among its troops on the other. With DU weapons the Pentagon postpones casualties and avoids responsibility for them.

A Pentagon document outlining its goals, called the *Defense Planning Guidance,* was leaked and then published in *The New York Times* on March 8, 1992. The document asserted complete U.S. world military and political domination, and threatened to punish any other nation that even aspired to rival U.S. power. The document implied this list of potential rivals included not only the latest demonized governments but even those major capitalist powers in Western Europe and the Pacific that were always allied to the U.S. as long as the USSR was their common enemy.

Any such broad plan for conquest requires at least some risk by the troops. Yet former Joint Chiefs head Colin Powell has made it clear that his military doctrine in the Gulf War—and it was shared by many of his colleagues—was to limit U.S. casualties for fear of losing political support at home. He would avoid battle unless the politicians could sell the aims of the war to the public. Then the military would go in with overwhelming force, hoping to win quickly and take almost no losses.[1]

That this could be Powell's public attitude shows how much has changed since World War I. There the first day of the British offensive at the Somme in France in August 1916 cost sixty thousand British casualties, including twenty thousand killed. The battle succeeded only in moving the British lines a few yards forward.[2]

The generals ordered troops to charge through machine-gun fire and gas attacks without worrying about popular resistance in the cities or disobedience at the front. It took all of three years of that great slaughter to incite revolution in Russia and four years to topple the Germany monarchy.

Times have changed. With vast profits from oil at stake in the

Gulf, the Bush administration was prepared to risk many GI lives—but managed to get away with only 147 U.S. troops killed in battle. The slaughter of the Iraqis was one-sided. In Mogadishu, Somalia, in 1993, the well-publicized deaths of only eighteen troops made the Clinton administration pull out.

That is where DU comes in. This dense material makes shells that penetrate and shields that block. It keeps casualties lower during battle, but imposes them later when the political costs are small.

The Vietnam Syndrome

During the U.S. war against Vietnam it started to become politically important for the brass to kept U.S. casualties low. And they were low compared with the horrors inflicted on the Vietnamese. But each death of a GI, each wound, raised the question in the minds of the rank-and-file troop: "What am I doing here?"

Whatever Washington politicians claimed, the U.S. military was in Vietnam to keep a colonial nation from fully liberating itself and from aligning with those countries that had thrown over capitalist property relations. No U.S. troops in Vietnam with their eyes open could believe they were saving Vietnamese "democracy" or that the Vietnamese people wanted them there.

Those of us who organized U.S. troops against the war in 1968 and 1969 saw the rapid growth of a powerful movement of rank-and-file GIs that would inevitably force the Department of Defense to change its whole strategy toward recruiting troops. And millions of youth at home came out against the war by the fall of 1969. This anti-war movement exerted a strong pull on the troops, especially the lower ranks.

An army reflects the society it is part of, without the subtleties. American capitalism is divided into classes; there are vast differences in privileges between rich and poor, but many gradations. With its sharply delineated chain of command, the military expresses those class differences crudely. Military attitudes also reflected the racism integral to ruling-class ideology in the United States since the days the slaveowners ran the country.

Sentiments against the Vietnam War were strong, and the growing opposition to it inside the military often took the form of rebellion by rank-and-file soldiers against their commissioned and non-commissioned officers. The favorite column in the GI newspaper I worked on, *The Bond,* was the one where troops nominated their commanders for "Pig of the Month."

By 1967, individual GIs were either deserting or outright refusing to go to Vietnam.[3] In August 1968, African American troops from Fort Hood, Texas, refused riot-control duty in Chicago.[4] By the early 1970s, entire units in Vietnam were refusing orders to go into battle. Sometimes after a sharp conflict with an officer, GIs might throw fragmentation grenades into their officers' tents. Even as the direct U.S. role in the war wound down, this form of resistance increased.[5] Called "fragging," this practice discouraged many officers from ordering aggressive patrolling.

This anti-war attitude among both the population and the troops was called "the Vietnam Syndrome." It was not a disease or a collection of symptoms, like Gulf War Syndrome. It was a healthy understanding by youth in general and young workers in the military that they had no interest in pursuing any war directed by Washington.

Toward a Volunteer Army

In 1973 the government decided to end involuntary conscription—the hated draft. The U.S. Armed Forces were to be completely volunteer. Now, twenty-four years later, the lower ranks of the U.S. military are filled with people who basically joined to get a job, training and education benefits, often because it appeared to be their only option. Some may have patriotic motives, but how many would look forward to one of those World War I trench warfare battles? Who would re-enlist?

For their relatives, indeed for most of the population, a battle with heavy casualties would arouse immediate protest. Therein lies the general staff's problem. They have to plan their high-tech battles so that no one sees U.S. troops being killed and injured. It must look like only the enemy can be hurt.

At least during the war.

If the troops grow ill or die in the months and years after the battle—as they would from DU poisoning—that has less importance for the generals. That becomes more of a problem for public relations rather than war or politics.

A Record of Contempt for the Troops

This contempt for the troops is nothing new for the Department of Defense. During the Cold War against the Soviet Union, the Pentagon experimented with radiation's impact on the Atomic Veterans, not even allowing them to talk publicly of their injuries and illnesses. And only a few hundred of the hundreds of thousands of Atomic Veterans have been compensated.

In Vietnam the Pentagon freely used herbicides containing Agent Orange to defoliate the Vietnamese countryside. This denied the revolutionary soldiers cover from the U.S. air war. It poisoned the Vietnamese environment and millions of Vietnamese. And it also poisoned thousands of U.S. troops.

The Pentagon continued to deny that the dioxin in Agent Orange was responsible for the health problems suffered by many U.S. veterans of the Vietnam War or for the congenital defects in their children. Finally in 1984 veterans who brought a class-action suit won a settlement out of court, which set up a modest fund that paid for a small part of their problems.

The military brass made the same choice regarding DU weapons. The Army was aware of the potential dangers—both to the environment and to its own troops—from low-level radiation emanating from the DU and especially from inhaled or ingested particles.

But using DU weapons added to the already huge advantage the U.S.-led Coalition had against Iraqi tanks. It helped the coalition destroy almost four thousand Iraqi tanks while taking almost no casualties—if you don't count those who breathed in DU oxide.

In the period building up to the Gulf War and at its beginning in mid-January 1991, a massive anti-war movement was underway in the United States. Hundreds of thousands of people demonstrated. Individuals refused to serve when their reserve units were called up. This movement developed more quickly than the similar movement against the war in Vietnam, which grew during 1965-1969 as the Vietnamese—with support from their allies—kept fighting despite their losses.

In the Gulf War, the low U.S. battle deaths, the managed news and seeming video-game war portrayed on CNN helped disguise the war's real costs. Before the anti-war movement could get a second wind, the war was over.

Casualties among U.S. troops from uranium poisoning or low-level radiation would not show up until long after Iraq was subdued and U.S. military domination of the Persian/Arabian Gulf region secured. Of course the Pentagon completely ignores the consequences to Iraqis, Kuwaitis and Saudis.

Gulf War Syndrome

The Pentagon has tried to maintain the illusion that it cares about its troops, that it doesn't just consider them cannon fodder. But when Gulf War veterans later started reporting medical problems, the Pentagon blamed wartime stress; that is, it blamed the soldiers themselves.

Not only those people interested in protecting the environment, or those wanting to protect U.S. enlisted people, or those who believe the world's population is threatened by this radioactive waste have an interest in banning DU. Those who want to arouse the population to stop new U.S. military adventures must make everyone aware how DU poisoning is part of the costs of war.

It is part of making the youth ask, as they did in Vietnam, "What am I doing here?"

One of the few U.S. generals who ever answered that question honestly was Maj. Gen. Smedley Butler, U.S. Marine Corps (ret.). He wrote in November 1935:

I spent thirty-three years [in the Marines] ... most of my time being a high-class muscle man for big business, for Wall Street and the bankers. In short, I was a racketeer, a gangster for capitalism. ... I helped purify Nicaragua for the international banking house of Brown Brothers in 1909-1912. I helped make Mexico and especially Tampico safe for American oil interests in 1914. I brought light to the Dominican Republic for American sugar interests in 1916. I helped make Haiti and Cuba a decent place for the National City Bank boys to collect revenues in. ... I helped in the rape of a half-dozen Central American republics for the benefit of Wall Street. In China in 1927 I helped see to it that Standard Oil went its way unmolested. ... Looking back on it, I feel I could have given Al Capone a few hints. The best he could do was to operate his racket in three city districts. I operated on three continents.[6]

Maj. Gen. Butler's exploits might be considered small potatoes today. Former Secretary of Defense Caspar Weinberger, in his 1996 book, *The Next War*, would have the Pentagon prepared for five war scenarios from Japan to the Gulf to Mexico,[7] with much greater spoils at stake. But the spoils from these operations go to only a tiny proportion of wealthy monopolists. They risk the lives of the rank-and-file troops, and provide nothing for their families and the working class they are part of.

The GIs should refuse to kill and die for a military that has these goals. And they should refuse to be exposed to depleted uranium.

References

1.   Powell, Colin and Joseph Persico, *An American Journey,* Ballantine Books, 1995, pp. 512-515.

2.   Winter, J.M., *The Experience of World War I,* Andromeda Oxford Limited, 1988, p. 92.

3.   Watts, Max, *U.S. Army—Europe, von der Desertion zur Wiederstand in der Kaserne,* Harald Kater, 1989, pp. 41-61.

4.   Stapp, Andy, *Up Against the Brass,* Simon and Schuster, 1970, pp. 145-168.

5.   Johnson, Haynes and George Wilson, *Army in Anguish,* Pocket Book, 1972, p. 92.

6.   Arevalo, Juan Jose, *The Shark and the Sardines,* Lyle Stuart, 1961, p. 249.

7.   Weinberger, Caspar and Peter Schwezer, *The Next War,* Regnery, 1996, Introduction.

9 | Military and Media Collaborate in Coverup of DU

The relationship between corporations, the Pentagon and the news media comprises a powerful trinity, with the Pentagon's military policies advancing the corporations' financial interests, and the media's corporate owners defining editorial policy.

LENORA FOERSTEL

In April 1994, Women for Mutual Security received an invitation to meet with members of the Iraqi women's organization in Baghdad. While in Baghdad, WMS delegates visited the Amiria bomb shelter. The shelter was considered safe for the eight hundred women and children who fled there during the Gulf War, yet a depleted-uranium projectile fired by a U.S. plane was able to penetrate the shelter's walls, killing every mother and child. Long after the mass burials of the victims, one can still see the imprint of their bodies pressed against the walls of the shelter.

A visit to a hospital in Baghdad revealed other insidious effects of the intensive Gulf War bombing campaign. In a special ward of newborn babies suffering from radiation diseases and mutations, babies had extra toes, fused fingers and missing ears. The young doctors attending the ward reported that the babies also had internal problems which had not been seen before the war. Many of the same symptoms seen among the Iraqi babies have appeared in the newborn of American soldiers who fought in the Gulf War.

Laura Flanders, journalist for *FAIR* magazine, published a report prepared by the U.S. Veterans Administration covering a state-wide survey done on 251 families of Gulf War veterans living in Mississippi. A study of their children conceived and born since the war shows that sixty-seven percent were born with severe eye defects or no eyes and ears. They also suffer from blood infections and respiratory problems.

New studies demonstrate that low-level radiation can cause genetic instability and cancer in the children of exposed parents. This means that the exposed persons may or may not die of cancer, but their offspring have a greater chance of inheriting the mutated cells.[1]

In 1991, a document was released by the Department of Defense stating: "The Defense Department and its contractors should address environmental concerns during the development, production, and maintenance of weapons systems."[2] Although the Department of Defense recognizes the environmental hazards of DU, it continues to include DU in ammunition, aircraft, and armored vehicle designs. Cruise missiles, like the Tomahawk, made by Hughes Aircraft Co., incorporates DU penetrators. "Cruise missiles have become one of the prestige items in the world arms market because of their accuracy and the fact they can be launched from air, land and sea" (Washington Post, Sept. 4, 1996, A23). The Pentagon boasts about the performance of the Tomahawk stating that, "It will go through a few feet of concrete, it will destroy a bunker, it will go through floors of an office building" (ibid).

While the media played up the new military technology being used in the Gulf War as "smart weapons," they did not report the death of some two hundred thousand people slaughtered by the allies, mainly by the U.S. and British forces.

Although the media claims to be free and independent, it has become a "second front" for the U.S. government. On military matters, journalists tend to serve as a second front against official enemies. This occurs because of a compliant press willing to accept arbitrary control and official misinformation. Even in the face of such media cheerleading, the American public is often unwilling to have their taxes increased or to sacrifice their sons and daughters in order to protect distant oil fields, air bases or corporate investments.

Pentagon Controls the Media
In order to orchestrate public opinion, the Pentagon has taken action to ensure that the kind of uncontrolled press access allowed during the Vietnam War would not be repeated in future military campaigns. In 1984, the Department of Defense commissioned a study of military press coverage, overseen by Brigadier General Winant Sidle, who as the military's chief of public affairs in Vietnam, had warned of a press "conspiracy." Sidle recommended the establishment of a "pool system" of controlled and supervised press access to military action, and in 1984 the Department of Defense Media Pool was formally created.

The first opportunity to implement the new pool system came with the 1989 invasion of Panama. The press pool plane was five hours late for the invasion, held up in order to keep the press out of Panama City when U.S. troops arrived. When reporters were finally allowed into the capital city, military escorts barred them from first-hand observation of combat areas. The full impact of this new system of military press control was to emerge several years later during the planning of Operation Desert Storm in the Persian Gulf. Here the military made sure that the roving reporters tolerated during the Vietnam War would be avoided through the system of press pools under tight military escort.

From the moment President Bush committed troops to Saudi Arabia, he had no intention of allowing the press to give a true picture of the war. On the home front, for the first time in memory, Americans saw messages such as "Cleared by U.S. Military," or "Cleared by Israeli Censors" on their television screens or newspapers.

In January 1991, a group of magazines, newspapers, radio stations and individual journalists brought suit in federal court challenging the Pentagon's restrictions on press coverage of the Gulf War. The suit claimed that the press controls imposed during the Gulf War could not be justified on national security grounds. The suit sought an injunction against hindering members of the press in their coverage of U.S. combat forces or prohibiting the press from areas where U.S. forces are deployed or engaged in combat, unless legitimate security reasons could be demonstrated. Before the suit could be carried out, Iraq withdrew from Kuwait and U.S. forces were withdrawn from Iraq. With press pool restrictions no longer enforced, the case was moot and the suit was dismissed.

The Gulf War was considered by most in the press to be the worst-covered major U.S. conflict of the twentieth century. There was broad consensus that the "pool" system had been inappropriately used by the government to control the news and shape American political opinion about the war.

The relationship between corporations, the Pentagon and the news media comprises an interesting and powerful trinity. The financial interests of corporations are advanced by the military policies of the Pentagon. The corporate owners of the major media in the U.S., in cooperation with the Pentagon, define the editorial policy which serves their interests, feeding appropriate stories to journalists and middle managers. They recruit "experts" and top academics to add credibility to corporate studies, and give businesses a strong voice on campuses and in the public sphere.

The Big Lie About Kuwaiti Babies

An important class of "experts" are the public relations firms which are increasingly employed by governments to control the initial image in a military action. Kuwait hired Hill and Knowlton, one of the largest and most politically connected public relations firms in the United States, to convince Congress and the public of Iraqi atrocities in Kuwait.

A story was circulated that Iraqi soldiers had removed 312 Kuwaiti babies from their incubators, leaving them to die on hospital floors. Soon the story became a regular part of political speeches and was instrumental in influencing Congress to support Operation Desert Storm. Only after the Gulf War had ended did the truth emerge. The entire baby atrocity story was fabricated by Hill and Knowlton.[3]

None of this deception seemed to bother the press. In fact, CBS News quickly hired General Schwarzkopf to host their war documentaries and engaged General Tom Kelly, the Pentagon's military spokesman during the Gulf War, to assist in its news decisions. NBC then hired Peter Williams, the enforcer from the Bush Administration's censorship system, and Richard Haass, National Security Council staff member.

Even today, headlines continue the second front against Iraq, relying on statements by Swedish Ambassador Rolf Ekeus, who chairs the U.N. Special Commission on Iraq. Ekeus, with the support of C.I.A. Director John Deutch, accuses Iraq of using warheads containing deadly substances. Conveniently, Ekeus and Deutch never mentioned the use of DU projectiles against Iraqi citizens during the Gulf War.

It is estimated that 50,000 Iraqi children died during the first eight months following the U.S. bombing from a variety of diseases seldom seen before the war. There were dramatically increased rates of kidney failure and cancer. Many of the same symptoms seen in Iraqi children have also appeared in the American and British soldiers who fired those projectiles from their tanks and planes. When it occurred in our soldiers, the media was content to label these symptoms as the "Gulf War Syndrome," a mysterious ailment without a cause.

The Institute of Medicine, which is affiliated with the National Academy of Sciences, reviewed the Defense Department's evaluation of Gulf War Syndrome and concluded that the military, having failed to find a physical cause for the syndrome, should consider psychological causes as well. This report was carried throughout the U.S.

media. One wonders how the war veterans managed to "psyche" their newborn into developing birth defects.

The United Nations Special Commission on Iraq spends approximately $75 million each year monitoring Iraq's now largely dismantled weapons program, while eleven thousand Iraqi children die each month of malnutrition and Iraqi newborns suffer birth defects caused by DU. Thirty percent of the money used to keep the UN Special Commission going, about $25 million, comes from Iraq's frozen assets in the United States.

'Surplus People'

We have entered into a period of time where a vast amount of the world's population is considered by the corporations and the military to be "Surplus People." Among the surplus are the Iraqi people, Palestinians, Africans, Native Americans, and even a large number of U.S. soldiers. International corporations are now determining western foreign policy and have set into motion military action against countries which are considered a threat to corporate interests.

These corporations have helped to develop a whole new generation of high technology weapons of war and have given the U.S. military the ability to dominate important communications and information processing technologies. The military today can boast of its superior control of space surveillance, direct broadcasting, and its unparalleled ability to integrate complex information systems. However, neither military officials nor the Pentagon seem able to identify the causes of Gulf War Syndrome.

By late August 1996 the Defense Department acknowledged that it knew as far back as November 1991 that chemical weapons had been stored at an Iraqi ammunition depot that U.S. troops demolished just months earlier. We are told that the Pentagon did not release this information because they failed to realize that U.S. troops had been at Kamisiryah in southern Iraq, and there was "not yet any public concern about the mysterious ailment known as Gulf War Syndrome" (Washington Post, Aug. 29, 1996: 9). Concealing information is not new for the Pentagon, and we are reminded of the many years of official secrecy and disinformation before the public was informed of the use of Agent Orange in Vietnam.

A vast portion of the American public appears to be unconcerned about U.S. foreign policy and military action. Media disinformation plays a large role in keeping the U.S. public complacent. Perhaps another reason for public silence is the belief that their economic security depends on jobs within the military-industrial complex. One out of every ten Americans works for the arms industry. This includes the Pentagon's civilian bureaucracy, intelligence organizations, defense laboratories, research centers, and military industries, as well as the millions of people who make up the armed forces.

As we take steps to expose the use of toxic weapons affecting the health of the world's peoples, we must also take action to convert our military economy into a civilian economy. Only through conversion can we address the drastic needs of our civilian population while removing the dependence on wars to fuel corporate profits. Equally important is the recognition that a true democracy can only exist if there is a free press.

The architects of media control prevent investigative journalism. A democracy can only succeed if its government has an independent source of information about its weaknesses and its citizens have sufficient knowledge to judge their government's performance. In this way, government is made responsible to its citizens. In the United States, the increasing control of the media by the Pentagon and the corporations makes a true democracy impossible. The American people have been kept ignorant of the horrible effects of wars, sanctions and the use of new military weapons which use depleted uranium to subdue Third World nations.

References

1. Bukowski, G.; D. Lopez and F. McGehee, eds. *Uranium Battlefields Home and Abroad*: Depleted Uranium Use, Citizens' Alert and Rural Alliance for Military Accountability, March 1993, p. 48

2. *Ibid.*, p. 51

3. Middle East Watch, "Kuwait's 'Stolen' Incubators: The Widespread Repercussions of a Murky Indicent," *White Paper,* Volume 4, Issue 1, February 6, 1992, p. 5

10 | Burying the Past,
Protecting DU Weapons for Future Wars

The Committee concludes that it is unlikely that health effect reports by Gulf War veterans today are the result of exposure to depleted uranium during the Gulf war.
—Final Report: Presidential Advisory Committee
on Gulf War Veterans Illnesses (PAC)[1]

TOD ENSIGN

With one sentence, a blue-ribbon panel of scientists and public health experts denied that the extensive use of depleted uranium during the Gulf War contributed, in any way, to the chronic health problems that have been reported by over ninety thousand veterans.

The Clinton administration created its PAC in May 1995 in response to growing criticism by Gulf War vets about the way their concerns were being handled by the Pentagon and the Veterans Administration.

President Clinton was undoubtedly happy to be able to showcase the PAC's Final Report on January 7, 1997, since it allowed him to broadcast his concerns about ailing vets while at the same time requiring him to do almost nothing about their problems. The report also boosted the Pentagon's efforts to keep one of its favorite new weapons—depleted uranium, free from any restrictions on future use.

Early in its report, the panel acknowledges that, "many of the health concerns of Gulf War veterans may never be resolved fully because of the lack of data." It dryly ticks off some of the problems; missing medical records, absence of baseline (pre-war) health data, inaccurate and incomplete data on troop locations and incomplete data on health risks that could have been anticipated.[2]

Although it concedes these deficiencies, the panel nonetheless was not deterred from concluding that eight risk factors in the Gulf War—chemical weapons, biological weapons, vaccines, pyridostigmine bromide (PB-an experimental nerve-gas antidote), infectious diseases, oil-well smoke and fires, petroleum products and depleted uranium, were not "causal[ly] link[ed]" to the health problems reported by Gulf vets.

The Pentagon was quick to claim a victory with the report's conclusions. "This is a very important finding and one on which the committee deliberated long and hard," crowed Assistant Defense Secretary for Health, Stephen Joseph, M.D.[3]

The process whereby the PAC determined that depleted uranium is not responsible for Gulf War illness is our concern here. A close examination of how this decision was made raises several important questions.

The PAC conclusion depends on a finding that it is impossible to test DU-exposed veterans today so that their risk from such exposures could be calculated. Dan Fahey discusses in some detail the Army Environmental Policy Institute's 1995 report on DU in his contribution to this book. That report makes a strong argument for the early testing of military personnel who may have been exposed to DU, e.g., "Measuring the quantity of DU a soldier internalized, as soon as practical after initial exposure, would improve the Army's ability to subsequently determine the significance of the exposure."[4]

The PAC report acknowledged that a large number of soldiers were potentially at risk from DU weapons: "U.S. service personnel also could have been exposed ... if they inhaled DU dust particles during incidental contact with vehicles destroyed by DU munitions or if they lived or worked in areas contaminated with DU dust from accidental munitions fires. Thus, unnecessary exposures of many individuals could have occurred."[5]

A month before Iraq invaded Kuwait, the Army's Armament, Munitions, and Chemical Command received a detailed report on DU weapons from a well-established military contractor, Science Applications International Corporation. It read in part: "Combat conditions will lead to the uncontrolled release of DU—Aerosol (airborne) DU exposures to soldiers on the battlefield could be significant with potential radiological and toxicological effects."

While acknowledging that it may be impossible to measure such exposures, the SAIC continued: "We are simply highlighting the potential for levels of exposure to military personnel during combat that would be unacceptable during peacetime."[6]

It is indisputable that the Army command knew before fighting commenced in the Gulf that GIs were at risk from exposure to DU weapons and that timely monitoring was medically prudent.[7]

Since there's no evidence that the Pentagon ever conducted any DU monitoring in the Gulf during or just after the war—when it would have done the most good—the PAC had no choice but to try to determine if it would be useful to monitor veterans years after the fact. Unfortunately, their investigation of this issue was half-hearted and tainted by relying on scientists with conflicts of interest.

Biased Experts: Bad Science?

The PAC clearly understood that many Gulf veterans distrust the Pentagon and other federal agencies because of the way they've responded to their health complaints. For this reason, the PAC's Final Report was willing to bruise egos at the Pentagon by recommending: "Any further investigation of possible chemical or biological agents during the Gulf War should be conducted by a group **independent** of DoD."[8] (emphasis added).

Yet, this same panel was willing to rely **solely** on advice from scientists employed by the nuclear bomb-making industry in reaching its conclusion that medical monitoring of Gulf vets today for DU contamination would serve no useful purpose.

In general, the PAC's evaluation of the DU issue was cursory. It took testimony on the issue at only one of its eighteen public meetings at Denver on August 4, 1996. There, only two scientific witnesses were heard on the DU monitoring issue.

Dr. George Voelz, a career scientist from the Los Alamos Labs, creator of the world's first atomic bomb, led off. Voelz's presentation on the health consequences of exposure to uranium minimized any long-term effects. He stated that the human body would excrete in one day sixty to seventy percent of the uranium particles absorbed in the blood via the kidneys. He estimated that an additional twenty percent would lodge in the bone, the body's principal storage site. The remaining ten percent would travel to other organs, primarily the liver.

According to Voelz, the decay rate (half-life) for these radioactive nuclides is about fifteen days. In other words, their radioactivity would be cut in half each succeeding fifteen-day period.

Dr. Voelz estimated that about two percent of the radioactive particles would remain in the bone for several years although he didn't think that these deposits would cause health problems. As an example, he mentioned the excessive rates of lung cancer among uranium miners. This excess, he claimed, is due not to uranium but because the miners inhaled radon gases and were exposed to other radioactive products such as radium, thorium and vanadium. He added that epidemiological studies haven't identified a "significant risk" of kidney disease for miners.

"Studies of the health effects of workers exposed to uranium are meager and inconsistent," he concluded. "At these dose levels [i.e., what Gulf vets received] they provide little epidemiological support for kidney damage or excessive malignant tumors. The latest BIER IV Report [a federal radiation standard-setting group] reached similar conclusions."[9]

The good doctor's testimony raises several questions—none of which were asked by either the PAC members or their staff. If the earlier studies on workers are, in fact, "meager and inconsistent," shouldn't he and other scientists await the completion of adequate studies before drawing conclusions about the health risk of DU at the expense of Gulf veterans?

Second, Voelz never explained how he had determined the dose levels to which Gulf vets were exposed. If no monitoring was done in the Gulf, on what basis did Voelz estimate them? Presumably, some vets might have been exposed to high enough levels in the Gulf that even Dr. Voelz would concede that they were at risk. Third, did researchers at BIER actually evaluate fallout from DU weapons or armor plating?

The meeting's transcript reports that only one question was asked of Voelz. A staff member asked whether he thought DU exposure could harm the reproductive process in male GIs so that they could pass birth defects through their sperm. Without bothering to establish any scientific credentials on reproductive effects, Voelz answered; "I don't think any of the uranium doses [what doses, Dr. Voelz?] have any chance of producing that. Look at [where] the uranium is--in the kidney and bone. The rest is pretty low level." When I asked PAC staff whether Voelz possessed such qualifications, I was told, off the record, that he did not.

The second witness was Dr. David Hickman, a health physicist employed by another branch of the nuclear bomb-making indus-try--the Livermore Radiation Laboratory in California. At Livermore, he conducts *in-vivo* (whole body) measurement of radioactive particles in nuclear workers. This sophisticated technology can help determine the radioactive levels of uranium particles which may have lodged in the lung or other parts of the body.

Dr. Hickman described in detail how scientists measure low energy protons which are emitted from contaminated workers. Many nuclear-industry workers receive *in vivo* monitoring once or twice a year at the cost of $500-1,000 per exam.

At this point, the PAC's chairwoman popped the $64,000 question. Was it feasible, she wondered, to use these whole-body counting techniques on Gulf vets today to determine if they've been harmed by depleted uranium?

Hickman responded that he didn't believe that such testing would be useful. "The equipment is designed to detect photons (between) 100-200 KEVs. It would not detect photons you need to detect for depleted uranium."[10]

To make sure no one missed the point, PAC staffer Mike Kowalok returned to the issue with Dr. Hickman. "[Since] Gulf war veterans' exposures to depleted uranium were not likely to be chronic and second ... [they're] not reporting renal [kidney] effects ... is it appropriate ... to provide *in vivo* counting to a population of Gulf veterans five or six years ... after exposure?"

Being the well-trained witness he is, Dr. Hickman wasted no time knocking Kowalok's slow, hanging curve ball clear out of the park. "If we're talking insoluble [particles] the lung would be involved. ... It is not really a good technique to utilize six years down the road. It really isn't a very ... sensitive technique," Hickman opined. "Plus ... if you're not seeing effects that would be characteristic of the radionuclide (picking up on Kowalok's debatable assertion about no kidney effects) why go monitor for it?"[11] End of subject.

To further buttress its conclusion that *in vivo* monitoring cannot now be used to test vets for DU contamination, the Final Report cites a "personal communication" from Dr. Richard Toohey, Director of the Radiation Internal Dose Information Center of the Oak Ridge Associated Universities (ORAU) in Tennessee.[12]

According to Jackie Kittrell, a Tennessee attorney who has worked for years on behalf of radiation victims: "ORAU scientists constantly appear as expert defense witnesses in radiation injury cases throughout the country. In fact, until the 1980s, the entire budget of ORAU was provided by the Department of Energy. Since World War II, they've taken in at least $500 million from DoE and AEC [Atomic Energy Commission], its predecessor."[13]

When I asked PAC staff about the appearance of bias in favor of nuclear-bomb industry scientists, they countered that non-governmental scientists were also consulted. They also argued that nearly all nuclear scientists work, in some way, for the federal government, the nuclear power industry or military contractors.

In fact, there are some highly respected authorities on radiation hazards, such as Dr. John Gofman, author of *Radiation and Human Health*, Dr. Arjun Makhijani, director of the I.E.R.R., and Dr. Michio Kaku, a contributor to this collection, who might have reached different conclusions about the hazards of DU to Gulf vets than did the scientists picked by the PAC.

An Insider's View of the Army

One other witness who testified at the Denver hearing made some interesting revelations about the Army's handling of the DU issue. Dr. Stephen Shelton, a civil engineer at the University of New Mexico, spent three years as research director of the Army Environmental Policy Institute's study of depleted uranium (see discussion in Dan Fahey's article).

Shelton told the panel that although Congress had asked the AEPI to find ways to reduce the inherent toxicity of depleted uranium, it is impossible to do so. Commenting on the Army's claim that it had done an "excellent" job of handling the environmental hazards of DU, Shelton stated: "I fully concur with [this] from the time the Army takes control of DU [until] it goes out the muzzle of a weapon."

He expressed concern about changes in Army policy on DU hazards after he left the AEPI. "I tried to project ... that we were open and wanted to talk." A national conference on DU where, he proposed, environmental groups like the Depleted Uranium Network could be heard, was shelved after his departure.

The Doha Accident: A Missed Opportunity

Professor Shelton also told the panel that he had requested that his AEPI research team be sent to Doha, Kuwait, to conduct an on-site investigation of the accident site. He also wanted to inspect a nearby area which had been used as a target range for at least a third of all the DU munitions fired in the Gulf. Since his team had spent many months studying every aspect of the DU issue, they would seem to be well-qualified to conduct the Doha probe. Nonetheless, Shelton's request was denied.[14] Maybe the Army was nervous that the AEPI scientists would take the investigation too seriously.

At any rate, a group from the Army's Center for Health Promotion and Preventative Medicine (CHPPM) did eventually visit Doha. Unfortunately, there is no mention of what they learned there in the PAC's Final Report.

Anecdote: Professor Shelton told the panel that he had persuaded the Army to use "catchboxes" at its U.S. firing ranges to collect spent shells and thus reduce contamination. Unfortunately, no one bothered to install such boxes in Kuwait or Iraq.

The VA Rejects Whole Body Counting

The Veterans of Foreign Wars (VFW), one of the largest veterans service organizations, adopted a resolution at its August 1996 national convention calling on the DoD and VA to use whole-body counting as a standard diagnostic procedure to test vets for depleted uranium. (Gulf War vet Dan Fahey, who serves as a VFW post commander in Santa Cruz, California, was a primary proponent of this resolution.)

Just days after the PAC report was released in January 1997, Jesse Brown, the Secretary of Veterans Affairs, wrote the VFW national staff advising them that the VA cannot support whole-body counting. He gave three reasons: the cost, the scarcity of facilities which can perform the tests, and that, "these tests are not effective for screening."[15] He cited no scientific evidence for this conclusion.

Air Force Use of DU Ignored

Nowhere in the PAC's report is there any discussion of the Air Force A-10 planes which fired nearly a million 30mm DU rounds during the war. Why wasn't the PAC interested in the shipping and handling of this enormous arsenal? We'll probably never know whether Air Force munitions personnel or bomb loaders have experienced any elevated health effects which may be related to the toxic weapons they handled.

Lessons Learned by the Military

There is a long-standing tradition in the American military of conducting post-battle assessments which are then later distributed as "lessons learned." The subject of depleted-uranium armor and munitions however, appear to be an exception to this rule, at least publicly. On the subject of depleted uranium the guiding principle seems to be the less said the better.

A basic Army reference guide, *Weapons Systems*, published in 1996, provides detailed descriptions of both the MIA2 Abrams tank and the A2 Bradley Fighting Vehicle without ever mentioning that both fire DU rounds and that the Abrams is equipped with DU armor plating. The book opts instead for vague references to "special armor" and "improvements in lethality." One version of the Bradley which has been renamed "Operation Desert Storm" is described as enjoying "high survivability."[16] (This writer will buy a steak dinner for the first Army enlistee who reports being told by the recruiter when signing up for Armor that he or she will be working around depleted-uranium plating and munitions!)

Recently, Army Chief of Staff General Dennis J. Riemer was interviewed by *Army* magazine about the service's combat readiness. "We are on the leading edge of a whole new way of warfighting," Riemer stated. "Improvements in combat systems will provide enhanced warfighting capabilities."[17]

Depleted-uranium armor and munitions are highly valued by today's Army commanders because it gives them, at least for the time being, a tactical advantage over non-DU equipped armored units.

Scientific Research on DU is Low Priority

According to the PAC Report, the federal government is currently funding 107 different research projects on various substances to which Gulf War illness has been attributed. Only two of these studies are concerned with depleted-uranium exposure. Combined, the two studies are following fewer than forty Gulf vets who either have embedded DU fragments in their bodies or were exposed to large doses of DU smoke when "friendly fire" DU rounds hit their tanks or Bradleys.[18]

Even this small group of veterans haven't received the medical monitoring or followup they were promised by the VA. According to a Gannett News story, only eight of the thirty vets have been given whole-body radiation counting tests. The VA doctors refused to discuss any findings with Gannett's reporters. Instead, they issued a general description of their multi-year monitoring effort and stated that none of the vets showed evidence of kidney disease.

One of the vets interviewed by Gannett's reporters, Jerry Wheat of Los Lunas, New Mexico, was hit with twenty pieces of DU shrapnel while driving a Bradley vehicle. When Wheat was sent to the VA's DU clinic in Baltimore, "They told me there was no danger and not to worry. I didn't even know what DU was," he recalled. Since Wheat's father worked at the Los Alamos weapons labs, he was able to confirm that his fragment samples were DU. The VA has denied Wheat's request that he receive a whole-body evaluation.

Equally disturbing is a disclosure in a separate Pentagon report unearthed by Gannett's reporters that states that fifteen of the thirty DU vets have "elevated levels of uranium in their urine."

Dr. Frances Murphy, VA director of environmental services, stressed to Gannett that their Baltimore program is designed for medical surveillance—not scientific research. Yet, she added, "There's no evidence from the testing that any significant systemic effect or adverse health effect could be detected."[19]

Too Little, Too Late

Nearly six years after the shooting stopped in the Gulf, the VA finally published a guide for its medical staff on DU-related health problems in December 1996. Unfortunately, it follows the government's "party line" on this issue. For example, it tells VA doctors that "the only practical [way] ... to assess uranium exposure clinically is to measure urine [for] uranium." It adds that other measurement techniques (e.g., whole-body counting) are "not appropriate for routine clinical use."[20]

While the guide expresses "concern" about vets who may have inhaled or ingested DU particles, it offers no mechanism whereby VA doctors can identify and evaluate these at-risk veterans. Instead of screening its data-base of 69,000 Gulf vets seen at its medical centers, the VA relies on its medical staff to voluntarily report "suspect" cases to the Baltimore DU center. Given their current workloads and lack of knowledge about DU, it's unlikely that this will be of much use to DU-exposed veterans.

To add insult to injury, the guide recommends the PAC's Final Report, discussed earlier, as a source of information on DU!

Can an Old Dog Learn New Tricks?

The PAC reported little success with its effort to pressure the Pentagon to be more aggressive in protecting the health of GIs in future wars. The panel recommended that, "Prior to any [future] deployment, the DoD thoroughly evaluate the health of a large sample of troops to enable better post-deployment medical epidemiology." The PAC labelled the Pentagon as "not responsive" to this proposal."[21]

Veterans and grass-roots environmental organizations must build a movement that holds the Pentagon accountable for past injuries from DU and pushes for a worldwide ban on these weapons for the future. Otherwise, the outrage felt by ten of thousands of people about these weapons will fade away.

References

1. *Presidential Advisory Committee on Gulf War Veterans' Illnesses, Final Report*, 174 pages, U.S. Government Printing Office, Washington, D.C., December 1996.

2. *Ibid.*, Executive Summary.

3. U.S. Department of Defense News briefing, Information Access Co. M2, Presswire, January 9, 1997.

4. *Op. cit., PAC Report,* p. 97.

5. *Ibid., PAC Report*, p. 99.

6. Danesi, M.E., *Kinetic Energy Penetrators Long Term Strategy Study*, Appendix D, AMCCOM, Picatinny Arsenal, New Jersey (1990), pp. 4-5.

7. *Health & Environmental Consequences of Depleted Uranium Use in the Army*, AEPI, June 1995, at p. 119. Also see, *Operation Desert Storm: Army Not Adequately Prepared to Deal with Depleted Uranium Contamination*, GAO/NSIAD 93-90 (1993).

8. *Op. cit. PAC Report*, Executive Summary.

9. Transcript, PAC meeting, Denver, CO, August 4, 1996.

10. *Ibid.*

11. *Ibid.*, at pp. 270-272.

12. *Op. cit.*, PAC Report, footnote 259.

13. Interview, J. Kittrell, January 22, 1997.

14. *Op. cit.* Transcript, PAC meeting, Denver

15. Copies of correspondence, author's files.

16. *Weapons Systems*, U.S. Army, Government Printing Office, Washington, D.C., (1996) pp. 157-158.

17. *Army* magazine, Association of U.S. Army, October 1996, pp. 20-21.

18. *Op. cit., PAC Report*, Appendix F.

19. Brewer, Norm and Hanchette, John, "Some Vets Say They Have Not Been Monitored for Radiation Exposure," *Gannett News Service,* March 12, 1996.

20. *Depleted Uranium: Information for Clinicians,* DU Followup Program, Baltimore VA Medical Center, December 1996.

21. *Op. cit., PAC Report*, p. 19.

11 | 'National Security' Kept
Atomic Veterans' Suffering a Secret

Of the hundreds of thousands of Atomic Veterans exposed to radiation by the military, at most 455 have received compensation.

PAT BROUDY

This article will cover the uses of depleted uranium before and during the Gulf War, the exposures of military and civilian personnel and the resultant coverup of the records of the "Atomic Veterans" exposed to ionizing radiation during the Cold War, as well as the expectation of the same treatment of the Gulf War veterans.

Separation of the slow-neutron-fissionable uranium 235 (U-235) isotope from the major isotope, uranium 238 (U-238), was necessary to build the uranium bomb detonated over Hiroshima, Japan, and other gun-type uranium weapons. Natural uranium is almost 99.3 percent U-238 and only about 0.7 percent U-235. To obtain a few kilograms of U-235 leaves more than a ton of U-238 and remaining U-235 waste.

DU-waste removal discussed 1957

What to do with about a billion pounds of DU waste was discussed in meetings as early as 1957. One of the earliest uses of DU was as a substitute for U-235 in the test firings of the Hiroshima gun-type weapons at Los Alamos, New Mexico, in 1945.

A more important early use was as the "tamping" material between the high explosives and plutonium core of implosion bombs, such as the first Fat Man bomb design used at Alamogordo, New Mexico; Nagasaki, Japan; and twice at Operation CROSSROADS. A large mass of U-238 acted both to hold the core together until it could fission more efficiently and to reflect neutrons back into the core for more fissions. The plutonium core of Fat Man was only the size of a grapefruit, but the U-238 tamper and explosive lens surrounding it increased the bomb diameter to five feet.

In addition, about 20 percent of the Fat Man TNT-equivalent explosive yield of twenty-one thousand tons was from fast-neutron fission of U-238, because large quantities of fast neutrons are produced in a fission explosion.

This capability of U-238 to fast fission led to its use in thermonuclear bombs to create more explosive yield. The reaction became fission of a small trigger fission bomb to create the heat and pressure for fusion of hydrogen-containing components, then fission of U-238 by fast neutrons produced in copious amounts by both the fission trigger and fusion reaction.

A negative aspect was production of large amounts of fission products in the fission-fusion-fission reaction from the large amount of DU employed to enhance total explosive yield significantly compared to the large fusion yield. This greatly increased fission product inventory was essentially the opposite of the "clean bomb" development intent.

Resultant heavy fallout from tests such as Shot Bravo, during 1954 in the Pacific, caused beta burns and overexposure of Japanese working on the "Lucky Dragon" fishing boat, Americans on Navy ships caught in the fallout, Marshall Islanders exposed on Rongelap Island, as well as American military personnel on Rongerik Island.

Besides nuclear bomb munitions, other military uses were found for DU. Armor-piercing shells made of DU or with DU claddings were developed as well as hardening of armor with DU cladding. Burn tests of DU munitions alone, as well as DU munitions in shipping containers, in lightly armored Bradley fighting vehicles, and turrets and hulls of Abrams tanks, were conducted at the Nevada Test Site to determine hazards. These uses were prevalent in the Gulf War, the cause of "friendly fire" deaths and injuries.

Thus DU was produced in great quantities during U-235 enrichment operations at Oak Ridge, Tennessee, and large numbers of both civilian and military personnel were exposed during World War II during these operations and subsequent fabrication and operations at Los Alamos, including manufacturing of fission bomb tampers and components for hydrogen bombs, there and at other locations. Thousands of these personnel have been exposed to DU and its adverse health effects.

Military personnel exposed to DU during the Gulf War have developed a variety of illnesses that may have been caused by the synergistic effect of additional exposure to airborne petroleum products, adverse reaction to vaccines, and possibly exposure to chemical or biological warfare agents released by Iraq. Our thoughts go back to Atomic Veterans exposed to ionizing radiation, DU, and probably other toxins throughout atmospheric and underground nuclear testing.

Hundreds of thousands exposed; hundreds awarded

Although the Department of Veterans Affairs when queried about the numbers of military involved in nuclear-related activities admits to approximately 250,000 from 1945 to 1963, the VA Committee on Environmental Hazards (chartered by Congress in 1984, P.L. 98-542), in 1993 estimated another approximately 543,000 exposed to ionizing radiation post-1963 to 1970 (mandated by P.L. 102-578, 1992). However, since that figure included 60,000 underground military personnel, and since underground testing continued to 1992, we can only assume there may be several hundred thousand more exposures.

On July 18, 1994, Secretary of Veterans Affairs Jesse Brown wrote a letter to Hon. John D. Rockefeller in which he stated: "...[O]ur records also show that service connection on a presumptive basis was granted in 414 cases." He was referring to the "presumptive laws," P.L. 100-321 and 102-578, in which fifteen cancers are listed. It is not necessary under those laws to prove causation and radiation dose.

However, on April 23, 1996, I was informed by the Compensation and Pension Service of the VA that "fewer than 450" had been awarded benefits under P.L. 98-542, which does require a dose reconstruction costing the claimant about $4,000, if he could find someone to do a dose reconstruction these many years after the fact.

I was informed on June 20, 1996, that the figure for the presumptive laws is now 405, which is less than the 414 quoted Sen. Rockefeller by the secretary of Veterans Affairs two years earlier. Adding those two figures, 405 and "less than 50," we arrive at a figure of 455, giving the benefit of the doubt to the VA. So, out of 800,000 (not counting exposures from 1970 to 1992) we arrive at this embarrassing figure of 455 awards granted by the Veterans Administration for ionizing radiation exposures caused by nuclear testing.

The Defense Nuclear Agency on March 3, 1995, forwarded to me a breakdown of its costs for the "less than 50" awards under P.L. 98-542 (which requires dose reconstructions by both the Defense Nuclear Agency and the claimant). The total, representing the years 1978 to 1994 is $110,098,939. This amount includes Defense Nuclear Agency costs for dose reconstruction ($13,598,939) and funding for the Nuclear Test Personnel Review Program ($96,500,000). None of these figures represents the unknown monetary costs to the veteran or his survivors. No amount of money can assuage grief occasioned by their government's deception and intrigue.

Atomic Veterans of the Cold War exhibited many of the same illnesses borne by Gulf War veterans and their families upon return from Desert Storm, as well as sterility, stillbirths and mutagenic effects suffered by their children. Unlike the Atomic Veterans, the Gulf War veterans were able to talk about their illnesses and those of their families. The Atomic Veteran was sworn to secrecy and told he would be court martialed or sent to prison if he discussed his experiences during the Cold War period. It was just recently that Secretary of Defense William Perry released these men from their vows of silence.

Because they did not speak about their experiences or illnesses, and the government destroyed or classified their military and medical records, the subject was unknown to most of the American people. Even the wives of the men were not told by their husbands of this awful chapter in our history. Children's textbooks were barren of the subject, so even today, millions in this country do not know of this shameful chapter in our history. And so the men died, the awful secret buried within their patriotic hearts.

Both groups of veterans and their families are victims of the same voodoo technology, some as recently as the last underground nuclear test four years ago, where military personnel worked underground in toxic atmospheres. Because of the coverup of documents to "prove" exposures, less than 500 Atomic Veterans/survivors have received benefits from the Veterans Administration under existing laws. The same fate is in store for the Gulf War veterans. The health of these veterans and their families has been compromised forever in the name of "national security."

References

1. Smyth, Henry DeWolf, Chairperson, Department of Physics, Princeton University. *Atomic Energy for Military Purposes*. Written at the request of Maj. Gen. L.R. Groves, USA, Princeton University Press, 1946, pp. 32, 66, 67.

2. *Minutes*, Third Session, January 18, 1957, Fifty-Second Meeting of the General Advisory Committee to the U.S. Atomic Energy Commission, pp. 11, 39.

3. Jones, Vincent C., *United States Army in World War II*, Center of Military History, U.S. Army, Washington, D.C., 1985, p 510.

4. *Nuclear Weapons Databook*, Volume I, pp. 24, 26, 27, 28, 32.

5. Finding of No Significant Impact, U.S. Army, Depleted Uranium Testing in Area 25 at the Nevada Test Site.

6. *Power Reactor Based on Fused Salt Technology—C-84 Aircraft Reactors*, Oak Ridge National Laboratory, January 17, 1957, cover, pp 2,5.

7. Letter from General Advisory Committee to the U.S. Atomic Energy Commission, February 1, 1957, to Mr. Lewis L. Strauss, Chair, U.S. Atomic Energy Commission, p 2.

12 | A Bizarre Recycling Program
—the Arrogance of Power

The same malevolent mentality that permitted horrendous radiation experiments to be performed on poor people, the mentally retarded, pregnant women, soldiers, and prisoners without their knowledge and consent—has now created the new victims of depleted uranium.

ALICE SLATER

The world is awash in radioactive waste. We simply haven't a clue where to put it. The latest harebrained scheme in the U.S. is to ship the lethal carcinogenic garbage from nuclear weapons and civilian nuclear power plants, by rail and by truck, from the four corners of the continent, and bury it in a hole in the ground in Nevada at Yucca Mountain.

Citizens groups, like the proverbial boy with his finger in the dike, have been holding off the onslaught of this devastating disposal solution, preventing the legislation from passing in the Congress. Deadly plutonium remains toxic for 250,000 years and there is no way of guaranteeing that the Yucca site could prevent radioactive seepage into the ground water over this unimaginable period of time. Remember that all of recorded history is only 5,000 years old!

Meanwhile we are importing foreign fuel waste and scheduling it for "reprocessing" and "enrichment" for eventual resale to feed the reckless nuclear power industry. Stymied in this country where they are unable to build hazardous new reactors, companies like Westinghouse have redoubled their efforts to peddle their poisonous products abroad, spreading not only more lethal nuclear waste, but creating nuclear bomb factories in ever more countries who want to play with the big boys by developing their own source of bomb material with each new siting of a civilian power reactor.

The most difficult part of building a nuclear weapon is obtaining the plutonium. The mechanical technology is widely known today. All nuclear power plants produce weapons material. Some reactors, such as the light water reactors proposed for North Korea, make the process of developing bomb-grade plutonium more complicated than others. But eventually they can all deliver the lethal goods.

Enchanted by the "density" of depleted uranium and the "hardness" of its alloys, some evil genius in the pay of the Pentagon thought to make bullets from it that can penetrate tank armor in a bizarre recycling program that enabled the government to make a dent in the five hundred thousand tons of depleted uranium waste amassed since the Manhattan Project. Don't be misled by the term "depleted uranium." Like "spent fuel" from civilian reactors, depleted uranium is highly toxic and carcinogenic and has a half life of some 4.4 billion years.

"Half life" is another euphemism that distances us through our language from grasping the deadly seriousness of what we are doing to our planet. For example, while the half life of plutonium is twenty-six thousand years, this lethal poison has a fully toxic life of about 250,000 years until all the radioactivity decays. So you can imagine—or can you—the life span of toxic depleted uranium with its "half life" of over four billion years!

While our brilliant military was dreaming up its scheme of penetrating Saddam's tanks with "hard" depleted uranium, they neglected to calculate the impact this material would have on our own soldiers. "Friendly fire" killed thirty-five U.S. soldiers and wounded seventy-two others during the Gulf War while disabling more U.S. tanks than the Iraqis did. Spewing three hundred tons of DU ammunition over Iraq, the U.S. left a growing legacy of respiratory problems, liver and kidney dysfunction, and birth defects among the newborn children of U.S. vets. (A Veterans Administration study of 251 Gulf War veterans families in Mississippi found that sixty-seven percent of the children born to the vets since the war have severe illnesses, with effects ranging from missing eyes and ears to fused fingers.)

And similar medical reports are coming from Iraq with an increase of leukemia and congenital birth defects from eight percent before the war to twenty-eight percent today.

This callous disregard for human well-being is sadly typical of government policy during the nuclear age. In Portsmouth, Ohio, where we have been leaching radioactive poisons into the rivers and streams for fifty years to produce uranium, the U.S. Enrichment Corporation is recycling spent fuel for overseas sale. I saw photos of a two-headed cow, children with three fingers, with one ear. And the people seem to be helpless against the onslaught which continues to this very day.

In Karaul, Kazakhstan, a small village near the former Soviet test site at Semipalatinsk, I saw similar birth defects among the unfortunate children there who had the misfortune to be born downwind from Soviet nuclear testing.

Trying to get our government to admit that radioactive bomb factories and power plants are harmful to living things is like the long battle waged against the tobacco companies who continue to claim that there is no connection between smoking, cancer, and other life-threatening diseases. This is the same malevolent mentality that permitted thousands of horrendous radiation experiments to be performed on poor people, the mentally retarded, pregnant women, soldiers, and prisoners without their knowledge and consent—the disenfranchised guinea pigs of the nuclear age to whom we must now add the new victims of depleted uranium.

The shocking radiation experiments were conducted by some of our leading universities and institutions which even today sit as trustees over the national laboratories of death at Los Alamos and Livermore. In New York, Brookhaven National Laboratory, with its two nuclear reactors, has been declared a superfund site. The lab told eight hundred local homeowners not to drink their well water now contaminated with radioactive tritium and strontium-90 which is "migrating" into the Long Island aquifer, the sole source of drinking water in the area. Epidemiologist Jay Gould reports a higher incidence of cancer within fifty miles of every nuclear reactor across the country.

Brookhaven Laboratory is governed by Associated Universities, Inc., a consortium of our most prestigious eastern universities including Harvard, Columbia, Yale, and Princeton. They have failed to take responsibility for the harm and havoc to human health and the environment which is occurring today under the aegis of their trusteeship. Similarly, the University of California adds its respected imprimatur to the lethal brainstorms from Los Alamos and Livermore including MIRVs, hydrogen bombs, and Star Wars.

$4 Trillion on Nuclear Madness
Since 1945 we spent $4 trillion on nuclear madness and this year [1996] we are still spending $25 billion on our nuclear program. Over $3 billion of these funds is allocated to so-called "science-based stockpile stewardship" which will enable our mad Dr. Strangeloves to continue to design new nuclear weapons. Indeed, this deadly "stewardship" program will have a cost of $40 billion over the next 10 years.

The long sought Comprehensive Test Ban Treaty, which was finally signed by President Clinton at the UN on September 24, 1996, was a Pyrrhic victory for activists who heard nation after nation condemn the nuclear powers for having gutted the meaning of the treaty by their elaborate computer-simulated virtual-reality testing programs which will enable weaponeers to design new nukes for space and earth penetrators—"to get Saddam in his bunker." And these computers are not laptops. The new terraflop computer is as big as a house; the National Ignition Facility planned at Livermore is the size of a football field!

Meanwhile we have over four thousand contaminated sites in the U.S. alone. In Idaho I saw rusting tin cans filled with plutonium from nuclear submarine waste sitting in raw open earth pits on top of an aquifer in an earthquake zone! The Navy ships its spent fuel clear across the country by rail, from New York to Idaho, creating this macabre storage "solution." And they continue to build new submarine reactors, creating even more waste.

In Amarillo they store plutonium pits from dismantled bombs on top of the world's largest freshwater aquifer—the Oglala—which supplies drinking water to 16 states. In Portsmouth, Ohio, on the Ohio-Kentucky border, the U.S. Enrichment plant pours its toxic filth into the rivers and streams poisoning the poor people of Appalachia. Downwinders in Utah with higher incidences of breast cancer and leukemia continue to suffer from nuclear testing in Nevada.

Uranium miners in Arizona and workers at the leaking Hanford tanks in Washington live shorter lives than average with higher cancer rates than the general population. Indeed every site where nuclear activity occurs, both military and civilian, has a saga of woes from the effects of lethal radioactivity. Further, most sites, worldwide, are located on the lands of indigenous people or in poverty-stricken rural communities. It is an immoral tale of environmental racism.

Time for a 'Bronx Project'

And now that we have inherited mountains of radioactive waste that remains lethally toxic for some 250,000 years, what are the great scientific minds at our national laboratories focused on? Space nukes, bunker busters, depleted uranium bullets and armor, third generation hydrogen bombs in virtual reality computer simulations—while paying lip service to disarmament measures by agreeing to stop underground nuclear explosions while they go merrily, madly on their way building still more bombs, thinking up even grander schemes of nuclear terror—instead of applying themselves to cleaning up the poisonous legacy of the nuclear age.

Our world needs a Bronx Project. Just as we had a Manhattan Project to build the bomb we need to put some resources and energy behind an effort to figure out how to clean up the bomb's remains. We need a commitment like the one that was made to put a man on the moon in ten years. While not as glamorous as the Manhattan Project, the Bronx Project would perform an invaluable service by seeking ways to render plutonium less long-lived so we can guard it until it is harmless to future generations. This is a man-made substance and we have yet to take a hard look at unmaking it—or at least making it less lethal over time.

We need to tell the boys to put away the toys of war and clean up the mess they made. And if today's unreconstructed cold warriors are too addicted to new weaponry instead of good housekeeping, then we ought to at least get them to stop making any more of it. We need to keep it all in place as safely as possible instead of moving forward with wild transportation schemes by air, by sea, by rail, and by road, across all the ocean lanes and flight paths of the world for reprocessing, centralized storage, and other lunatic schemes to spread the stuff around, poisoning more people under cover of secrecy which weakens the very foundation of our democracy.

The Cat Is out of the Bag
Our ability to govern ourselves has been eroding as a result of the unprecedented secrecy and cover-up engendered by the nuclear age. Scarcity of information has disempowered the people. Well the cat is out of the bag. Iraq, Iran, India, Pakistan, Israel, North Korea, Japan, Germany—all have the means to get the bomb. South Africa, Brazil and Argentina actually had it and gave it up.

It is no longer a secret that any country with a nuclear reactor can get the bomb. For this reason, the recently signed Comprehensive Test Ban Treaty requires a designated group of forty-four nations to sign it before it "enters into force." Those are the very forty-four nations that have nuclear reactors and can make a bomb. So let's get all the facts out on the table. The radiation experiments, the depleted uranium illness, the nuclear dumpsites, the spills, the leaks, the health statistics, the real long-term costs of nuclear power compared to clean energy from our sun, the wind, the tides—let the people decide.

A sane, informed citizenry would call for an immediate cessation of the production of any new nuclear material, leaving all existing nuclear waste as close to the point where it is generated, as safely as possible, under international guard. We would call for a Global Alternative Energy Agency to promote clean sustainable energy the way the International Atomic Energy Agency now touts for the nuclear power industry pushing for the proliferation of nuclear reactors abroad. We would call for a new generation of physicists to develop the Bronx Project.

Just as the Hebrew children born in slavery had to wander in the desert for forty years so that no one born in servitude would enter the promised land, we need to have young physicists work on the Bronx project. We must guard against the possibility that scientists who developed nuclear bombs would be given opportunities to pervert the new goal of eliminating nuclear waste by devising deadly new schemes for spreading contamination. We must prevent developments such as the latest crackpot scheme of making toxic weapons out of depleted uranium, leaving a lethal legacy not only for innocent civilians in Iraq, but for our own soldiers and their progeny as well.

[Based on a talk given September 12, 1996, at the United Nations Church Center in New York]

Metal of Dishonor

The following photo section provides a glimpse of the widespread impact of the entire uranium cycle. From the testing and development of nuclear bombs to the production, testing and use of depleted-uranium weapons to the dumping of nuclear waste, the nuclear industry has endangered the health of millions of military personnel and civilians around the world.

GIs watch the most publicized atomic test, "Smoky," on August 27, 1957. From 1945 to 1963, the Pentagon exposed more than 250,000 military personnel to ionizing radiation during nuclear tests. Hundreds of thousand more have been exposed since. The health of these veterans "has been compromised forever in the name of national security. Only 455 individuals have ever received government compensation." *(See Chapter 11) U.S. Army photograph.*

The Pentagon's use of radioactive material reached new heights during the 1990s, employing for the first time in combat munitions and armor made with depleted uranium during the Gulf War. Operation Desert Storm/Desert Shield consumed over 940,000 30-millimeter uranium-tipped bullets and more than 14,000 large caliber DU rounds (105–millimeter and 120–millimeter).

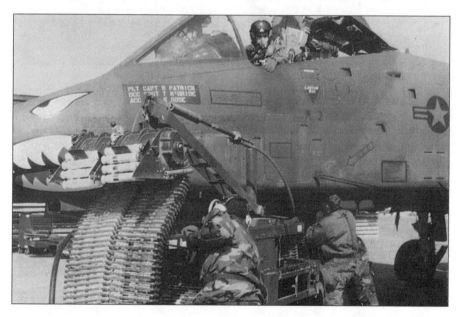

The Fairchild A-10A Thunderbolt II, also known as the Warthog, wields a GAU-8/A Avenger 30mm seven-barrel cannon capable of firing 4,200 DU rounds per minute. Each 30mm round contains a 300-gram DU penetrator core. *U.S. Air Force photograph*

The M1A1 tank fires 120–millimeter anti-tank rounds which contain a 10.7-pound depleted uranium penetrator core. The dense DU core increases the firing range of the M1A1 tank to between 3,000 and 3,500 meters (up to two miles). The Bradley Fighting Vehicle, the M1 and M60 series tanks, the XM8 Armored Gun System and the M1A2 Abrams tank also use DU artillery ranging in size from 25mm to 120mm. *Photo courtesy of Grace Bukowski,* Uranium Battlefields Home and Abroad: Depleted Uranium Use of the U.S. Department of Defense, *March 1993*

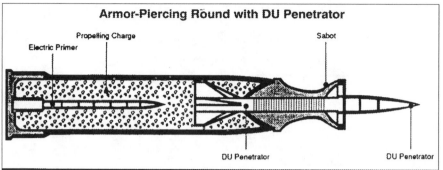

Armor-Piercing Round with DU Penetrator

Electric Primer
Propelling Charge
Sabot
DU Penetrator
DU Penetrator

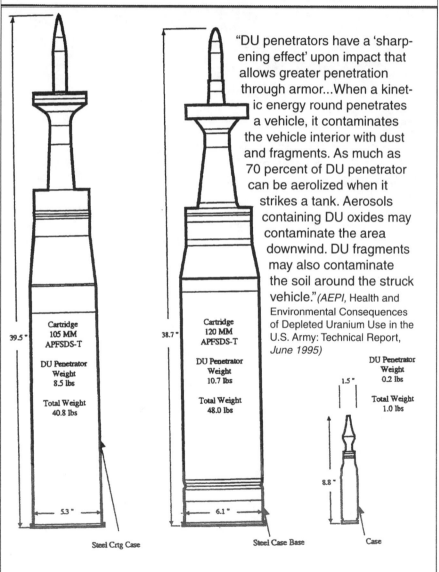

39.5 "

Cartridge
105 MM
APFSDS-T

DU Penetrator
Weight
8.5 lbs

Total Weight
40.8 lbs

5.3 "

Steel Crtg Case

38.7 "

Cartridge
120 MM
APFSDS-T

DU Penetrator
Weight
10.7 lbs

Total Weight
48.0 lbs

6.1 "

Steel Case Base

"DU penetrators have a 'sharpening effect' upon impact that allows greater penetration through armor...When a kinetic energy round penetrates a vehicle, it contaminates the vehicle interior with dust and fragments. As much as 70 percent of DU penetrator can be aerolized when it strikes a tank. Aerosols containing DU oxides may contaminate the area downwind. DU fragments may also contaminate the soil around the struck vehicle." *(AEPI,* Health and Environmental Consequences of Depleted Uranium Use in the U.S. Army: Technical Report, *June 1995)*

1.5 "

DU Penetrator
Weight
0.2 lbs

Total Weight
1.0 lbs

8.8 "

Case

U.S. aircraft firing DU rounds strafed more than sixty miles along the "Highway of Death." Thousands of retreating Iraqi military and civilian vehicles, including ambulances and buses, were destroyed, killing thousands of Iraqi civilians and soldiers. Although this attack was a serious violation of international law, scenes such as the one above have increased the world demand for depleted uranium weapons. *International Action Center photograph reprinted from* The Fire This Time, *by Ramsey Clark, published by Thunder's Mouth Press in 1992*

Basra, southern Iraq: Depleted uranium weapons not only increased U.S. firepower and destructive capabilities, they poisoned the environment in regions of Iraq, Kuwait, and Saudi Arabia for generations to come. Because the U.S.-led forces used DU weapons in 1991, hundreds of thousands of Iraqi civilians may be suffering the untreated effects of exposure to radioactive contamination of the land and water.

International Action Center photograph reprinted from, War Crimes: A Report on United States War Crimes Against Iraq *by Ramsey Clark, Maisonneuve Press 1992*

"...Our troops were used as human guinea pigs for the Pentagon. Thousands must have walked through almost invisible clouds of uranium dioxide mist, not realizing that micron-sized particles were entering into their lungs." (M. Kaku, chapter 17)

"When the wind blows, those particles blow. We had storms, wind storms, every day in Iraq. They were blowing everywhere."(C. Picou, chapter 6)

Photograph courtesy of Carol Picou, Retired Sergeant First Class, U.S. Army

"Recovery and maintenance soldiers working in and around DU contaminated vehicles can inhale or ingest resuspended DU particles. If DU enters
the body, it has the potential to generate significant medical consequences. The risks associated with DU in the body are both chemical and
radiological" (AEPI report, June 1995)

This photograph demonstrates how tens of thousands of GIs from the U.S.
and other Coalition member nations were exposed to depleted uranium.
Iraqi vehicles and other targets were hit by DU weapons. The DU burned,
and GIs breathed a fine aerosol mist of DU particles. Eighty-two percent of
U.S. Gulf veterans queried say they entered Iraqi vehicles. No one informed these GIs of the health hazards. *Photograph courtesy of Carol Picou, Retired Sergeant First Class, U.S. Army*

Note the similarities in congenital defects of these children: one of a Gulf War veteran; one from southern Iraq; and one born to a Marshall Islands woman exposed to atomic fallout. Can this be just a coincidence?

Gulf War veteran and his child. *Photo courtesy of Derrick Hudson*

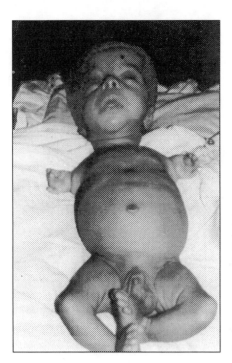

Iraqi child.
Photo courtesy of Prof. Sigwart-Horst Guenther

Marshall Islands child.
Photo courtesy of Glenn Alcalay

U.S. Department of Veterans Affairs in a state-wide survey of 251 Gulf War veterans in Mississippi reported that 67% of their children conceived since the end of the war were born with severe illnesses or birth defects.
Laura Flanders Nation *March 7, 1994*

The scar on Ellen Boas's neck indicates repeated surgery for thyroid cancer. She is one of fifty thousand Marshall Islanders the U.S. government intentionally exposed to radioactive contamination from which the Atomic Energy Commission gathered data about the impact on humans (chapter 15). *Photo courtesy of Glenn Alcalay, by Fernando Pereira, Greenpeace photographer killed when French government agents bombed the anti-nuclear protest ship, Rainbow Warrior.*

In the U.S. military Black, Latino and other people of color are disproportionately at risk on the front lines. During the Vietnam War this meant a far higher level of deaths, injuries and delayed combat-stress syndrome. According to Department of Defense Manpower Data, during the Gulf War almost half the troops stationed in the Gulf region were Black and Latino. It follows that they suffer a high incidence of Gulf War Syndrome. The impact on physical and mental health of this war and past wars is reflected in the statistic that over one third of the homeless in the U.S. today are veterans.

From uranium mining to the testing of nuclear and radioactive weapons to the dumping of nuclear waste, the Indigenous peoples of North America have suffered the effects of each stage of the uranium cycle. More than fifty percent of all the uranium in the U.S. is located on tribal reservation lands. More than half of the uranium miners working from 1946 to 1968 died from cancer and respiratory diseases, including the father of the Navajo family from Cove, New Mexico, shown above. Only fifty claims from the Navajo miners and their widows have ever received any government compensation.
Photograph courtesy of Dan Budnik

Tons of radioactive mine waste remain exposed on reservation lands like this United Nuclear Waste site in Blue Water, New Mexico. The Abandoned Mines Land Office has estimated that on the Navajo Reservation alone there are still over one thousand unreclaimed uranium mines. Many of these open pits are filled with water, inviting children to swim and animals to drink. *Photograph courtesy of Dan Budnik*

Former U.S. Attorney General Ramsey Clark, speaking at the Sept. 12, 1996, meeting at the UN Church Center in New York City. Seated from left to right are Alice Slater, Dr. Jay Gould, Dr. Michio Kaku and Anna Rondon. This initial meeting of the Depleted Uranium Education Project drew more than three hundred individuals and the endorsement of dozens of Non-Governmental Organizations interested in combating the threat of depleted-uranium weapons.

"We need your help. We must accept this challenge and persevere for the duration in this struggle. We must stop DU now, and sanctions and militarism and nuclear weapons and plutocracy which wrings its wealth from the suffering of the poor." (R. Clark, Chapter 2). *International Action Center photograph*

Section IV:

Indigenous Peoples Victimized by Military Radiation

13 | Uranium Development on Indian Land

In remote areas of the Navajo Reservation there are still over one thousand unreclaimed uranium pit mines open, filled with water, inviting children to swim and animals to drink.

BY MANUEL PINO

Uranium development on Indian land parallels the history of the nuclear industry in the United States. When the race to build atomic weapons began in secrecy during World War II, nuclear weapons research had been established in New Mexico, right in the heart of Indian country. Six Pueblo nations in northern New Mexico are within thirty miles of the Los Alamos Scientific Laboratory, where the first atomic bomb was developed. The remote desert spot called Trinity, New Mexico, where on July 16, 1945, the first atomic bomb was tested, is withing sixty miles of the Mescalero Apache Nation. The Grants Mineral Belt—which would ultimately become the largest uranium belt in the world—was located on or near the Navajo nation and Laguna and Acoma Pueblo lands.

A majority of uranium produced on Indian land between 1950 and 1968 went to one source: the Atomic Energy Commission of the United States. The supply was found in the Grants Mineral Belt of the Southwest, in the midst of Navajo and Pueblo lands. Because the government was the sole purchaser of uranium mined during the early years—and because the government neglected to regulate the health and safety of miners—a large percentage of Navajo, Laguna and Acoma miners have developed cancer and other related illnesses. The U.S. government gave the mining companies financial incentives to increase productivity, and repeatedly reminded the Indian miners of their patriotic obligation, stating that U.S. security was at stake.

In those early years of production, uranium development was a pick and shovel operation. The Indian miners were virtually "miners' canaries," who were sent into the crude, unventilated mines called "dog holds" immediately after dynamite blasting. There they breathed radon gas and silica-laden dust.

Miners would eat their lunches in close proximity to the mines and blasting; they would also drink contaminated water that dripped from the mine walls. They would carry uranium home to their families on their shoes and clothes that would be washed with the family laundry.

Past evidence indicates that miners were never fully informed or warned of the health and safety hazards involved in uranium mining.

For example, a 1953 letter from Duncan A. Holaday, an official with the federal Division of Occupational Health, to Allan Look, with the U.S. Bureau of Mines, indicated that there was a high concentration of radioactive dust in the Jackpile Mine on the Laguna Reservation. The concentrations were so high that two minutes of exposure could give a person the maximum amount they were allowed to receive in a day. Holaday wrote, however, "We have not worn respirators in the mines primarily because we actually do not spend many days a year in high concentrations. Also, the psychological effect on the miners probably would not be very good."

This letter is an example of the lies Indian people have had to live with in the thirty years uranium was developed on Laguna land. Despite evidence such as this and repeated warnings from Public Health Service physicians, mining companies and government agencies refused to acknowledge that there was danger. A majority of American Indian miners today who have developed cancer as a result of these violations feel that since the government had created the market for uranium, it is liable for damages to the health of those who worked mining it.

Two decades after mining began and only after deaths began to mount among miners did the federal government impose radiation exposure standards on the uranium mines, in spite of relentless opposition from mining companies. These standards, along with environmental protection legislation and the over-supply of high-grade ore worldwide led to the demise of uranium production on Indian land.

A little-known fact outside of energy circles is that Indian nations own one half of the country's privately owned uranium. If the industry becomes revitalized the energy companies will come to Indian nations with their lucrative development proposals.

Today American Indians are left with tons of exposed radioactive mine waste on their lands. Rainwater has leached uranium by-products and toxic metals into underground water, with potentially long-lasting consequences. The Abandoned Mines Land Office of the tribe has estimated that in many remote areas of the Navajo Reservation there are still over one thousand unreclaimed mines. These small uranium pit mines remain open, filled with water, inviting children to swim and animals to drink.

At Laguna Pueblo, the Jackpile Mine covers nearly three thousand acres, which remained untouched for seven years after mining stopped in 1982. Then the tribe itself began the reclamation process. The reclamation at Jackpile, which grew to be the largest open pit mine in the world in its thirty years of operation, is a first-time experiment. Jackpile is the only strip mine in the world where reclamation has been attempted.

The Laguna Pueblo people live in the village of Paguate, which is located only two thousand feet from the mine site. Now they are questioning the so-called successful reclamation project. Many residents of Paguate feel that since this is a first-time attempt at reclamation, monitoring and followup studies are necessary. There are also growing concerns by both mining and non-mining populations over the growing incidents of cancer and cancer-related illnesses.

Both the Navajo and Laguna people are working on trying to amend the 1990 Radiation Exposure Compensation Act, which does not at present include compensation for open-pit uranium miners or uranium mill workers.

The legacy of uranium mining continues. There is still work to be done concerning monitoring reclamation of mines and mills. As true owners of this land that we have seen destroyed before our very eyes, we hope and pray to the Creator that the federal government lives up to its promises. We Native nations provided the resources for development. We hope the U.S. government takes responsibility for its commitment to nuclear weapons and nuclear power, and will not ignore this damning evidence, deny the truth, mislead our people, and jeopardize our health and even life itself.

14 | Uranium, the Pentagon and Navajo People

Out of five hundred claims from Navajo uranium miners' widows, only fifty received any compensation—a $75,000 check. Now there are two mines proposed to open up in the same vicinity of a test range for cruise missiles near Gallup, New Mexico.

ANNA RONDON

In our Navajo creation story we have always learned that uranium—the Navajo call it "cledge" from the underworld in our creation stories—was to be left in the ground. It is a yellow substance, we knew that from our legends. We were told from the gods in our songs and our creation stories that we had a choice, a choice between uranium and the yellow corn pollen that we pray with every morning and carry in our medicine bags. The yellow corn pollen possesses the positive elements of life in our belief.

We chose that way, which is the beauty way of life. Uranium was to remain in the ground. If it is released, as all other native indigenous cultures around the world believe, it would be a serpent. It will bring you evil, death, and destruction, and we are at that brink today. That is a little background on the spiritual natural laws that we have known and we join the people here today to create an alliance, a world-wide movement to educate the public, the international community.

On our reservation back in 1941 a mineral called carnotite was found. Those from the United States Department of the Interior, Bureau of Indian Affairs, had discovered it. They in turn told the Department of Defense and the Atomic Energy Commission that carnotite was within the Carrizo Mountains, which are by Shiprock, New Mexico, on our reservation. Carnotite is an element that contains both vanadium and uranium. They mined and used the vanadium to create a hard steel alloy for battleships. They mined it from 1942 to 1945.

They also used the uranium. Eleven thousand tons of uranium were mined between 1942 and 1945. The Manhattan Project—which we all know now as the project to create the atomic bomb—was then a secret project that made use of the uranium. From 1943 to 1945 the Manhattan Project Engineering District contracted with Union Mines Development Corporation to mine additional carnotite and use the vanadium for U.S. battleships.

From 1946 to 1968 thirteen million tons of uranium were mined. Fifteen hundred uranium miners were used on that work. Today more than half these miners have passed away from cancer and respiratory diseases.

In 1990 the United States Congress passed the Radiation Exposure Compensation Act (RECA) that created a $200 million trust fund. Are we going to continue exposing people from around the United States to uranium radiation? Because the trust fund is only two hundred million dollars. Out of five hundred claims of the Navajo, from Navajo widows, from the miners, only fifty received any compensation in the form of a $75,000 check.

Now, it is very hard for the Department of Justice to come up with the additional funds to pay the widows of the miners and the surviving miners. Right now, the RECA is going through amendments so it will make it easier for the miners and also the millers and community people that live around uranium tailings and mill tailings.

They make it so difficult for us to have the evidence, to bring the medical documents. Did they smoke? Were they married? In our way we don't have marriage licenses. In those days in 1943, we had traditional ceremonies. So we're feeling victimized today.

Right now there is a Radiation Victims Political Action Committee being formed under Cooper Brown who helped the Marshall Islanders get compensation from the federal government. If you look at the United States government record, you would have to conclude it is not going to be giving out millions of dollars to future victims of radiation exposure.

From 1954 to 1968, four uranium mills were constructed. The tailings from over one thousand underground and open pit mines still remain on our reservation with children playing in the tailings. Sure they have signs that say "Beware," but most of our people still don't understand or read English.

The homes are being built from tailings. Six hundred homes are already being lived in that were made from the tailings—uranium tailings—the actual rock that comes from the mines.

Back in 1979, some ninety-five million gallons of water contaminated with radiation broke from a dam in Churchrock. It was the worst nuclear accident in United States history. We are still living with that contamination. Our livestock are still being contaminated.

Right now, Hydro-Resources Incorporated, a subsidiary of Uranium Resources Incorporated out of Australia is proposing to open up two uranium infusion mines, using the same process used to mine oil and gas, where they shoot down into the groundwater with chemicals and suck up the uranium. They say it is more environmentally safe and sound. That's what they are telling us.   Now   the Nuclear Regulatory Commission members are the ones that are reviewing the final environmental impact statement, but these people are monitoring their own, they are the watchdogs, they are the political arm for the corporations and the terrorists, the United States Army, the Department of Defense.

We have two mines proposed to open up in the same vicinity of a test range for cruise missiles. Gallup, New Mexico is here [pointing to map]; this is Churchrock that's where the proposed mine is; and this is Crownpoint. Right here at Fort Wingate they are going to test-launch cruise missiles, eighty to one hundred per year till the next century.

The environmental impact statement says it is not going to harm anyone, we're going to have evacuation plans, but there's a school right in that area, Fort Wingate. That's also where the United States Army held us hostage in the 1800s.

The madness is going beyond our control as indigenous people, so we join you in this movement. The summit we are going to focus on for the next year is to ban uranium mining. We would also like to join the Ban Depleted Uranium Campaign; no nuclear waste to be transported but kept where it is until we can find other ways to dispose of it—not to let it be recycled for bullets. We would step up the public-information campaign about nuclear issues at local, state, regional, and international levels; create new alliances and strengthen current alliances that we have now; and share total tactics that work, some solutions that have been proven to work.

One action that we propose to do will be on July 25, 1997. We are going to do community actions locally, for the first bomb that was dropped on the Bikini Islands. We chose that day in solidarity with the South Pacific Islanders. So if you can, somehow wherever you are from, look into indigenous issues, get them on your agenda. We cannot be forgotten.

[From a talk given September 12, 1996, at the United Nations Church Center in New York]

15 | Nuclear Testing, Government Secrecy and the Marshall Islanders

[Rongelap] is safe to live on but is by far the most contaminated place in the world, and it will be very interesting to go back and get good environmental data. ... While it is true that these people do not live ... the way Westerners do, civilized people, it is nevertheless also true that these people are more like us than the mice.
—*AEC Director of Health and Safety Merril Eisenbud*[7]

GLENN ALCALAY

The half-million Gulf War veterans enmeshed in the macabre net of continuing U.S. government secrecy and coverup are not unique and follow a long lineage, including the 250,000 "atomic veterans," the Utah downwinders near the Nevada Test Site, the Vietnam veterans exposed to Agent Orange, and the 23,000 American citizens involuntarily used as human guinea pigs in plutonium injection and other equally grotesque experiments in the last half century.

An especially odious and infamous chapter of official Washington secrecy was the Tuskegee syphilis experiment conducted for nearly forty years by the U.S. Dept. of Public Health among four hundred African-American sharecroppers.

Such a history of secrecy and coverup makes it seem obvious that to get to the root of the causes of Gulf War Syndrome, it will be necessary to carry out a study independent of the government. To see just how far the government will go in its callous mistreatment of Cold War victims, just look at the story of the Marshall Islanders and U.S. hydrogen bomb testing.

Bravo: the U.S.'s Largest Hydrogen Bomb
Included in this litany of unsuspecting fodder for U.S. military and nuclear dominance in the Cold War are the fifty thousand people of the Marshall Islands located in the obscure Micronesian archipelago between Hawaii and the Philippines. Their land was seized by the U.S. as booty after World War II.

The Marshall Islanders have made the supreme sacrifice under the aegis of nuclear colonialism in terms of the unfolding drama (including psychological stress) associated with the acute and latent effects of ionizing radiation, the long-term contamination of their once-pristine island ecosystems, and the forced sociological disruption of several island communities. Australian author Nevil Shute drew his inspiration for *On the Beach* from the Marshall Islanders' 1954 rendezvous with their radioactive dystopia.

Less than one year after the end of WWII—and with the radioactive rubble of Hiroshima and Nagasaki still fresh in the collective consciousness—the U.S. converted the Marshallese atolls of Bikini and Enewetak into nuclear-weapons laboratories in order to further its nuclear monopoly far from American shores. Between 1946 and 1958 the U.S. exploded sixty-seven atomic and hydrogen bombs in the islands for the dual purpose of perfecting thermonuclear warhead design, as well as obtaining crucial data about the effects of radioactive fallout on human populations.

In early 1954, at the height of McCarthyism, the electrocution of the Rosenbergs, and the U.S. offer (subsequently turned down) to the French of using tactical nuclear weapons in their quagmire of Vietnam, the U.S. unleashed the massive Castle series of megaton-range hydrogen bombs at Bikini Atoll. The largest and dirtiest of the 1954 series was code-named "Bravo," a 15-megaton behemoth hydrogen bomb that was one thousand times the size of the Hiroshima atomic bomb.

Bravo rained lethal radioactive fallout over thousands of unsuspecting islanders (and Air Force weather personnel) under circumstances which remain mysterious. Edward Teller designed Bravo. At that time Teller had been instrumental in denying his former colleague Robert Oppenheimer security clearance that destroyed a reputation (and life) over the decision to build the hydrogen bomb. Bravo was intended to produce maximum fallout over an immense area. Indeed, the Atomic Energy Commission established an international network of radiological monitoring stations prior to Bravo in anticipation of collecting worldwide fallout data.

After the fallout from Bravo "accidentally" blanketed several populated islands, the U.S. claimed that last-minute "wind shifts" had been the culprit in the widespread nuclear contamination. Twenty-eight years and many cancers later, including at least thirty-four radiogenic diseases,[1] Air Force weather personnel stationed on a nearby island reluctantly came forward to challenge the official explanation. "The wind was blowing straight at us for days before, during and after the test," admitted Gene Curbow, the senior weather technician at the time. "The wind never shifted."[2]

A 1954 Defense Nuclear Agency document on Bravo had confirmed Curbow's assertion. Just six hours before the Bravo detonation "winds at 20,000 feet were headed for [inhabited] Rongelap to the east."[3] Although the Department of Energy (DOE) admitted in 1978 that at least fourteen islands, many of which were inhabited, were hit with "significant fallout" during the nuclear tests in the Marshalls, it is widely believed that many more islands were contaminated with radioactivity.[4] When asked why he had waited until 1982 to reveal his knowledge of this important information, Curbow replied sheepishly, "It was a mixture of patriotism and ignorance, I guess."[5]

The people of Rongelap Atoll—one hundred miles downwind of where Bravo was exploded at Bikini—were especially hard-hit, and were evacuated from their home islands two days after Bravo, following the absorption of massive doses of high-level fallout.

Following the Rongelap evacuation, the Atomic Energy Commission considered repatriating the islanders to their home atoll in order to gather vital fallout data at the height of the Cold War. In 1956, Dr. G. Failla, chair of the AEC's Advisory Committee on Biology and Medicine, wrote to AEC head Lewis Strauss: "The Advisory Committee hopes that conditions will permit an early accomplishment of the plan [to return the Rongelap islanders]. The Committee is also of the opinion that here is the opportunity for a useful genetic study of the effects on these people."[6]

Recently, another document on Bravo from previously classified minutes of an AEC meeting revealed in the most bare-knuckled manner the actual rationale for conducting the follow-up Marshallese radiation studies by researchers from the Brookhaven National Laboratory on Long Island, New York. In January 1956, two years after Bravo, Merril Eisenbud, the AEC Director of Health and Safety, addressed the radiation problems in the Marshalls:

> Now that Island [Rongelap] is safe to live on but is by far the most contaminated place in the world, and it will be very interesting to go back and get good environmental data. Now data of this type has never been available. While it is true that these people do not live, I would say, the way Westerners do, civilized people, it is nevertheless also true that these people are more like us than the mice.[7]

It appears that the AEC was guilty of both negligently disregarding the well-being of the Marshallese and then lying about its actions. On February 24, 1994, Rep. George Miller (D-Calif.), then-chair of the

House Committee on Natural Resources, convened a hearing on Bravo. Recalling weather data that demonstrated prior knowledge that islanders would receive substantial fallout, and that winds had not unexpectedly "shifted," Rep. Miller declared that "We have deliberately kept that information from the Marshallese. That clearly constitutes a coverup."[8]

Low-Level Ionizing Radiation: No Threshold

Although the health risks associated with ionizing radiation continues to divide the scientific establishment, the real controversy revolves around the question of low-level radiation exposure. This question continues to haunt the Marshallese because of their daily uptake of radionuclides through the foodchain and their chronic background exposures.

One of the most eloquent statements on this topic was enunciated by Karl Z. Morgan, the founder of the field of health physics and the former Director of the Health Physics Division of the Oak Ridge National Laboratory from 1943-72. Writing in the September 1978 *Bulletin of the Atomic Scientists*, Morgan stated that when radiation passes through the human body, four principal events can occur:

1. the radiation passes through or near the cell without producing any damage;

2. the radiation kills the cell or renders it incapable of cell division;

3. the radiation damages the cell but the damage is repaired adequately, or;

4. the cell nucleus (or library of information) is damaged but the cell survives and multiplies in its damaged form over a period of five-to-seventy years and forms a clone of cells that is eventually diagnosed as a malignancy.[9]

Morgan further stated that "only this last event relates to somatic damage such as cancer from low-level exposure. It seems obvious that if the cell nucleus is damaged and some information is lost or if a similar series of events leads to a malignancy, there can be no dose so low that the risk is zero."[10] In other words, Morgan postulated that there was no so-called "threshold dose" and that even the smallest dose of radiation can produce deleterious effects in stark contrast with the alleged "safe doses" of low-level radiation peddled by the nuclear industry and the EPA/OSHA.

Women and Reproduction in the Marshall Islands

For the Marshallese, the debate about the effects of ionizing radiation is far more than an academic exercise. As expected, it is universally believed that the health and environment of the Marshall Islanders have been adversely affected in the aftermath of the nuclear weapons testing program in their islands. This perception has become part of the social fabric of Marshallese society, and is now culturally reproduced in the subsequent generations following the nuclear tests in the 1940s and 1950s.

Bella Compoj of Utirik Atoll—one of the island populations caught in the 1954 Bravo fallout—relates her encounter with the U.S.'s largest hydrogen bomb test:

> When we returned to Utirik after three months on Kwajalein [following the evacuation after Bravo] I recall seeing a woman named LiBila and her skin looked as if someone had poured scalding water over her body, and she was in great pain until she died a few years after "the bomb."

> Also, after our return to Utirik, Nerik gave birth to something resembling the eggs of a sea turtle, and Flora gave birth to something like the intestines of a turtle which was very sticky like a jellyfish. Soon afterwards, many other women would be pregnant for about five months and then they turned out not to be pregnant after all. I too thought that I was pregnant and after three months I found I was not. This was quite new for the women here, and this rarely happened before "the bomb."[11]

Researchers from the Brookhaven National Laboratory have flip-flopped over the years concerning the question of the impact of the nuclear tests on women and their progeny. For example, a Brookhaven report issued six years after Bravo stated that

> During 1958 [i.e., four years after Bravo] six miscarriages and stillbirths were recorded in the exposed Rongelap group, but none were reported in this group for 1959. ... **The data on pregnancy terminations show an increased incidence of miscarriage in the exposed group** (emphasis added).[12]

Twenty years later, in the 1980 Brookhaven annual report, a reversal was made concerning the incidence of congenital anomalies among the exposed Rongelap women:

> Vital statistics suggest that mortality and fertility rates have been about the same in the exposed as in the unexposed people. During the first four years there appeared to be an increase in incidence of miscarriages and stillbirths in the exposed Rongelap women, but this observation was uncertain in view of the small numbers involved.[13]

The problem with the inherent conclusions of the Brookhaven researchers is that, in fact, Brookhaven has never undertaken a systematic study of the perceived problems facing Marshallese women and their fertility. That is, if Brookhaven (and the U.S. government by extension) were an honest broker with respect to the latent effects of radiation exposure in the Marshall Islands, they would have impartially stated that the "jury was still out" over this question until systematic research was conducted. In fact, Brookhaven has concerned itself with only the narrowest parameters of health injury from radiation in the Marshalls, in particular the damage to the thyroid gland from the uptake of radioactive iodine (I-131) and the consequent abnormalities associated with an impaired thyroid gland.

In light of the swirling debate about so-called "jellyfish babies" in the Marshall Islands, I conducted a pioneering one-year independent health study of women and reproduction in the islands. Between 1990-91, I collected detailed health and statistical data from the women of childbearing age on ten outer atolls in the Marshall Islands in relationship to their proximity to Bikini Atoll. That is, it seemed reasonable to compare and contrast the reproductive histories of the island women closest and furthest away from Bikini, the site of the infamous 1954 Bravo hydrogen bomb explosion.

The results of my independent health study provided the first glimpse into potential problems facing women in the Marshall Islands. The results of the independent study revealed that women who reside closest to Bikini Atoll (and who consequently received a higher dose of radioactive fallout from Bravo) had a statistically higher incidence rate of congenital anomalies (miscarriages and stillbirths) than Marshallese women who live furthest away from Bikini. That is, there was a consistent dose-response effect in relation to the distance from Bikini: Women who lived nearest the former nuclear test site at Bikini had the highest incidence rate for reproductive problems, and women who lived the farthest from Bikini had the least number of problems associated with pregnancy and birth.[14]

Obviously, there may be other explanations for these findings among Marshallese women, but at a minimum the possibility of teratogenic effects associated with the long-lived transuranic isotopes of strontium-90, cesium-137, americium-243 and plutonium-239 must be prudently considered.

Conclusion

The nuclear age lesson from the not-so-balmy bowels of the Pacific is that the U.S. has consistently down-played or covered-up the seamier side of America's obsession with the atom. Forty-three years after Bravo, the Marshallese are still scratching their heads trying to discern a radiogenic disorder from the myriad health problems they face as a newly developing republic.

Like the countless numbers of American citizens who have been sacrificed upon the alter of the Cold War by their own government, the Gulf War veterans remain in purgatory concerning their health (and their children's health) as a consequence of possible exposure to varying levels of ionizing radiation from depleted uranium artillery shells used against Iraq in 1991. Also unknown are the possible synergetic effects associated with exposure to chemical or biological weapons also experienced in the Gulf War.

What is called for is an international campaign concerning the bio-hazards of depleted uranium to prevent future exposures to the newest and most insidious Frankenstein of the nuclear age.

At the very least, an independent and non-governmental health study must be immediately undertaken to ascertain the extent of possible health injury among the 500,000 Gulf War veterans. Whatever the cost for such a study must be factored into the total cost of "winning" the Gulf War—the first post-Cold War atrocity fought over oil reserves and natural resources. Perhaps the Kuwaiti Royal Family might be tapped for the cost of the proposed study?

Because of continuing U.S. government secrecy and intransigence, the Gulf War veterans are only the latest group of victims to be caught between the proverbial rock and a hard place, and only our continued vigilance and campaigning will bring about any degree of justice and sought-after answers for those who have become most recently ensnared in the talons of the U.S. eagle's imperial policy.

References

1. Nuclear Claims Tribunal, *Annual Report to the Nitajela,* Majuro, Marshall Islands, January 1997, p. 26.

2. Miller, Judith, "Four Veterans Suing U.S. Over Exposure in '54 Atom Test," *New York Times,* September 20, 1982, p. B15.

3. "Castle Series, 1954," Report from the Defense Nuclear Agency, DNA 6035F, Washington, D.C., April 1, 1982, p. 202.

4. "Radiological Survey Plan for the Northern Marshall Islands," Report of the Department of Energy, Washington, D.C., August 22, 1978, p. II-3.

5. "Four Veterans," *op. cit.*

6. Failla, Dr. G., chair of the AEC's Advisory Committee on Biology and Medicine, from minutes of the 58th meeting of the AEC's Advisory Committee on Biology and Medicine, November 17, 1956, p. 10.

7. Atomic Energy Commission (AEC), Minutes of Advisory Committee on Biology and Medicine, AEC, New York, January 13-14, 1956, p. 232.

8. Lee, Gary, "Postwar Pacific Fallout Wider Than Thought," *Washington Post,* February 24, 1994, p. A20.

9. Morgan, Karl Z., "Cancer and Low-Level Ionizing Radiation," *Bulletin of the Atomic Scientists,* September 1978, p. 31.

10. *Ibid.* p. 31.

11. Alcalay, Glenn, "The Sociocultural Impact of Nuclear Weapons Tests in the Marshall Islands," unpublished field report, February-April 1981, pp. 1-2.

12. Conard, Robert A., et al., "Medical Survey of Rongelap People Five and Six Years After Exposure to Fallout," Brookhaven National Laboratory, BNL 609 (T-179), Upton, New York, 1960, p. 17.

13. Conard, Robert A., et al, "Review of Medical Findings in a Marshallese Population 26 Years After an Accidental Exposure to Radioactive Fallout," Brookhaven National Laboratory, BNL 51261, Upton, New York, 1980, p. 86.

14. Statement of Glenn Alcalay Before the Presidential Advisory Committee on Human Radiation Experiments, March 15, 1995, Washington, D.C., pp. 4-5.

16 | Declaration of the Indigenous Anti-Nuclear Summit

Albuquerque, New Mexico, September 5-8, 1996

For more than fifty years, the legacy of the nuclear chain from exploration to waste has been proven, through documentation, to be genocidal and ethnocidal and a most deadly enemy of Indigenous Peoples.

During September 5-8, 1996, over thirty Native organizations gathered for the first Indigenous Anti-Nuclear Summit in Albuquerque, New Mexico. The purpose of the Summit was to develop a unified Native-directed strategy to oppose the genocidal impacts that the nuclear industry has had upon the communities and nations of Indigenous Peoples.

Since the dawn of the nuclear industry, Indigenous Peoples throughout the world have suffered disproportionate higher death and illness rates than any other population. Here in the United States, we have worked unprotected and ill-advised in uranium mines; our homelands and ecosystems are contaminated by radioactive tailings of thousands of abandoned mines; our peoples are continuously exposed to lethal doses of radiation from processing and refining plants. In remote villages of Alaska, we have been used like test rats in radioactive (Iodine 131) experimentation. To further complicate the lives of Indigenous Peoples, our lands serve as "test sites" for hundreds of nuclear bombs and our communities continue to be targeted locations for nuclear waste storage and dump sites.

It became most evident at the Summit that Indigenous Peoples and/or our lands are adversely affected at every phase of the nuclear power and weapons chain. There it was concluded that a well organized and sustained anti-nuclear campaign, lead by Indigenous Peoples, could have a major impact upon the nuclear industry. The first and most important part of the campaign strategy is to send a clear message to the nuclear industry as well as tribal, state and national governments, that Indigenous Peoples will no longer tolerate the continual genocidal and ethnocidal effects of the nuclear industry.

—The Seventh Generation Fund,
in a letter to the International Action Center

Declaration of the Indigenous Anti-Nuclear Summit:

We, the Indigenous Peoples gathered here for this Summit, standing in defense and protection of our Mother Earth and all our relations, do hereby unanimously express our total opposition to the nuclear power and weapons chain and its devastating impacts and deadly effects on our communities.

The Indigenous Anti-Nuclear Summit brought together a network of Indigenous Peoples from different areas of Mother Earth that are negatively impacted by the nuclear chain. These impacted areas of the nuclear chain include: Uranium mining in the Grants Mineral Belt, that has had devastating health and environmental impacts on Navajo and Pueblo peoples in New Mexico; the uranium mining industry has actively targeted northern Saskatchewan where the mining exploration process has already had negative implications on the culture of Chipewayan, Metis, Dene, Blood and other Indigenous Peoples in the region; conversion fuel fabrication and enrichment have impacted Indigenous Peoples in Oklahoma who live near the Sequoyah Fuels Uranium Processing Plant, and among Indigenous People, whose way of life depends upon the Columbia River where Hanford Nuclear Reservation is located (Washington/Oregon); power plant operation at the Prarie Island Power Plant has manufactured deadly waste impacting the Mdewankanton Dakota; and storage has been a tool of divide and conquer among Indigenous Nations targeted for the United States Department of Energy's Monitored Retrievable Storage proposals.

Although we are varied in languages and beliefs, we have the common ground of being Indigenous Peoples who have no desire to give up the traditional laws that the Creator gave us and accept the deadly, unsustainable ways the colonists have tried to force upon us. We are not asking anyone else to accept our ways; however, we are exercising our right to live our sustainable lifestyles in our own lands.

The nuclear industry—which has waged an undeclared war—has poisoned our communities worldwide. For more than fifty years, the legacy of the nuclear chain from exploration to waste has been proven, through documentation, to be genocidal and ethnocidal and a most deadly enemy of Indigenous Peoples.

United States federal law and nuclear policy have not protected Indigenous Peoples, and in fact have been created to allow the nuclear industry to continue operations at the expense of our lands, territory, health and traditional ways of life. This system of genocidal and ethnocidal policies and practices has brought our people to the brink of extinction and among some Indigenous Peoples it is believed that if they die, all life on Earth will stop. Therefore, we demand an immediate stop to these crimes against our peoples, communities and future generations by the nuclear industry, its stockholders and nuclear governments including the United States, Japan, France, Canada and China.

We demand all levels of governments, including tribal, state, national and international, do whatever possible to stop all uranium exploration, mining, milling, conversion, testing, research, weapons and other military production, use and waste disposals onto and into Mother Earth.

We further demand increased research and development, funding allocations and utilization of sustainable energy such as solar, wind and appropriate technologies that are consistent with our natural laws and respect for the natural world (environment).

We particularly call upon tribal governments to measure their responsibilities to our peoples, not in terms of dollars, but in terms of maintaining our spiritual traditions, and assuring our physical, mental and spiritual well being. It is our responsibility to assure the survival of all future generations.

We invite you to join us by:

1. At the Summit, October 13, 1996 (Unplug America—Give Mother Earth a Rest Day) and July 25, 1997 (Anniversary of the Rio Puerco Nuclear Accident and Nuclear Testing by the French in the Pacific at Bikini Atoll) were designated as national days of acknowledging the devastating impacts of the nuclear industry against Indigenous Peoples. We encourage you to create an event in your community that brings awareness and attention to these critical issues.

2. Recognizing that the proposed transportation of nuclear waste will affect numerous communities throughout the United States, we encourage you to contact your local representatives and let them know that you place health and safety as a priority and that you believe it is their job to protect human rights and oppose transportation through your region.

3. If you live in a state that currently depends upon nuclear power plant(s) for energy we encourage you to contact your representative to phase out nuclear power plants and implement sustainable energy production methods (i.e., solar energy, wind energy, etc.).

4. You are invited to join as a co-signatory of this declaration. For more information please contact N. Butler at (415) 512-9025 or write 568 Howard Street, Third Floor, San Francisco CA 94105.

5. Please circulate this declaration—through newsletters, mailings, tables at events, etc.

Organization Signatories
Citizen Alert Native American Program
Columbia River Educational, Economic and Development Fund
Diné CARE
Ejit Iep Jeltok Women's Club
International Indian Treaty Council
Nuclear Free Future Campaign—Indigenous Land
Greenpeace
Rural Alliance for Military Accountability
The Seventh Generation Fund
Tribal Environmental Watch Alliance
Water Information Network

Section V:

What Risks from Low-Level Radiation?

17 | Depleted Uranium: Huge Quantities of Dangerous Waste

U.S. troops were used as human guinea pigs for the Pentagon. Thousands must have walked through almost invisible clouds of uranium dioxide mist, not realizing that micron-sized particles were entering into their lungs.

DR. MICHIO KAKU

The use of depleted uranium for military purposes is a deplorable development that, if unchecked, could have serious consequences. The widespread use of DU in the Gulf War can be directly linked to the Gulf War Syndrome. Although most of the publicity has gone to plutonium-239, uranium-235, and uranium-233 (the only substances in the universe which can sustain an uncontrolled chain reaction), the dangers of waste uranium-238 are much more pervasive, simply because there are huge quantities of waste U-238 lying around and because most people do not think it is that dangerous. Now that DU is being used in warfare, steps must be made to prevent its use.

It has been known for over three hundred years that U-238 harms people's health. For example, Bohemian miners in what is now the Czech Republic would often come across pitchblende ore in their work. Pitchblende ore contains uranium-238. Because of its unusual weight, it would often be used as doorstops in Europe. It was also used to create beautiful colors in ceramic glazes. However, the Bohemian miners would often come down with a mysterious "mountain disease."

We now know that this mountain disease is really lung cancer, caused by the radioactive emissions of radon gas, a standard byproduct of radioactive decay. Even today the emission of radioactive radon gas and the dispersal of uranium particulates poses a health risk. In the American Southwest, there are hundreds of millions of tons of waste uranium "tailings" left over from the mining and milling of uranium ore. Unscrupulous contractors would sell the uranium tailings to Native Americans, who would then use them to build their adobe homes. It was also sold to developers, who would use the waste uranium for landfill for suburban housing tracts.

It is one of the great unpublicized scandals in this country that Native Americans would breathe the radon gas and uranium particulates, both as miners in unventilated mines, as well as residents in their own radioactive homes. Illness and death have ravaged those in the Native American community who came in contact with uranium waste. But most of the publicity went to several middle-class housing tracts (like Grand Junction, Colorado), which were actually built on top of waste uranium. Much to the embarrassment of the old Atomic Energy Commission, measurements of the radioactive waste uranium showed high levels of radiation and radon gas, so the basements of many of these homes had to be dug up at the taxpayers expense.

Even today, uranium ore poses a problem. During the scandals related to human radiation experimentation, it was revealed two years ago that several million pounds of uranium dust were dispersed over an area near Cincinnati, near suburban homes, in an experiment conducted by the U.S. government to determine the dispersal of radioactive materials in the atmosphere in populated areas. Not long ago, there was a truck accident where uranium "yellow cake" (uranium ore after being processed) spilled onto an interstate in the Midwest. Local, state, and federal officials argued for days as to who was responsible for cleaning up this radioactive mess, even as cars drove through the dust left by the yellow cake ore.

Even in many homes in the Northeast, a persistent problem is radioactive radon gas that seeps into people's basements, contaminating the house. Radon gas is quite radioactive but is also an inert gas, so it will seep right through the cracks in people's walls and floors. It will also go right through activated charcoal in a gas mask as if it weren't even there, so gas masks provide no protection whatsoever.

Today the military has found a new use for waste uranium—as a weapon of war. Precisely because uranium is quite heavy as a metal, it has ideal armor-piercing capabilities against tanks and artillery. If you hold uranium, you are surprised how dense it is.

When I was in the infantry in the U.S. Army in 1968-1970, I had several personal demonstrations of armor piercing anti-tank weapons, and fired one round myself. The anti-tank weapon I fired in Fort Lewis, Wash., during advanced infantry training, was hand held and was contained in a lightweight tube placed on your shoulder. Because the tube contained its own rocket, there was zero recoil. The anti-tank missile had a metal plunger about an inch or so wide in its nose cone, which would puncture a hole in solid tank steel. This meant that hot gases would penetrate through that hole and flood the tank; anyone inside the tank would be instantly roasted alive by the hot gases.

Uranium metal, like many others, possesses the nasty characteristic that it will burn and aerosolize if heated, due to the metal-air reaction (oxidation). For example, the burning of plutonium metal during the machining process at the weapons plant in Rocky Flats, Colorado, created several plutonium fires which caused large amounts of plutonium oxide to be dispersed over the Denver area. Likewise, the firing of an Exocet cruise missile at a British warship during the Malvinas/Falklands war caused the metal deck of the ship to burn, which accelerated the ship's eventual capsizing.

Similarly, the metal-water reaction between zirconium and water during the Three Mile Island accident created the notorious hydrogen gas bubble which threatened to blow up the reactor. But because DU easily pulverizes and aerosolizes after puncturing the hull of a tank (the U.S. Army admits that up to seventy percent may be aerosolized), it also disperses widely into the environment, entering people's lungs, where it may stay for a considerable length of time as uranium dioxide. The danger there is that the particulates and their daughter radioactive products such as thorium, protactinium, and other isotopes of uranium itself, will continue to emit gamma, beta, and alpha radiation for decades to come.

The half-life of uranium-238 is 4.5 billion years, which is also the age of the solar system. The point here is that lung cells which are near the uranium dioxide particulate will be bathed with intense radiation for decades to come.

Approximately 350 tons of DU were used in the Gulf War. The number of DU rounds fired keeps changing as the Pentagon admits to additional use of this weapon. But up to a million rounds of DU may have been fired during the Gulf War. This means that our troops were used as human guinea pigs for the Pentagon. Thousands must have walked through almost invisible clouds of uranium dioxide mist, not realizing that micron-sized particles were entering into their lungs.

No one knows the true scope of the medical effects of releasing that much aerosolized uranium in the atmosphere, which was breathed by both our troops and the Iraqi people. But judging from the experience of uranium miners and Native Americans exposed to uranium tailings, we know that the symptoms can be disastrous. A micron-sized particle can stay lodged in the lungs for years and even decades, bathing the surrounding tissue with a constant stream of gamma, beta, and alpha radiation. Ciliary action, which normally ejects large particles, has difficulty expelling micron-sized particulates lodged deep in the lungs.

Eventually, the particulates may be assimilated into the blood system, where they will cause problems with other organs. The kidneys, lungs, and reproductive organs are especially vulnerable to this material. There is also the health danger to the crew which maintains the stockpiles of DU weaponry. The U.S. Army states that at the surface of the DU warhead, the radiation levels can be 250 millirems per hour. For someone stationed next to the warhead, this means about a chest X-ray per day.

By contrast, background radiation on the surface of the earth is 100 millirems per year, coming from cosmic rays and thorium in the ground. Thus, someone sitting next to the shells will absorb in just one hour 2.5 times the normal yearly exposure to radiation.

Ultimately, the Gulf War Syndrome will probably be traced to a variety of factors, simply because the Pentagon released so much firepower on the Iraqis during that war that large quantities of materials were sent into the atmosphere, including DU and chemicals stored in warehouses. However, when the final chapter is written, DU will have a large portion of the blame.

It is sometimes said that DU cannot be used in hydrogen bombs. This is incorrect. The hydrogen bomb is a multi-stage device, which uses DU in its last (not first) stage. In the first stage, we have the standard implosion of plutonium-239 which sets off the initial chain reaction, which releases a burst of X-rays. In the second stage, this expanding shock wave of X-rays heats up lithium deuteride, which then undergoes fusion. In the third stage, an expanding sphere of fast neutrons emerges from the lithium deuteride, which goes through a "blanket" of DU surrounding the bomb. The fast neutrons create a new wave of fissioning, which yields up to fifty percent of the final megatonnage of the bomb itself. Thus, DU is an essential part of any standard H-bomb.

An H-bomb without the DU blanket is called the neutron bomb. This weapon, because of its lower power output, is designed to disintegrate people with a burst of neutrons, but preserve property.

Second, DU can be used in breeder reactors to create plutonium for atomic bombs. Uranium inside a reactor is continually bombarded with neutrons, causing it to mutate, first to neptunium, then to plutonium. In this way, the U.S. has created huge inventories of plutonium by this "Midas Touch" of transforming waste uranium-238 into bomb grade plutonium.

Conclusions

In conclusion, I would like to make the following points:

1. It is deplorable that the U.S., faced with cleaning up millions of tons of radioactive uranium waste, is getting rid of that waste by firing it into other people's back yards. It sends a horrible signal to the world, that we are using their precious land and their people as garbage dumps for our own radioactive waste uranium, which will pollute their country for billions of years.

2. There should be an international movement to ban the use of DU in warfare. After the world saw the horror of mustard gas after World War I, there was a mass movement which sought to ban the use of gas warfare. Ironically, the troops releasing mustard gas would often find it coming back at them because of shifting wind currents. Similarly, the use of DU also adversely affects the country that releases it into the atmosphere.

3. The use of DU could stimulate a new arms race, as other nations purchase uranium on the open market and create DU warheads of their own. This will, in turn, spur new efforts to re-enforce our tanks and set off a new, costly cycle of war research.

4. The Pentagon should release all its classified information concerning the Gulf War Syndrome and DU. It is a national embarrassment that the Pentagon, even at this late date, is still withholding vital information about precisely what happened during the Gulf War.

5. The Pentagon should also pay for the medical examinations of all those individuals who might be victims of DU. If found to be contaminated, they should be compensated.

6. Ultimately, it will be the American people who pay for the wanton use of DU in warfare. Our own troops were sacrificed to the U.S. war machine during the Gulf War. The fact that the Pentagon has stonewalled all attempts to obtain an accurate and complete description of the Gulf War Syndrome is a shameful chapter in U.S. history.

[Developed from a talk given September 12, 1996, at the United Nations Church Center in New York.]

18 | Nuclear Testing, Power Plants and a Breast Cancer Epidemic

The anguish of the Gulf War veterans suffering from the ravages of DU is only a small part of the damage exacted by the American nuclear addiction. A cumulated total of twenty million premature deaths can be attributed to the post-war interaction of both chemical and radioactive pollutants.

DR. JAY M. GOULD

The illnesses affecting veterans of the Gulf War are all symptomatic of the same immune system deficiencies that have affected the atomic veterans deliberately exposed to the Nevada nuclear bomb tests, Native American miners exposed to uranium dust and indeed the many millions of victims who since the birth of the nuclear age in 1945 have inhaled or ingested radioactive fission products never before encountered in nature. When uranium and strontium-90 are ingested—especially because they have long half-lives—both have immediate and delayed adverse effects on the immune system's response capabilities. These effects were clearly indicated by classified animal experiments conducted by American nuclear scientists as far back as 1943.

The name for this condition is low-level radiation, which has little relation to background radiation from natural causes such as cosmic rays and radioactive minerals in the soil. Over the course of countless millennia, human immune defenses have developed the capacity to resist cancer from such natural sources, only to be overwhelmed in 1945 by the sudden introduction into a previously pristine atmosphere of huge amounts of man-made radiation.

The Department of Energy has recently admitted that in the haste to produce plutonium for the first atomic bombs, the Hanford nuclear weapons complex released 550,000 curies of radioactive iodine in 1945. In terms of picocuries, the unit now used to measure radioactivity in a liter of milk or water, this means that in 1945, one-hundred-fifty million Americans were unwittingly exposed to more than four billion picocuries per-capita of this lethal radionuclide, comparable to releases from the Chernobyl accident—the worst in human history.

This was followed by two decades of atmospheric bomb tests recently estimated by the Natural Resources Defense Council to be equivalent to exploding forty thousand Hiroshima bombs. The effects of this testing were revealed by a sudden epidemic increase in cancer among children five to nine years old. Since 1945, female breast cancer incidence has nearly tripled, and we have established that a significant number of the eighty million baby boomers born in the bomb-test years 1945 to 1965—literally the worst time in history—did in fact subsequently display evidences of the damage to hormonal and immune systems sustained in utero.

We can show that in the period 1945-1965 there had indeed been an anomalous forty percent increase in underweight live births, perfectly correlated with the rise in strontium-90 found in human bone and especially in baby teeth. In fact, it was the concern expressed by mothers, as in the Women's Strike for Peace movement that helped prod President John Kennedy and Premier Nikita Khrushchev to finally terminate above-ground nuclear tests in 1963. There was a brief period of improvement thereafter until fallout from civilian power reactors replaced bomb-test fallout, especially after the Three-Mile-Island and Chernobyl accidents of 1979 and 1986. Since 1979, the ominous rise in the percentage of underweight live births that first surfaced in 1945 has resumed.

Human Guinea Pigs
We have also recently learned from Department of Energy Secretary Hazel O'Leary that since 1945 the Pentagon has exposed twenty-three thousand unwitting human guinea pigs to the ingestion of fission products to test their immune response. The Department of Energy still refuses to release the results of these Nazi-like experiments, as well as refusing compensation to the victims.

These are among the great secrets of the Cold War, first revealed more than three decades ago by Linus Pauling, Rachel Carson and Andrei Sakharov, who were thereafter treated as scientific pariahs for becoming in effect the first nuclear whistle-blowers. According to his memoirs, Sakharov worried so about the biological effects of strontium-90 released in above-ground thermonuclear bomb tests that in 1958 he made two terrifying predictions we have validated.

Based on his own animal experiments, he predicted that there would be millions of premature deaths world-wide from the strontium-90 released in the superpower bomb tests. He also predicted that the man-made bomb test radiation would accelerate the mutation of all microorganisms, leading to future opportunistic infectious diseases that would particularly affect those whose immune response had already been compromised at birth by low-level radiation.

And in fact when baby boomers began to reach the age of thirty-five in the 1980s, one could for the first time in history observe that they began to die of the constantly mutating opportunistic infections like tuberculosis and AIDS, now increasingly resistant to traditional antibiotics, in accord with Sakharov's prediction. In the 1980s, young female baby boomers first began to contract breast cancer at ages younger than fifty—another sign of an impaired immune response.

Perhaps the most obvious indicator of Sakharov's prescience comes from a close examination of the official annual movements of the U.S. mortality rate, which the U.S. Public Health Service likes to brag has been cut in half, from eighteen deaths per thousand in 1900 to about nine today. However, almost all of this improvement came in the pre-nuclear period prior to 1945, when the annual rate declined on average by two percent each year. Since then the rate has flattened out, standing at 8.5 per thousand in 1982, and since rising slowly to 8.8 deaths per thousand in 1996.

I have calculated that if the U.S. mortality rate had continued to improve after 1945 as it did before, the mortality rate today would stand at six deaths per thousand, the level attained by Japan. The widening annual differences between the observed rates after 1945 and the expected rates based on the pre-1945 trend yields a cumulated total of twenty million premature deaths that can be attributed to the post-war interaction of both chemical and radioactive pollutants, which Rachel Carson had termed "sinister partners" in her equally prescient *Silent Spring*.

Breast-Cancer Epidemic

So it is clear that the anguish of the Gulf War veterans suffering from the ravages of DU is only a small part of the damage exacted by the American nuclear addiction.

All this and many similar radiation-induced epidemiological anomalies are the subject of *The Enemy Within*, which is designed as a handbook for anti-nuclear activists alarmed at the evidence offered that breast cancer risk increases directly with exposure to reactor releases into the air and water.

Gaining access to previously unpublished official age-adjusted breast cancer mortality rates for every county since 1950, my colleagues and I were able to uncover many surprises. The breast cancer epidemic is one of incidence, but not mortality. For the nation as a whole, the breast cancer mortality rate, adjusted for an aging population, rose by only one percent since 1950, but the risk of dying of breast cancer rises significantly for those living close to fifty-five out of the sixty nuclear reactor sites we studied. Those counties within fifty miles of a reactor that had above-average levels of rainfall and exposure to chemical pollutants were hardest hit by fallout from both bomb tests and reactor emissions, as predicted by Rachel Carson.

The nation's greatest increases in breast-cancer mortality (of the order of thirty-five percent) occurred in fourteen counties in which the seven oldest Department of Energy nuclear facilities had been built in the years 1943-1950. A forty percent increase was registered in Suffolk County on Long Island, New York, the largest increase of any large county in the nation, perhaps because it is the home of the Brookhaven National Laboratory, which after forty-five years is still discharging radioactive fission products into the local air and water.

Since I live in East Hampton, on the east end of Suffolk County, I may be permitted some personal observations on the national implications of this interesting fact. In 1993, I and my radiologist colleague E.J. Sternglass of the University of Pittsburgh Medical School, had been invited by the Long Island One in Nine Breast Cancer Survivors Coalition to serve as their scientific advisors. They were so enraged because the National Cancer Institute had told them that the Long Island breast-cancer epidemic was due to the dominant presence of "affluent Jewish women," they had organized their own door-to-door household study in West Islip. They found one blue-collar neighborhood in which every other home had been hit by either a breast-cancer diagnosis or death in the previous ten-year period.

Their homemade colored map of their results drew so much national TV attention that the New York State Cancer Registry was moved to release, for the first time ever, recent age-adjusted breast cancer incidence rates for every town on Long Island. When we examined these figures it became immediately obvious that the highest rates in Suffolk County were within fifteen miles of the Brookhaven Lab, especially in the towns of Brookhaven, Bellport, Yaphank and Shirley located just south of the twenty-five square miles of laboratory grounds in central Suffolk County. Since the Brookhaven Lab had been declared an Environmental Protection Agency Superfund waste site, I used this fact to warn of possible contamination of the Long Island aquifer. I was denounced for this by Brookhaven officials as a "fearmonger with a hidden agenda and without academic credentials," and a threat to property values. I found little local support.

The situation changed drastically in 1995 after two Brookhaven whistleblowers testified to scandalous mishandling of radioactive waste, and an admission from Brookhaven that there had indeed been a southward flow of contaminated groundwater affecting at least eight hundred private wells in Shirley. This resulted in an immediate drop in home values and the filing of a one-billion-dollar suit by the affected families, not only against Brookhaven but also the nine universities that share in the direction of the BNL nuclear program.

No Longer Enemy of the People

An affidavit on my epidemiological warnings now helped an East End non-profit fishing association to force the laboratory to stop (temporarily) discharging radioactive waste into the Peconic River, an act suspected of contributing to the decline of East End fishing. I was no longer "an enemy of the people" as in the Ibsen play, but was now seen as a defender of East End business and realty interests!

Early in 1996, while revising the galleys containing the details of this interesting turnaround, I had a visit from an emissary of the Methodist Church, which I can only regard as miraculous, judging from its outcome. Dr. Randolph Nugent, head of the General Board of Global Ministries of the United Methodist Church—with eleven million members worldwide—explained to me that after Chernobyl they were horrified to find incredibly high long-standing cancer rates around the Soviet test site in Kazakhstan.

Dr. Nugent had asked Dr. Helen Caldicott, founder of Physicians for Social Responsibility and the International Physicians for the Prevention of Nuclear War, and former Secretary of the Interior Stuart Udall whether there were similar high risk areas in the United States. He was referred to us. (In a *Nation* review of Mr. Udall's recent book *The Myths of August*, I had saluted him as "the highest placed public official with the courage and wisdom to tell the truth about our deceptive official nuclear policy.")

Dr. Nugent was surprised to hear that in my judgment Suffolk County—exposed so long to emissions from both Brookhaven and the troubled Millstone reactors just twelve miles to the north—had registered the nation's worst epidemiological record, but that we lacked the necessary clinical evidence that radioactivity levels in the water, soil and in humans increased with proximity to the reactors.

We would welcome a small planning grant to explore the possibility of making independent measures of such radioactivity levels.

We received the grant in June 1996, which coincided with Dr. Caldicott's decision to move to East Hampton. This permitted us to hold several public meetings there for joint appeals for matching grants. To my astonishment and delight, and thanks to the eloquence with which she linked the Brookhaven problem with her life-long commitment to rid the world of the nuclear threat, within two months we raised sufficient funds to permit my non-profit Radiation and Public Health Project to conduct a six-month independent prototype baby-teeth study that may establish beyond all possible doubt the danger of low-level radiation from reactor emissions.

The measures of strontium-90 in baby teeth will be carried out at the University of Pittsburgh Medical School, which in the past has successfully measured levels of lead in baby teeth to show a high correlation with learning disabilities. High levels of strontium-90 in baby teeth have been shown to be highly correlated with childhood leukemia near German nuclear reactors in studies sponsored by the Berlin International Physicians for the Prevention of Nuclear War.

We already have indications that long-lived strontium-90 found in private wells near Brookhaven is at least six times higher than in Brooklyn, which gets its drinking water from the Catskill watershed, far from possible contamination of the Croton system close to the Indian Point reactors in Westchester. A significant difference in baby teeth strontium-90 levels between Brooklyn and Suffolk would also explain the current significant difference in cancer levels.

Our baby teeth survey has been barely started, but it appears to have struck a sensitive nerve and we are already being offered baby teeth from concerned mothers living near reactors in Connecticut, Westchester and New Mexico. I do believe it will demonstrate that we need not be in thrall to a nuclear establishment that is willing to kill its own people in pursuit of unlimited power over others.

To prepare a baby tooth for the study: When it falls out, wash it with soap and water, wrap in tissue paper and send to RPHP, PO Box 60, Unionville, NY 10988. Telephone (914) 726-3380. Include detailed information on the child's birth date, address and telephone number and length of residence at that location. All personal information will be kept confidential and the results will appear in statistical tables that may help in identifying high and low-risk areas in the country.

19 | Nine-Legged Frogs, Gulf War Syndrome and Chernobyl Studies

Desert Storm veterans along with the people of Iraq and Kuwait were victims of one of the latest military experiments on human beings. I believe that the ignorance was culpable and criminal.

DR. ROSALIE BERTELL

I first heard about the military using depleted uranium for bullets from the Native Americans for a Clean Environment (NACE) in Gore, Oklahoma. Kerr Magee was operating a factory there, and in a liquid waste spill a young man, about twenty-one years old, was sprayed with the mixture and died. Many members of the public were also exposed, and were taken to the University in Oklahoma City for medical examination and feces analysis. It seems that the liquid waste contained primarily uranium and other heavy metals.

Local people had found this factory to be very polluting. When I visited the town to see what was happening and to decide whether or not I could help, they showed me rust marks scattered over the surface of their automobiles where the toxic corrosive spray released from the factory routinely had impacted on the paint. People complained of burning throats and eyes, some with even more serious complaints, but little systematic information which would show that the factory was the source of their problem.

I met a young boy who showed me a frog he had caught—the frog had nine legs. It was in a bottle of formaldehyde. I wanted to take it for some tissue and bone analysis but it was his prize possession and he would not part with it.

I learned that the Kerr Magee plant had been disposing of its waste by deep-well injection in this rural, primarily farming area. The people, becoming alarmed at this practice which threatened the water table, got a court injunction to stop it. In an action, which seemed to the local farmers to be a retaliation, Kerr Magee had applied to the Nuclear Regulatory Commission to call their waste an "experimental fertilizer" and just spread it over the top of the land. The stories were quite strong evidence that this so-called fertilizer was sometimes just released into the local river, or released in one place on the factory property, with no pretense even to spread it.

The young boy had found his nine-legged frog on the hill which served as the "experimental plot." Hunters had found a rabbit with two hearts, and the local taxidermist told me that he had tried to mount two deer heads and the fur came off in his hands in clumps. He had never seen anything like it in his whole career.

As local people became sick and started to complain, Kerr Magee bought them out, and took over their land. The Native people, who were determined to preserve their land, formed a Coalition of Whites and Natives Concerned, and began the long legal fight with the company. They learned about environmental assessment hearings, licensing hearings, etc. and began to seriously participate. They also undertook a human health survey of all families—there were about four hundred of them—living within four miles of the factory. Every family was included in the survey, which was very comprehensive and carefully administered.

The International Institute of Concern for Public Health agreed to analyze this data for the citizens. The outstanding illnesses in the area were respiratory and kidney problems. There were significantly more persons with respiratory illnesses downwind of the plant, and significantly more with kidney problems downstream of the plant.

We intended to do a clinical follow-up of this survey, and designed the study with the cooperation of the Occupational Health and Respiratory Units at the University Medical School of New Jersey. We were not able to obtain funding for this study. Nevertheless, with the health survey and a great deal of local perseverance, Kerr Magee moved out. A second multinational tried to take over the factory—I think it was General Dynamics—but it failed.

I learned much about uranium bullets during this research:

- They are incendiary; that is, after piercing the object they can burst into flame.
- They are fragmentary; they disintegrate into small fragments inside the body, and cannot be removed.
- They are more dense than lead, and can pierce a bullet-proof vest, or a light armored car or tank.
- Because the "enemy" might also use them, the military made uranium armor as a protection.
- They were cheap, because the depleted uranium was a waste product of the nuclear-bomb program.
- They were radioactive, which meant that even handling them was risky, but no one seemed to be worrying about this!

Research into Gulf War Syndrome

Six years after the Gulf War there is still deep controversy over the causes of the severe health problems observed in the veterans. Reluctantly, the U.S. government has been slowly releasing data on possible Iraqi chemical exposures of the veterans, but many physicians, some of whom have reported that their jobs are being threatened, have said that this information does not explain the variety of symptoms observed.

Shortly after the Gulf War, at the request of Staff Sergeant Carol Picou, San Antonio, Texas, who was herself a victim, Patricia Axelrod undertook research into the possible causes of this illness.

The research was jointly sponsored by the U.S. National Institutes of Health, Office of Women's Health. It was submitted to the Department of Health and Human Services on May 10, 1993, and was labeled, "for internal distribution only." The research was intended to be a guide to further research into the problem, so its limitation to internal distribution did not make sense.

Our journal, *International Perspectives in Public Health,* published the document in full in 1994.

At the time, the U.S. Department of Defense was treating this illness as Post Traumatic Stress Disorder (PTSD) and advising military doctors to treat it with muscle relaxants and sleeping pills, while ordering a mental illness assessment. Most of the information in Ms. Axelrod's *Guide to Gulf War Sickness* comes from interviews with Dr. Thomas Callender, a toxicologist; Dr. Barry Wilson, of Battelle Pacific Northwest Laboratories; and Commissioner Rudy Arredondo, Maryland's Commission on Black and Minority Health. Ms. Axelrod also interviewed many veterans and reviewed the journal articles and reports available in the public press. Information on leishmaniasis was provided by the World Health Organization.

Potential Causes of Gulf War Syndrome

In this complex situation, any or all of the following factors may have interacted to bring about specific symptoms in veterans. Obviously, the combinations of factors differ with individuals, hence it is likely that there is not one single explanation of the whole spectrum of symptoms. However, the following main categories are candidates for causal relationships with illnesses reported by veterans:

• Administration of three vaccines intended as protection against nerve and biological warfare agents. These were:

1. Pyridostigmine, normally prescribed for myasthenia gravis and known to have serious side effects, especially when the person taking it is exposed to heat. It is also known that exposure to pesticides and insecticides (Baygon, Diazinon and Sevin) should be avoided when taking pyridostigmine because they can accentuate its toxicity. Some women who took this drug during pregnancy and have breast-fed infants have seen side effects in their child.

2. Botulinum Pentavalent, an unproven vaccine intended to counteract botulism. It is unlicensed in the United States.

3. Anthrax, to protect against the disease anthrax. This was apparently selectively administered to troops during the war, and women receiving it were warned not to have children for three or four years.

• Depleted uranium was used for the first time in this war. It was incorporated into tank armor, missile and aircraft counterweights and navigational devices, and in tank, anti-aircraft and anti-personnel artillery. The scientific information on this deadly chemical has been reported in "Radium Osteitis With Osteogenic Sarcoma: The Chronology and Natural History of Fatal Cases" by Dr. William D. Sharpe, *Bulletin of the New York Academy of Medicine*, Vol. 47, No. 9 (September 1971). There was no excuse for this human experimentation because the effects of this exposure were known.

• Smoke and chemical pollutants released by the continuous oil-well fires. Levels of soot, carbon monoxide and ozone have been studied by an Environmental Protection Agency Task Force. The National Toxics Campaign, Boston, Massachusetts, found five different toxic hydrocarbon products in the smoke (1,4-dichlorobenzene, 1,2-dichlorobenzene, diethyl phthalate, dimethyl phthalate and naphthalene), any one of which could induce serious health effects.

• Old World leishmaniasis, a parasitic disease transmitted by the bite of many species of sand fly indigenous to the region.

Non-indigenous people who enter an infected area are known to be more seriously affected by this parasite than the inhabitants. If left undiagnosed, and therefore untreated, it can be fatal. Diagnosis requires bone and spleen biopsy, and the disease can have a three-year incubation period without causing symptoms. It can be transmitted by blood transfusion, and transmitted by a woman to her unborn child. Leishmaniasis was reported as widespread in Iraq and Saudi Arabia. This disease is thought to be responsible for the Pentagon ban, November 1991, against blood donations from Gulf War veterans. This ban was lifted, for unknown reasons, on January 11, 1993.

- Pesticides and insecticides were used extensively throughout the war to protect against pestilence. It is known that large quantities of DDT, malathion, fenitrorthion, propuxur, deltamethrin and permethrin were used. They are all toxic nerve agents, and many are suspected carcinogens and mutagens.

- Destruction by allies of Iraqi chemical, nerve and biological warfare weapons resulting in widespread distribution of these toxins in the environment. This problem has now been, at least in part, documented by the U.S. Department of Defense. They are focusing on this potential cause as if it were the only candidate cause.

- The electromagnetic environment which permeated the battlefield during the war. Veterans were exposed to a broad spectrum of electromagnetic radiation created by electricity generated to support the high-tech instruments, thousands of radios and radar devices in use. This intense electromagnetic field causes both thermal and non-thermal effects, and potentially interacts with the other hazardous exposures and stresses of the battlefield. Electromagnetic radiation can alter the production of hormones (neurotransmitters), interact with cell membranes, increase calcium ion flow, stimulate protein kinase in lymphocytes, suppress the immune system, affect melatonin production required to control the "body clock," and cause changes in the blood-brain barrier.

The Hazards of Low Level Radiation

In the past few years the information available on the health effects of exposure to low levels of radiation has increased. We are no longer dependent on the commercial or military nuclear researchers who since 1950 have claimed that studies of the effects of low-level radiation are impossible to undertake. The new information is unsettling because it proves the critics of the industry to have been correct as to its serious potential to damage living tissue.

There have also been significant new releases of findings from the atomic bomb research in Hiroshima and Nagasaki, the self-acclaimed "classical research" of radiation health effects. I will list these documents toward the end of this article, along with studies from the nuclear industry.

In reviewing these research papers one is struck by the high-dose response when the radiation is delivered slowly, with low total dose. The conventional wisdom has claimed that at low dose/slow-dose rate the body is well able to repair most of the harm caused by the radiation. Some nuclear apologists go so far as to claim such exposures are "beneficial."

Because the nuclear industry has always maintained that the effects of low-dose radiation exposure are so small that it is impossible to study them, they proposed extrapolating the effects from those observed at high dose, using a straight line to zero (zero dose, zero effect), together with "correction factors" for low dose/slow-dose rate.

The effect of this "correction" is to reduce the fatal cancer estimates calculated by D.L. Preston, then Director of the Radiation Effects Research Foundation at Hiroshima, using the new dosimetry, from seventeen fatalities per million people per rad exposure, to five fatalities per million people per rad exposure. The corresponding estimates based on actually observed rates for nuclear workers is between ten and thirty fatalities per million per rad. Obviously, for the adult healthy male, the dose-response estimate should be about twenty for fatal cancers per million per rad. The official estimate used by nuclear regulators is four fatal cancers for workers (or military personnel) and five fatal cancers for members of the public from one rad exposure to one million people. (One rad is about the dose of radiation received from a major diagnostic medical X-ray).

However, although we can make a strong case for increasing the "official" estimates of harm by a factor of four, this fails to deal with non-fatal cancers, depressed immune systems, localized tissue damage (especially the respiratory, digestive and urinary tracts), damage to skin, and reproductive problems. Radiation can cause brain lesions, damage to the stem cells which produce the blood and, when the radioactive material is carried in a heavy metal (uranium), it can be stored in bone, irradiating body organs and nerves within its radius.

Consequences of Chernobyl

Detailed studies of dose-response at the low dose/slow-dose rate level:

Dr. E. B. Burlakova has provided me with a copy of the book, of which she is editor: *Consequences of the Chernobyl Catastrophe: Human Health.* In one Chapter of this book, Dr. Burlakova and fourteen other scientists publish their findings on animal and human studies of the health effects of low dose/slow-dose rate, exposure to ionizing radiation. They examined carefully the following biological phenomena under ionizing radiation exposure situations:

- alkaline elution of DNA of lymphocytes and liver
- neutral elution and adsorption of spleen DNA on nitrocellulose filters
- restriction of spleen DNA by EcoRI endonuclease
- structural characteristics (using the ESR spin probe technique) of nuclear, mitochondrial, synaptical, erythrocyte and leukocyte membranes
- activity and isoforms of aldolase and lactate hydrogenase enzymes
- activity of acetycholine esterase, superoxide dismutase, and glutathione peroxidase
- the rate of formation of superoxide anion radicals
- the composition and antioxidizing activity of lipids of the above mentioned membranes
- the sensitivity of cells, membranes, DNA, and organisms to the action of additional damaging factors.

"For all of the parameters a bimodal dose-effect dependence was discovered, i.e. the effect increased at low doses, reached its [low-dose] maximum, and then decreased (in some cases, the sign of the effect changed to the opposite, or "benefit" effect) and increased again as the dose was increased" (Burlakova, page 118).

Dr. Burlakova has speculated that at the lowest experimental doses used in this research, the repair mechanism of the cells was not triggered. It became activated at the point of the low-dose maximum, providing a "benefit" until it was overwhelmed and the damage began again to increase with dose. This may well be the case.

However, the unexpected effects of low dose/slow-dose rate exposure to ionizing radiation can also be attributed to biological mechanisms, other than the direct DNA damage hypothesis usually used by radiation physicists. These secondary mechanisms are specific to the low-/slow-dose conditions. Three such secondary mechanism have been observed by scientists: the Petkau effect, monocyte depletion, and deformed red blood cells.

The Petkau effect was discovered by Abram Petkau at the Atomic Energy of Canada Ltd. Whiteshell Nuclear Research Establishment, Manitoba, Canada in 1972.[1] Dr. Petkau discovered that at 26 rads per minute (fast-dose rate) it required a total dose of 3,500 rads to destroy a cell membrane. However, at 0.001 rad per minute (slow dose rate), it required only 0.7 rad to destroy the cell membrane. The mechanism at the slow-dose rate is the production of free radicals of oxygen (O2 with a negative electrical charge) by the ionizing effect of the radiation.

The sparsely distributed free radicals generated at the slow-dose rate have a better probability of reaching and reacting with the cell wall than do the densely crowded free radicals produced by fast-dose rates. These latter recombine quickly. Moreover, the slight electrical charge of the cell membrane attracts the free radicals in the early stages of the reaction (low total dose). Computer calculations have shown that the attraction weakens with greater concentrations of free radicals. The traditional radiation biologist has tested only high-dose reactions, and looked for direct damage to the membrane by the radiation.

Monocyte depletion: Nuclear fission produces radionuclides which tend to be stored by humans and animals in the bone tissue. In particular, strontium-90, plutonium, uranium and the transuranics have this property. Stored in bone, near the stem cells which produce the white blood cells, these radionuclides deliver a chronic low/slow dose of radiation which can interfere with normal blood-cell production. A few less neutrophils or lymphocytes (the white blood cells which are most numerous, and are usually "counted" by the radiophysicist) are not noticeable. In the normal adult, there are about 7,780 white cells per microlitre of blood. Of these, about 4,300 are neutrophils and 2,710 are lymphocytes. Only 500 are monocytes.

If, for example, stem cells in the bone marrow are destroyed so as to reduce total white blood count by 400 cells per microlitre due to the slow irradiation by radionuclides stored in the bone, this would represent a depletion of only five percent in total white cells, an insignificant amount. If all of the depletion was of neutrophils, this would mean a reduction of only 9.3 percent, still leaving the blood count well in the normal range. The lymphocytes would also be still in the normal range, even though they were depleted by 400 cells per microlitre, or 14.8 percent. However, there would be a dramatic depletion of the monocytes by 80 percent. Therefore, at low doses of radiation, it is more important to observe the monocytes, than to wait for an effect on the lymphocytes or neutrophils (as is now usually done). The effects of serious reduction in monocytes are:

- Iron deficient anemia, since it is the monocytes which recycle about 37-40 percent of the iron in the red blood cells when they die;
- Depressed cellular immune system, since the monocyte secretes the substance which activates the lymphocyte immune system.[2]

Deformed red-blood cells: Dr. Les Simpson, of New Zealand, has identified deformed red-blood cells, as observed under an electron microscope, as causing symptoms ranging from severe fatigue to brain dysfunction leading to short-term memory loss. He has identified such cells in elevated number in chronic fatigue patients, and speculated that because of their bloated or swollen shape, they are obstructed from easily passing into the tiny capillaries, thus depriving muscles and the brain of adequate oxygen and nutrients. The chronic fatigue syndrome has been observed both at Hiroshima and Nagasaki, called bura bura disease, and at Chernobyl.[3]

In the official approach to radiobiology, only direct damage to DNA has been recognized as "of concern," and only high dose/fast-dose rate experiments or observations have been accepted for use in estimating the dose-response rate. As was noted, it is the "common wisdom" that effects of low doses/slow-dose rates cannot be studied, but must be extrapolated from the officially accepted high dose/fast-dose rate studies. This approach is rejected by the work of Dr. Burlakova, and the other research noted below.

Basing one's theory on claims that it is impossible to study the phenomenon is certainly a peculiar way to do science! This myth has now been clearly shown to have been rash and criminally negligent.

Unfortunately, the Desert Storm veterans were victims of one of the latest military experiments on human beings. The people of Iraq and Kuwait were also the victims of this misguided experiment. I believe that the ignorance was culpable and criminal.

Recent Reports on Low-Level Radiation

I would like to bring your attention to the following significant new reports on the effects of low-level radiation:

Health Consequences of the Chernobyl Accident, Results of the IPHECA Pilot Projects and Related National Programs, Scientific Report, World Health Organization, Geneva 1996.

Consequences of the Chernobyl Catastrophe: Human Health, E.B. Burlakova, ed. Co-published by the Center for Russian Environmental Policy and the Scientific Council on Radiobiology Russian Academy of Science, ISBN 5-88587-019-5, Moscow 1996.

Volume 137, Supplement, *Radiation Research 1994*, which published for the first time the dose-response data on cancer incidence rate observed in the atomic bomb survivors of Hiroshima and Nagasaki. Prior to this publication, only cancer death data was reported.

Biological Effects of Ionizing Radiation V (BEIR V), U.S. National Academy of Sciences, Washington 1990. This provides new radiation risk estimates based on the newly assigned doses of radiation in this atomic bomb survivor study.

Also available now are the long term follow-up of workers in the nuclear industry. This industry has now been operating more than fifty years in the United States and about fifty years in the United Kingdom. These include:

"Inconsistencies and Open Questions Regarding Low-Dose Health Effects of Ionizing Radiation", by R. Nussbaum and W. Kohnlein. *Environmental Health Perspectives*, Vol. 102, No. 8, August 1994.

RERF Technical Report TR9-87, by D.L. Preston and D.A. Pierce, Hiroshima 1987.

"The Effects of Changes in Dosimetry on Cancer Mortality Risk Estimates in Atomic Bomb Survivors" *Radiation Research*, Vol. 114, 1988.

"Mortality and Occupational Exposure to Irradiation: First Analysis of the National Registry for Radiation Workers" by G.M. Kendall. *British Medical Journal*, Vol. 304, 1992.

"Mortality Among Workers at Oak Ridge National Laboratory" by S. Wing. *Journal of the American Medical Association*, Vol. 265, 1991.

"Reanalysis of the Hanford Data, 1944-1986 Deaths" by G.W. Kneale and A. Stewart. *American Journal of Industrial Medicine*, Volume 23, 1993.

References

1. Graeub, Ralph, *The Petkau Effect, Revised Edition*, 1990, Translated from German by Phil Hill, and Published by Four Walls Eight Windows, New York, 1994. ISBN: 1-56858-019-3.

2. Bertell, R. "Internal Bone Seeking Radionuclides and Monocyte Counts," International Perspectives in Public Health, Vol. 9, 1993, pp. 21-26.

3. Simpson, Les, has published several papers in the New Zealand Medical Journal, and wrote a Chapter in the *Medical Textbook on Myalgic Encephalomyelitis* (MI), edited by Dr. Byron Hyde.

20 | DU Spread and Contamination of Gulf War Veterans and Others

The fallout range of airborne DU aerosol dust is virtually unlimited. These micro-particles can be inhaled and ingested easily and that makes them dangerous to human health.

LEONARD A. DIETZ

Abstract

We develop background information about depleted uranium (DU) and use it to describe a physical model of how on the battlefields in Kuwait and Iraq a large number of unprotected Gulf War veterans could easily have acquired dangerous quantities of DU in their bodies.

We examine how U-238, which comprises more than 99% of DU, decays radioactively, producing two decay progeny that are always present with it and add significantly to its radioactivity. The pyrophoric nature of uranium metal causes it to burn (oxidize rapidly) when heated by impact or in fires to form invisible aerosol particles that become airborne.

We refer to scientific measurements that have been made of the atmospheric wind-borne transport of uranium aerosols over distances up to 25 miles (42 km) from their sources. Stokes' well-known physical law helps to explain how airborne transport of DU particles can occur over large distances.

We describe how gamma rays and energetic beta particles become absorbed in body tissue and can traverse large numbers of body cells, potentially causing damage to genetic material in the nuclei of living cells. We describe a biokinetic model developed by the International Commission on Radiation Protection that explains how uranium microparticles can enter the body and spread to vital organs. The model predicts that an acute intake of uranium particles can result in urinary excretions of uranium for years afterward.

We review estimates of the tonnage of DU munitions fired during the Gulf War. Even if only one or two percent of a low estimate of 300 metric tons of DU fired had burned up, this would have produced 3,000-6,000 kg of DU aerosols.

This background information allows us to propose a plausible contamination model at a battle site. It consists of three steps:

1. a source of hundreds of kilograms of DU aerosols generated suddenly against concentrated Iraqi armor;

2. widespread rapid dispersal of DU aerosol particles by wind action;

3. inhalation and ingestion of DU particles by unprotected U.S. service personnel on the battlefield.

The U.S. military and its representatives claim that DU munitions are safe, but they have not publicly addressed health and safety issues that apply after DU munitions have been fired. Apparently the official view is that in a combat situation it is acceptable for unprotected personnel to be exposed to the combustion products of fired DU munitions and assume any health risks involved.

We mention that 22 U.S. service personnel have been reported to have suffered imbedded fragments of DU in their bodies from "friendly fire." More than five years after the Gulf War, few of these fragments have been removed and the long-term health situation for these veterans has not yet been determined.   We note the astonishingly high incidence of serious birth defects in families of Gulf War veterans in the State of Mississippi.

Finally, we mention how commonly used DU flight-control counterweights in aircraft and DU munitions can burn in intense fires and produce dangerous concentrations of airborne DU aerosol particles that can be inhaled and ingested.

Introduction

It has been reported widely in the press that numerous Persian Gulf War veterans have become ill with Gulf War Syndrome. During the war they were exposed to toxic chemicals, experimental drugs, insect repellents and depleted uranium or DU.[1] Uranium is known to be highly toxic both chemically and radiologically.[2]

It has not yet been determined to what degree DU may have caused their illnesses and genetic defects in their children conceived and born after the war. Few veterans were aware that DU munitions were used until after they were exposed to uranium and became ill. Some were told about the gamma emission from DU but no one was told about the health dangers of inhaling fine particles of uranium oxide dust generated when a DU penetrator hits armor.[3] Eight days after the shooting stopped, a directive from Army Headquarters gave the first instructions to troops on how to treat radioactively contaminated vehicles.[4]

The main purpose of this paper is to develop a physical model of how easily many Gulf War veterans could have acquired dangerous quantities of DU in their bodies. To accomplish this we review the pyrophoric nature of uranium metal and its radioactivity. We show how readily uranium aerosol dust can be transported great distances by wind action in the atmosphere, pathways that DU aerosol particles can take into the body and become absorbed, and the tonnage of DU munitions fired during the Gulf War.

This information is used to construct a contamination model that explains how large numbers of soldiers very likely became contaminated on the battlefields in Kuwait and Iraq. We show how the U.S. military views the safety of DU munitions, and we close by mentioning some of the known exposures of U.S. soldiers to DU and noting the high percentage of severe birth defects in children conceived and born in many families of Gulf War veterans.

The Pyrophoric Nature of Uranium Metal

The pyrophoric nature of uranium metal is well known.[2, 5] An estimate used by U.S. Army field commanders is that when a DU penetrator in a cannon round is fired at high velocity against armor, about 10% of it burns up and forms micrometer-size uranium oxide particles that can be inhaled or ingested.[6] However, a report by the Army Environmental Policy Institute (AEPI) describing research on hard target testing states, "As much as 70 percent of a DU penetrator can be aerosolized when it strikes a tank...."[7]

Uranium can burn in other ways to generate aerosol particles of uranium oxide. Because elemental uranium is pyrophoric, when DU metal is heated in air at a temperature of 500 deg. C it can oxidize rapidly and sustain slow combustion.[5] For example, the effects of fires at storage sites for DU munitions have been studied.[8] The burning of DU metal flight-control counterweights at airplane crash sites and the possibility of exposing large numbers of people to kidney poisoning (nephrotoxicity) by uranium oxide particles has been studied by Parker.[9]

In 1992 an El Al Boeing-747 crashed into an apartment building in Amsterdam, Holland, and burned intensely. Approximately 273 kg of DU in the tail of the 747 is unaccounted for; it burned and contaminated the surrounding area.[10]

Radioactive Decay of Uranium

We look briefly at the uranium decay series. Table I summarizes the isotopic composition of natural and depleted uranium. The isotopic compositions were measured in highly sensitive and accurate mass spectrometers at the Knolls Atomic Power Laboratory.[11]

Table I: Isotopic composition of natural and depleted uranium in atom percent.

	U-234	U-235	U-236	U-238
Natural Uranium	0.0055	0.7196	0.0000	99.2749
Depleted Uranium	0.0008	0.2015	0.0030	99.7947

A trace of U-236 from reprocessed nuclear fuel may be present in some of the DU stockpile. The alpha activity in DU is about 43% less than it is in natural uranium because there is less U-234 and U-235, but DU always occurs in highly concentrated form and this more than makes up for its lower alpha activity. In contrast, natural uranium occurs in concentrations of 1-3 parts per million by weight in soils, where it is locked up in nonmetallic form in minerals and is relatively inert to chemical action there.

Only the first three isotopes in the uranium decay series or chain headed by U-238 are important in determining the radioactivity of DU.[12] Uranium-238 decays into thorium-234 (Th-234), which decays into protactinium-234 (Pa-234), which decays into U-234, etc. down the decay chain. The 246,000-year half-life of U-234 is too long for it to decay much during our lifetimes and produce significant numbers of decay progeny.

The U-238 decay chain is broken during the chemical reduction of uranium hexafluoride into DU metal and is broken again during the melting and processing of the metal into a penetrator. To determine the maximum time it takes to regain equilibrium in the partial decay chain, we assume a solid sample of uranium that initially contains only the U-238 isotope, i.e. no decay progeny. Using Bateman's equations,[13] we calculate the growth of Th-234 and Pa-234 activities as a function of elapsed time in weeks. The results are given in Table II.

Table II: Radioactivity (disintegrations/second) in 1 gram of U-238
with no decay progeny initially present.

Half lives used:

U-238 = 4.47 x 10^9 years
Th-234 = 24.10 days
Pa-234 = 1.17 minutes, 6.69 hours (two decay states)
U-234 = 2.46 x 10^5 years.[14]

Scientific notation is used, i.e. 2.46 x 10^5 = 246,000.

Weeks	U-238 →	Th-234 →	Pa-234 →	U-234
0	12,430	0	0	0.000
1	12,430	2,270	2,150	0.000
5	12,430	7,890	7,840	0.001
10	12,430	10,770	10,750	0.004
15	12.430	11,830	11,820	0.007
20	12,430	12,210	12,210	0.010
25	12,430	12,350	12,350	0.013
30	12,430	12,400	12,400	0.017

After 25 weeks, Th-234 and Pa-234 have reached 99.4% of the decay
rate of U-238 and for practical purposes have reached secular
equilibrium with U-238, their parent isotope. Secular equilibrium
means that the decay progeny of U-238 are being replaced at the
same rate they are decaying; after 25 weeks all three isotopes are
decaying at approximately the same rate. This is a maximum time; in
reality, equilibrium will be reached much faster, since these two
isotopes can never be separated totally from U-238. The isotope
U-238 emits alpha particles and also emits some gamma rays. Its
decay progeny Th-234 and Pa-234 each emit beta particles and
gamma rays. An alpha particle is a fast helium atom with its two
electrons removed, a beta particle is a high-speed electron and a
gamma ray is like an X-ray.

Substantial Radiation Six Months After Manufacture
From this analysis we conclude that in a solid sample of DU, six

months at most after manufacture of a DU penetrator, or DU armor for a tank, or DU particles in a person's body, substantial additional radiation in the form of beta particles and gamma rays always will be present. In fact, most of the penetrating gamma radiation and all of the penetrating beta radiation from DU comes, not from uranium, but from the decay progeny of U-238.[15] In a year, only one-thousandth of a gram (1 milligram or mg) of DU generates more than a billion alpha particles, beta particles and gamma rays.

The U.S. Army has investigated the generation of DU aerosols in armored vehicles hit by DU cannon rounds. Their investigators report "... that personnel inside DU struck vehicles could receive a dose in the tens of milligrams' range due to inhalation."[16] This exposure results in an acute dose of uranium.

Gamma rays become absorbed in body tissue as follows. If their energy exceeds 40 keV, part of the gamma-ray energy is transferred to an atomic electron, setting it in high-speed motion (1 keV = 1000 electron volts energy). The remaining energy is carried off by a new gamma ray. This process, called the Compton effect, repeats until the gamma ray has an energy below about 40 keV where the photoelectric effect dominates and the remaining energy can be transferred to a photoelectron.

For example, using Gofman's method,[17] one can calculate that an 850 keV gamma ray absorbed in body tissue will produce a packet of high-speed Compton electrons and a fast photoelectron that on average can traverse 137 body cells. By contrast, according to Gofman, X-rays commonly used in medical diagnosis have a peak energy of 90 keV and an average energy of 30 keV[17] A 30 keV X-ray in body tissue can be converted into a photoelectron of this energy, which on average can traverse only 1.7 cells. Ionization along the tracks of high-speed electrons in tissue can cause damage to genetic material in the nuclei of cells.

Thus, a high energy gamma ray from Pa-234 is much more penetrating than a typical medical X-ray and can damage far more living cells. The many 2.29 MeV beta particles emitted by Pa-234 are extremely penetrating in body tissue (1 MeV = 1 million electron volts energy). Referring to the experimental data given by Gofman,[17] each one of these beta particles can traverse more than 500 body cells.

Alpha, beta and gamma radiations produce the same biological effects on cells and organs, and much of their radiation damage to body tissue can accumulate over the time of exposure.[18] Therefore, it seems reasonable that not only the continuous radiation of body tissue by alpha particles from U-238, but the energetic beta particles and gamma rays from its decay progeny Th-234 and Pa-234 must also be considered when assessing possible cancer risk and genetic damage.

Airborne Transport of Uranium Particles

The fallout range of airborne DU aerosol dust is virtually unlimited. These micro-particles can be inhaled and ingested easily and that makes them dangerous to human health. Environmental assessments for sites which process DU or test fire DU munitions typically downplay the potential for widespread fallout of DU particles.

For example, one such environmental impact study in 1992 by the U.S. Army Ballistics Research Laboratory[19] states, "Because of the mass and density of the DU particle, it only travels short distances when airborne. These two factors alone preclude the off-site release of DU." This is not true for micrometer-size particles of uranium metal or its oxides. In fact, the transport of airborne DU aerosol particles was well known long before the Army Ballistics Research Laboratory environmental impact study was written, since in 1976 it had been measured up to a distance of 8 km.[20] What may not have been fully appreciated in 1976 was that DU aerosol particles could be transported by wind action over much greater distances.

In 1979 the author worked at the Knolls Atomic Power Laboratory (KAPL) in Schenectady, New York. While trouble-shooting a radiological problem, he and his colleagues in the mass spectrometer component accidentally discovered DU aerosols collected in environmental air filters exposed at the Knolls site.[21] The origin of the DU contamination proved to be the National Lead Industries plant in Colonie, 10 miles (16 km) east of the Knolls site, on the western boundary of the city of Albany, NY. A local newspaper reported that National Lead was fabricating DU penetrators for 30-mm cannon rounds and airplane counterweights made of DU metal.[22]

A total of 16 air filters at three different locations covering 25 weeks of exposure from May through October of 1979 were analyzed; all contained trace amounts of DU. Three of these air filters were exposed for four weeks each at a site 26 miles (42 km) northwest of the NL plant. This is by no means the maximum fallout distance for DU aerosol particles.

Totally unrelated to the discovery of DU in KAPL air filters, in

February 1980, a court order by New York State forced National Lead Industries to cease production, because they exceeded a New York State radioactivity limit of 150 microcuries for airborne emissions in a given month.[22] The plant closed in 1983 and is now being decontaminated and dismantled.

The 150 microcuries corresponds to 387 g of DU metal. For comparison, one GAU-8/A penetrator in an aircraft 30-mm cannon round contains 272 g of DU metal.[5]

DU Particles Borne Miles by Wind

Using a special fission track analysis technique, 26 uranium-bearing particles were extracted from several air filters exposed at KAPL and were analyzed separately for their uranium isotopic content.[11] Four particles contained pure DU. They were approximately 4-6 micrometers in size; three were irregularly shaped and the fourth was a 3.8 micrometer diameter sphere. Probably it solidified from a molten state as uranium dioxide. The other 22 particles were enriched uranium associated with the radiological trouble-shooting problem.

This widespread trace contamination of DU in the atmosphere was less than 1% of allowable limits. Its presence in the air filters did not concern us nearly as much as the sizes of the DU particles that were borne 10 miles by the wind from Albany to KAPL. The four DU particles were near the upper end of the respirable size range, which is about 5 micrometers. Respirable means that particles will pass through the upper respiratory airway to the lung and become deposited in various interior regions of the lung, where many will remain for many years. A 5-micrometer uranium dioxide particle can cause a high, localized yearly radiation dose from energetic alpha particles to lung tissue; it is a radioactive hot spot in the lung.[23]

The density of uranium metal is 19 grams per cubic centimeter; for uranium dioxide it is 11 grams per cubic centimeter, equal to the density of lead. How can a uranium dioxide particle with this density, or a uranium metal particle with a density 1.7 times that of lead remain airborne long enough to be transported by wind 26 miles (42 km)? It might seem a daunting challenge to answer this question, but a complicated physical theory is unnecessary.

Just as a parachute jumper in a free fall through the lower atmosphere quickly reaches a constant terminal velocity of approximately 120 mph, so too a micrometer-size uranium particle falling under gravitational attraction through still air will reach a constant terminal velocity that is determined by its size, density, geometrical shape and air viscosity.

Stokes' law provides an accurate and convincing scientific explanation of how micrometer-size DU particles can remain airborne for many hours. This physical law is well known to scientists and engineers who study fluid dynamics. It was published in 1846 and 1851 by Sir George Stokes, and is described in introductory textbooks on fluid flow.[24] It is given by the expression

$$V = \frac{2G\,R^2\,(S\text{-}A)}{9\,C}\text{ , where}$$

R^2 means R squared,

$G =$ 980.4 centimeters per second squared is the acceleration of gravity,

$R =$ the radius of the sphere in centimeters,

$S =$ the density of the sphere in grams per cubic centimeter,

$A =$ 1.213×10^{-3} grams per cubic centimeter is the density of air at one atmosphere and 18 deg. C,

$C =$ 1.827×10^{-4} poise is the viscosity of air at one atmosphere and 18 deg. C.

The terminal velocity V is in centimeters per second if G, R, S, A and C are in the units shown. Stokes' law allows one to calculate the terminal velocity of a microsphere of uranium metal or uranium oxide of known radius and density falling through still air.

Stokes' law is valid for fluid flow described by a Reynolds number of 0.1 or less.[24] Experiments confirm this upper limit.[25] The dimensionless Reynolds number Re for a sphere is given by

$$Re = \frac{2\,R\,A\,V}{C}\text{ ,}$$

where the terms are defined above. A 10 micrometer diameter uranium metal sphere falls at 5.7 cm/sec in still air and Re = 0.038, which is much less than 0.1. Therefore, Stokes' law is accurate for all respirable spherical uranium metal or oxide particles 10 micrometers or less in diameter falling through air. Table III lists the fall rates for a range of particle sizes.

Table III: Terminal (constant) velocities for uranium dioxide spherical particles in still air. Diameters are in micrometers.

diameter	cm/sec.	ft./hour
5.0	0.82	97
4.0	0.52	62
3.0	0.30	35
2.0	0.13	15
1.0	0.033	4
0.5	0.0082	1

Irregularly-shaped microparticles will fall more slowly than a sphere of the same density and weight. Depleted uranium particles one micrometer or smaller are virtually floating in air and can remain airborne for a very long time. The 3.8 micrometer dia. spherical uranium dioxide particle analyzed at KAPL had a fall rate of 56 ft./hr. It had to reach a height of only 200 ft. in the warm exhaust plume from the National Lead plant for a gentle breeze averaging 3 mph to carry it 10 miles (16 km) to KAPL.

Fallout range can be increased greatly by two more natural phenomena. First, frictional forces in the air or emission of an alpha particle from a uranium atom will electrostatically charge a DU particle. For example, it is well known that a high velocity ion striking a metal oxide surface will dislodge a pulse of secondary electrons from the surface.[26]

An alpha particle is a high velocity helium ion, and it will generate a large number of secondary electrons below the surface of an uranium oxide particle as it passes through the surface. Many of the momentarily-free electrons just below the surface will escape from an airborne uranium oxide particle, leaving it in a positively-charged state.

Like an electrostatic precipitator collecting dust in a room, an electrically-charged uranium dioxide particle and an oppositely-charged dust particle will attract each other and join together.

The average density of the two particles together will be substantially less than 11 grams per cubic centimeter and the fallout range will be greatly increased.

Fallout particles of DU also can become attached to sand or dust particles on the ground and then become resuspended in the air by wind or vehicle action and transported to new locations.[27] Desert sand in the Persian Gulf region is extremely fine.[28] Second, random motions of the atmosphere of a few cm/sec are of the same order of magnitude as the terminal velocities of micrometer particles of DU oxide or metal falling through air.

Pathways of DU and Its Radiation into the Body

Routes of intake or pathways of uranium particles into the body include the respiratory tract, the gastrointestinal tract and the skin, through abrasions or wounds. The International Commission on Radiation Protection (ICRP) has developed a biokinetic model that describes the behavior of uranium within the human body.[29] The model takes into account aerosol particle size, chemical form, and the excretion rates of absorbed uranium from individual vital organs and bones. Radioactive particles reach the gastrointestinal tract by ingestion and by transfer from the respiratory tract. The model shows that for an acute intake of uranium aerosol particles of uranium dioxide or U_3O_8 (yellowcake), urinary excretion of the inhaled uranium can continue for years.

Exposure to gamma rays emitted from DU is another pathway into the body. Crews are exposed to the equivalent of one chest X-ray for every 20-30 hours they spend in an Abrams tank armed with DU ammunition.[30] The U.S. Army measured a gamma dose rate of 250 millirems per hour at the surface of a penetrator.[31] This dose rate is consistent with the 233 millirads per hour dose rate for an unspecified mass of DU listed on a U.S. Department of Labor Material Safety Data Sheet issued to Nuclear Metals, Inc.[32] For gamma rays, the rad and rem dose units are equal. At body contact, the 250 millirems per hour is equivalent to a dose rate of up to approximately 50 chest X-rays per hour. Whole penetrators or large fragments of penetrators fired from tank cannon and left on a battlefield have this amount of surface radioactivity.

Estimates of Tonnage of DU Munitions Fired

The actual tonnage of DU munitions fired during the Gulf War is difficult to ascertain. During the war all battlefield news was censored and the expenditure of DU by A-10 attack aircraft was classified.[33] It has been estimated that these aircraft fired about 95% of the DU munitions used during Desert Shield and Desert Storm.[34] The U.S. Army now claims that "More than 14,000 large caliber DU rounds were consumed during Operations Desert Shield/Desert Storm. As many as 7,000 of these rounds may have been fired in practice. Approximately 4,000 rounds were reportedly fired in combat. The remaining 3,000 rounds are losses that include a substantial loss in a fire at Dohoa, Saudi Arabia."[35] (This should be Doha, Kuwait.—L.D.)

The 14,000 rounds contained about 60 metric tons of DU. William Arkin estimates from documents released under the Freedom of Information Act that approximately 300 metric tons of DU littered the battlefields of Kuwait and Iraq after the war.[34] The LAKA Foundation estimates the total as 800 tons.[36] Allowing for DU projectiles missing their targets, even if only one or two percent of the lower estimate of 300 metric tons burned up, then 3,000,000-6,000,000 grams of DU aerosol particles could have become airborne over the battlefields—a huge amount.

Contamination Model

We can now propose a plausible model of how veterans became contaminated with DU during the Gulf War. It consists of a sequence of three steps:

1. **Source**: in a local area of a battlefield, hundreds of kilograms of micrometer-size DU particles were generated suddenly by cannon fire from U.S. airplanes and tanks at concentrated formations of Iraqi armor. Thermal columns from burning tanks and vehicles then carried aloft these localized plumes of DU aerosol particles.

2. **Dispersal**: Clouds of DU aerosol particles were dispersed far and wide by wind action over the battlefield and, based on the KAPL measurements, the fallout range of these uranium micro-particles could be up to 25 miles (42 km) or more.[11]

3. Inhalation and Ingestion: Unprotected U.S. service personnel could inhale and ingest huge numbers of DU particles into their lungs and bodies, where much of the DU could become absorbed in vital organs and bones. The ICRP biokinetic model explains how uranium aerosol particles can enter the body and become absorbed.[29]

The U.S. Army and the Veterans Administration have shown an unwillingness to investigate health issues associated with the toxicity and radioactivity of inhaled and ingested DU aerosol particles that have become absorbed in the body. Both have refused to test large numbers of veterans for the presence of DU in their bodies; so far only a handful have been tested. According to Laura Flanders, as of January, 1995, at least 45,000 soldiers deployed to the Persian Gulf during the war are suffering from symptoms connected with their service.[37]

Workers in DU industrial processing plants and people living in communities surrounding these plants also have been contaminated by fallout of DU particles.[22] How rapidly contamination takes place depends on the magnitude of the airborne concentration and particle size of the uranium dust. The smaller the particle, the easier it can enter the body.

In written testimony prepared for a 1982 New York State hearing on NL Industries, Dr. Carl Johnson, a principal investigator of the National Cancer Institute Project, stated that some of the workers at the NL plant had concentrations of uranium in their urine as high as 30 picocuries/liter (77 micrograms of uranium/liter). He said this concentration level indicated a very heavy body burden of uranium.[38]

How the U.S. Military Views the Safety of DU Munitions
In a letter to Senator Sam Nunn, a representative of the U.S. Air Force stated that "...these projectiles are no more hazardous to store, transport, or employ than those composed of lead or copper."[39] This view is echoed in the U.S. Army report to Congress that states, "The health risks associated with using DU in peacetime are minimal. This includes risks associated with transporting, storing and handling intact DU munitions and armor during peacetime."[40]

Neither the Air Force nor the Army has publicly presented an analysis of the health risks to soldiers and to others who inhale or ingest radioactive fallout particles of DU, or the health risks of living in an environment contaminated with DU after these munitions have been fired: these are the real safety issues they ignore. Furthermore, a General Accounting Office report to Congress states, "...[A]rmy officials believe that DU protective methods can be ignored during battle and other life-threatening situations because DU-related health risks are greatly outweighed by the risks of combat."[41]

The Army must know that it would be extremely difficult to provide breathing masks that can efficiently remove all of the respirable DU particles from air breathed by soldiers. Even if highly efficient air filters are used by troops, their surroundings will still be contaminated. The surface of the ground, vegetation, equipment, uniforms and other garments contaminated with DU particles will become secondary sources of airborne DU aerosols whenever they are disturbed or moved, thereby presenting an insurmountable radiological containment and decontamination problem on the battlefield.

In the AEPI report,[42] the Army judges it an acceptable risk if its personnel become exposed in an unprotected fashion to the combustion products of fired DU munitions on the battlefield or elsewhere. This report contains much technical information about DU, but many of the assertions and conclusions in the report are not supported by the technical and scientific data presented. A rebuttal to the AEPI report pointing out some major inconsistencies in the Army report has been published by the Military Toxics Project.[43]

Exposure of U.S. Soldiers and Illnesses in Their Families
Thirty-six U.S. soldiers, including 22 with embedded fragments of DU in their bodies, have sought or reported for medical treatment.[44] They were in vehicles hit by DU munitions. Another report states there were 35 casualties and 72 wounded in crews of U.S. tanks and Bradley Fighting vehicles in so-called "friendly fire" incidents.[45] This includes the 36 above and is the total number of service personnel officially admitted to have been exposed to significant quantities of DU aerosol dust and DU fragments during the fighting.

On an NBC Dateline program,[6] Sgt. Daryll Clark describes how he and twelve others were in an advanced position in the desert when someone radioed them that 20 Iraqi tanks were approaching his forward radar unit. He called for air support, and shortly a flight of A-10 Warthogs arrived and destroyed all of the tanks with DU-tipped 30-mm cannon rounds.

Clark describes how he and the men with him were coughing and choking on smoke from the burning tanks, but mixed with it was DU aerosol dust, which he and the others breathed. He has had chronic respiratory problems since the war, and his daughter Kennedy was born in September 1992 with purple welts called hemangioma covering not only her face and body, but some internal organs as well. Kennedy has serious breathing problems and was born without a thyroid. Clark stated that a geneticist told him that he could have ingested some radiation and that it could affect sperm cells. Almost three years after his exposure to DU, Clark's urine tested positive for uranium.

Army nurse First Sgt. Carol Picou also is featured in the NBC documentary. She and seven other women in her medical team were in a forward position, ahead of the main U.S. forces and surrounded by burning Iraqi tanks and vehicles when they stopped and became exposed to DU from the burning destroyed Iraqi armor. Doctor Thomas Callender of Lafayette, Louisiana, has examined Picou and said on the program that her outcome bears a striking similarity to other individuals who had exposures to ingested radioactive elements. Picou has been given a medical discharge.

The seven medical personnel with Picou and the 12 soldiers with Clark probably became contaminated with DU. These 21 soldiers are not included in the official list of those recognized by the U.S. government as having been exposed to DU. Given the large tonnage of uranium penetrators in cannon rounds that were fired on the battlefields in Iraq and Kuwait, it is likely that many thousands of other soldiers also became contaminated with DU. The U.S. Army and the Veterans Administration balk at giving urinalysis tests and *in vivo* tests (whole-body counting of gamma rays) to measure the amount of DU in the lungs and other body organs of Gulf War veterans.

An astonishingly high rate of birth defects in the families of Gulf War veterans is especially troubling. For example, Laura Flanders reports that the Veterans Administration conducted a state-wide survey of 251 Gulf War veterans families in Mississippi.[46] Of their children conceived and born since the war, 67% have illnesses rated severe or have missing eyes, missing ears, blood infections, respiratory problems and fused fingers. Flanders goes on to say that the birth defects are consistent with the effects of radiation from DU and infection from sand fly bites. Others blame experimental vaccines, chemical warfare pills, the insect repellent DEET and smoke from oil well fires for causing birth defects.

Conclusion

We have shown how easily micrometer particles of DU can spread over a large region and poison many people both radiologically and chemically. The promotion and sale of DU munitions by U.S. arms manufacturers (with U.S. government approval) and by other arms manufacturers to the armies and air forces of many nations will guarantee that in future conflicts thousands of soldiers on both sides will inhale and ingest acute doses of DU aerosols, and many in armored vehicles struck by DU penetrators will receive dangerous doses of non-removable uranium shrapnel in their bodies.

The human cost of using DU munitions in conflicts is not worth the perceived short-term advantages, especially if it results in U.S. veterans and others becoming ill and in genetic defects in their offspring. A comprehensive epidemiological study should be made of all Gulf War veterans and their families, searching for evidence of residual DU in their bodies and for causes of genetic defects in their children. The health issues associated with DU munitions should be investigated and evaluated by independent medical and scientific experts separated completely from the Department of Defense, Veterans Administration, National Laboratories, U.S. military services and their contractors.

References

1. Depleted uranium basically is natural uranium in which the U-235 isotopic content has been reduced from 0.7% to 0.2%. It is a waste product of uranium enrichment plants.

2. *Handbook of Chemistry and Physics*, The Chemical Rubber Co., 50th ed., 1969-70, p. B-55. This has been a standard reference text for generations of scientists and engineers. It is updated every two years.

3. "Operation Desert Storm: Army Not Adequately Prepared to Deal With Depleted Uranium Contamination," U.S. General Accounting Office Report GAO/NSIAD-93-90, Jan. 29, 1993.

4. Headquarters U.S. Army Armament, Munitions and Chemical Command memorandum on DU, March 7, 1991, to Persian Gulf commanders, photocopy in the book, *Uranium Battlefields Home and Abroad: Depleted Uranium Use by the U.S. Department of Defense*, Bukowski, G. and Lopez, D.A., March, 1993, pp. 91-94.

5. Lowenstein, P., "Industrial Uses of Depleted Uranium," photocopy in *Uranium Battlefields Home and Abroad: Depleted Uranium Use by the U.S. Department of Defense*, Bukowski, G. and Lopez, D.A., March, 1993, pp. 135-141.

6. Reported on National Broadcasting Co. (NBC TV) *Dateline* program, "Deadly Fire," Feb. 22, 1994.

7. "Health and Environmental Consequences of Depleted Uranium Use in the U.S. Army: Technical Report," prepared by the Army Environmental Policy Institute at the request of the U.S. Congress, June 1994, p. 78.

8. Mishima, J.; Parkhurst, M.A.; and Hadlock, D.E., *Potential Behavior of Depleted Uranium Penetrators under Shipping and Bulk Storage Accident Conditions*, Battelle Pacific Northwest Laboratory, Richland, WA, Report PNL-5415, March 1985, p. 138.

9. Parker, R.L., "Fear of Flying," *Nature*, Vol. 336 22/29 December 1988, p. 719.

10. Van der Keur, Henk, "Uranium Pollution from the Amsterdam Plane Crash," *Konfrontatie*, February 1994; translated by Wendie Kooge and Kemp Houck.

11. Dietz, L.A., CHEM-434-LAD, "Investigation of Excess Alpha Activity Observed in Recent Air Filter Collections and Other Environmental Samples," Jan. 24, 1980, p. 7; unclassified technical report, Knolls Atomic Power Laboratory, Schenectady, NY 12301; obtained under the Freedom of Information Act. Copies available upon request from Cathy Hinds, Director, Military Toxics Project, P.O. Box 845, Sabattus, ME 04280, or from Grace Bukowski, Citizen Alert, P.O. Box 5339, Reno, NV 89513.

12. Bukowski, G. and Lopez, D.A., *Uranium Battlefields Home and abroad: Depleted Uranium Use by the U.S. Department of Defense*, March 1993, p. 59.

13. Bateman, H., "The Solution of a System of Differential Equations Occurring in the Theory of Radioactive Transformations," *Proc. Cambridge Phil. Soc. 16*, p. 423 (1910).

14. Half-lives are from Nuclides and Isotopes Fourteenth Edition Chart of the

Nuclides, 1989, GE Co. Nuclear Energy Operations, 175 Curtner Ave., M/C 397, San Jose, CA 95125.

15. *Handbook of Chemistry and Physics*, p. B-535, *op. cit.*

16. "Health and Environmental Consequences of Depleted Uranium Use in the U.S. Army: Technical Report," p. 119, *op. cit.*

17. For a detailed description of the physics and method used in calculating average Compton electron and photoelectron energies, their ranges in body tissue, and estimating the number of living cells traversed by these highspeed electrons and by beta particles, see J. W. Gofman's book, *Radiation-Induced Cancer from Low-Dose Exposure: an Independent Analysis*, 1990: 1st. ed., Committee for Nuclear Responsibility, Inc. Book Division, P.O. Box 11207, San Francisco, CA 94101, Chapters 32 and 33.

18. Schubert, J. and Lapp, R.E., *Radiation: What It Is and How It Affects You*, Compass Books Edition, Viking Press, 1958, pp. 66, 8, 16 and 18.

19. Report No. NV-89-06, "Environmental Assessment for the Depleted Uranium Testing Program at the Nevada Test Site by the United States Army Ballistics Research Laboratory," U.S. Dept. of Energy, Nevada Field Office, Las Vegas, Nevada, March 1992, p. 12.

20. Dahl, D.A. and Johnson, L.J., LA-UR-77-681, "Aerosolized U and Be from LASL Dynamic Experiments," Los Alamos Scientific Laboratory, 1977, p. 2.

21. Dietz, L.A., CHEM-434-LAD, *op. cit.*

22. Hines, B., "Colonie Uranium Plant Closes as Radiation Continues Unchecked," Schenectady Gazette, Feb. 6, 1980, photocopy in *Uranium Battlefields Home and Abroad: Depleted Uranium Use by the U.S. Department of Defense*, by G. Bukowski and D.A. Lopez, May 24, 1991, p. 120.

23. Dietz, L.A., "Estimate of Radiation Dose from a Depleted Uranium Oxide Particle," in *Uranium Battlefields Home and Abroad: Depleted Uranium Use by the U.S. Department of Defense*, by Bukowski, G. and Lopez, D.A., May 24, 1991, pp. 153-155.

24. Massey, B. S., text book, *Mechanics of Fluids*, 6th Ed.,Van Nostrand Reinhold, 1989, p. 172.

25. Fox, R. W. and McDonald, A. T., text book, *Introduction to Fluid Mechanics*, 4th Ed., Wiley, 1992, p. 444.

26. Dietz, L.A. and Sheffield, J. C., "Secondary electron emission induced by 5-30 keV monatomic ions striking thin oxide films," *Journal of Applied Physics*, Vol. 46. No. 10, October 1975, pp. 4361-4370.

27. For a discussion of resuspension of radionuclides, see *Enewetak Radiological Survey*, U.S. Atomic Energy Commission, Nevada Operations Office, Las Vegas, NV, Report NVO-140, Vol. I, Oct. 1973, pp. 507-523.

28. Korényi-Both, Col. A.L., MD, Ph.D, "Al Eskan Disease-Persian Gulf Syndrome," synopsis of a medical report.

29. International Commission on Radiation Protection Publication 54, book, *Individual Monitoring for Intakes of Radionuclides by Workers: Design and Interpretation*, Pergamon Press, 1988.

30. Bukowski, G. and Lopez, D.A., *Uranium Battlefields Home and Abroad: Depleted Uranium Use by the U.S. Department of Defense*, March 1993, p. 50.

31. Skogman, D.P., Headquarters, U.S. Army Armament, Munitions and Chemical Command, Rock Is., IL 61299, May 24, 1991, photocopy of document in *Uranium Battlefields Home and abroad: Depleted Uranium Use by the U.S. Department of Defense*, by Bukowski, G. and Lopez, D.A., p. 98.

32. Bukowski, G. and Lopez, D.A., see pp. 131-132 for photocopy of Material Safety Data Sheet, *op. cit.*

33. Osterman, J., "Potential Hazards of Depleted Uranium Penetrators," a Pentagon report to Congressman Les Aspin, Chm. House Armed Services Comm., photocopy in *Uranium Battlefields Home and Abroad: Depleted Uranium Use by the U.S. Department of Defense*, by Bukowski, G. and Lopez, D.A., pp. 86-89.

34. Arkin, W.M., "The desert glows: with propaganda," *Bulletin of the Atomic Scientists*, May 1993, p. 12.

35. Summary Report to Congress, "Health and Environmental Consequences of Depleted Uranium Use by the U.S. Army," prepared by the U.S. Army Environmental Policy Institute, June 1994, p. 10.

36. The LAKA Foundation: Dutch national center for critical documentation on nuclear energy; No. 2 in a series of fact sheets on the Gulf War, June 1994.

37. Flanders, L., "A Lingering Sickness," *The Nation*, Jan. 29, 1995, pp, 94, 96.

38. Bukowski, G. and Lopez, D.A., p. 35, *op. cit.*

39. Washabaugh, Lt. Col. W.M., U.S. Air Force, Congressional Inquiry Div., Office of Legislative Liaison, letter to Sen. Sam Nunn, Chm. Senate Armed Services Comm., Nov. 8, 1990.

40. Summary Report to Congress, p. 3, *op. cit.*

41. "Operation Desert Storm," p. 4, *op. cit.*

42. "Health and Environmental Consequences of Depleted Uranium Use in the U.S. Army: Technical Report," *op. cit.*

43. "Radioactive Battlefields of the 1990s, the United States Army's use of Depleted Uranium and Its Consequences for Human Health and the Environment," by the Military Toxics Project's Depleted Uranium Citizens' Network, January 16, 1996.

44. Summary Report to Congress, p. 2, *op. cit.*

45. Helmkamp, J.C., "United States Military Casualty Comparison During the Persian Gulf War," *Journal of Occupational Medicine*, Vol. 36, June 6, 1994, p. 614.

46. Flanders, L., "Mal de Guerre," *The Nation*, March 7, 1994, p. 292.

[This paper was first written July 19, 1996. It is reproduced here with permission]

Section VI:

Environmental Cost of Gulf War to Iraqis and Others

21 | Gravesites: Environmental Ruin in Iraq

The chain of death created by the Gulf War is an awesome thing. But the really scary part comes later—now—when we find that things which looked alive are really dead or doomed.

BARBARA NIMRI AZIZ

It was a sunny spring afternoon in North Iraq in 1996. I stood on a gently sloping verge overlooking meadows of what was supposed to be young wheat. A cover of green tinged with a soft yellow extended as far as one could see in all directions and, from a distance, it appeared to be an undisturbed pastoral setting. On the surface, it looked serene.

Had I traveled four hundred kilometers just to escape the ugliness of Baghdad and the constant sight of beggars there? Did I come to this green landscape to shut out those endless complaints about food prices, and the now tedious questions put to me as a visiting journalist about when the UN sanctions might end? As much as I could, I had addressed those issues. Now I was pursuing my own agenda—to investigate agricultural production.

Why should the United Nations economic sanctions, imposed in August 1990 and still strictly enforced, hamper local food production? I wanted to know. So I travelled to the northern wheat-growing area around Mosul, as well as to small family farms both north and south of Baghdad.

With me on that tour in the north were agronomists from the agricultural office in Mosul. This was the administrative center for the entire northern governate. This region was Iraq's breadbasket—a grain-growing center for the country of nineteen million people. The Iraqis were to show me the farms, and when we pulled off the road and walked up the slope, I waited for them to lead me to fields where wheat grew. Yet the men did not move beyond where we stood when I asked to see the wheat.

"This is it," said the officer quietly, looking at the ground. "This is the crop."

I looked down at the growth at my feet, then around the hill, and finally at my Iraqi hosts. I was confused.

"I do not believe this is a wheat field."

I was stunned that I had blurted this out; I felt embarrassed. It was as if I had accused the men of deception.

Mohammed Sheet is chief plant protection officer for Mosul, a trained agronomist. Neither he nor his assistants responded to my observation. What were they to reply?

I broke into the awful silence and asked if we could move deeper into the field, as if our proximity to the road somehow was responsible for the sickly growth around us. They obliged and we walked five hundred meters up the slope. It was the same. I said nothing. "Yes, this is also wheat," said the official. It was no different from what grew at the first site. Now all of us were silent, gazing at the ground, as if standing on a grave.

Recovering from the shock, I apologized. I knew what ripe, healthy grain fields look like and I could recognize young stands of wheat. Elsewhere in the world, I had witnessed bad crops, too, places where seventy percent was lost due to drought, and I had observed thin fields planted with bad seed or crops eaten back by pests. But I had never seen anything as bad as this.

I asked Mr. Sheet to point out which was the wheat plant. He bent down and touched some of the grass shoots visible among the growth. Hardly more than shreds had reached the surface. The grass was just no more than four inches high, whereas a normal crop should be eighteen inches by this time of the year. Low yield is one thing. But this wheat was so badly infested, it was virtually destroyed. Moreover, this tragedy seemed to be no accident.

The growth at our feet was largely mustard weed and another thick plant I found very ugly. Both were weeds. Together they almost obliterated the wheat. Wide, prickly leaves of the second weed covered most of the ground. There was no possibility of separating these from the food crop. Not now, nor when the fields would be harvested. These weeds had also consumed most of the precious, limited fertilizer which the farmers had applied here.

Weeds of course are a threat everywhere. If not controlled, they destroy. They cannot be cut out by hand or machine; today only chemicals can control them.

Herbicides and pesticides could have saved some of that wheat. But they were unavailable. Why? They are embargoed by the UN along with other agricultural products and machinery. For years they have been almost absent from Iraq so that the current level of infestation is a result of accumulated neglect. And only with permission from the UN Sanctions Committee in New York can those essential chemicals be obtained. But permits are not forthcoming. This year, as in the past, the critical time for spraying had passed before the Food and Agricultural office in Baghdad received UN approval to import the essential chemicals.

The crop was lost. And the farmers knew it. Indeed, before leaving Mr. Sheet's Mosul office for these fields, I had personally witnessed dozens of farmers, anxious and angry, pleading with the government bureaucrats for some pesticide.

The Really Scary Part

The chain of death created by the Gulf War is a scary thing. I'm not talking about black skies over the blazing oil wells of Kuwait, or charred remains of soldiers on the sand or the incinerated families who had sought protection in a bomb shelter. Those are familiar images of death, recognizable, and however painful, they are finite. With the end of hostilities, they disappear.

The really scary part comes later—now—when we find that things which looked alive are really dead or doomed.

I refer to a chain of deadly pollution, the kind that creeps up on us, first with vague complaints, then with the persistence of strange illnesses, then with more testimonials of similar symptoms. We slowly recognize that disparate reports which first appear unrelated are, in fact, connected.

We have the sickening sense of something spreading, without limits, of something embedded so deep within the system that it's unreachable. Our inquiries are met with denials. So, to begin, all we seek to do is confront it. We just want to stand on the gravesite as if it were a known, finite place.

This is our feeling, I think, as we hear more and more documentation regarding Gulf War Syndrome and its link to the use, by the Pentagon, of depleted uranium weaponry during the 1991 war. Evidence is mounting, and those soldiers who find themselves stricken are growing in number, networking and uniting in a swelling movement of people who refuse to accept government disclaimers that these soldiers might be the victims of some new dangerous materials the Pentagon used.

While a public movement to ban depleted uranium grows and attracts more media attention in the U.S., in Iraq there is barely a whisper about what the human effects of exposure to depleted uranium within Iraq might be. Of course many Iraqis were killed outright by the weapons that blew apart their vehicles and their bunkers. Those who survived the onslaught and fled must have ingested and carried with them the fumes and dust created by the bombardments. There is also the uranium waste—three hundred tons of it, according to reports—left on the battlefield.

Today the entire population of Iraq is besieged by diseases. We know that waterborne parasites and bacteria and malnutrition in Iraq are responsible for many recognizable diseases, and for wasting and death. But what about reports of a sharp rise in spontaneous abortions, cancers, and other "new diseases"? The Iraqi Ministry of Health is systematically documenting some of these health problems.

However, as far as I am aware, only Dr. Siegwart Guenther of the Austrian Yellow Cross International is systematically studying evidence of possible Gulf War Syndrome inside Iraq and the high incidence across the country of abnormal births. It is possible that the Iraqi government is also assembling facts in this area but is withholding information so as not to create even greater panic than already exists among its public. Iraq also lacks adequate diagnostic instruments to undertake the needed research. Or, like the Pentagon, it may seek to play down the inexplicable illnesses of its soldiers.

Iraqi Scientists Most Concerned About Radiation

Nevertheless, those most concerned about radiation and other kinds of pollution are probably Iraqis. Their entire population is probably afflicted. And essential comparative studies of strange illnesses in the Iraqi population would best be gathered by their own scientists. Iraq has, or had, a highly trained community of biologists, environmentalists, energy specialists, cancer researchers, etc., most of whom earned advanced degrees in the United States or Great Britain. With access to the entire country, they are capable of conducting the needed research.

Until the embargo and war, these scholars were in the international scientific community; they published widely and they took part in international scientific gatherings.

Because of the embargo, however, their work and their findings are unknown to us. These men and women are now denied professional contact with their peers overseas. Their government can no longer afford to sponsor their travel; but more importantly, the international embargo effectively extends into this area of scientific exchange. Today Iraqis find they can neither obtain invitations to consult with others abroad nor visas to attend conferences. (See Aziz, "Scientists Outside History," *Natural History,* September 1996, pp. 14-17.)

This is happening when health and environmental conditions inside Iraq are deteriorating, and bad conditions generated by the war are spreading, creating a catastrophe of accelerating proportions and unknown ramifications. This is the time when data from within the country are essential, and when Iraqis are well placed to offer first-hand data and important comparative material.

The Pentagon, which has been trying so hard to suppress information about the extent, occurrence and possible source of Gulf War Syndrome among its own personnel, would doubtless want to keep any Iraqi source silent on the matter as well. Even a scientist researching the hazardous effects of the war finds herself or himself effectively blocked from reporting important relevant findings.

Dr. Huda Ammash is one of those Iraqi scientists who should be speaking to her international colleagues. She is presently an environmental biologist and professor at Baghdad University; but she studied in the United States and obtained her Ph.D. from the University of Missouri.

Working with governmental departments of agriculture, health, and environment, Ammash is now undertaking research in Iraq. When I met her in 1995, she kindly shared her report with me. She is most concerned with the enormous energy emission and light energy from the massive bombing in the forty days of war in 1991 and the resulting ionization.

"We know that ionization causes radiation," she said. "It is now diffused throughout the entire airspace of Iraq and has likely spread to our neighbors as well, possibly as far north as the southern border of Russia."

Dr. Ammash calculates that "the prolonged effect of this ionization is, over a period of more than ten years, equal to one hundred Chernobyls."

Dr. Ammash and others note that "an outbreak of meningitis in children concentrated in one Baghdad locality is highly unusual and may be a manifestation of high ionization levels. It has never been seen in Iraq before and, under the circumstances of the embargo, Iraq can provide no immunization against it." She notes the alarm among doctors she interviewed who report that "ninety-nine percent of the victims of this disease are children." Ammash accumulated reports that show cancer increasing at rapid and abnormal rates; child leukemia is especially rampant with some areas of South Iraq showing a four-fold rise in these few years. Breast cancer in young women (age 30 and under) is also many times higher than in 1990 in certain parts of Iraq.

In addition, the Iraqi environment is subject to a mass of other chemical and microbial pollutants released into the atmosphere because of indirect results of the war. Ammash points out, for example, how "damage to bombed and crippled industrial plants resulted in the leakage of millions of liters of chemical pollutants—black oil, fuel oil, liquid sulfur, concentrated sulfuric acid, ammonia, and insecticides—into the atmosphere. Fumes created by the bombardment of more than 380 oil wells produced toxic gases and acid rain."

Bombardment of chemical factories damaged their gas purification units and thus created tremendous air pollution as well. If these filters can't function, dangerous gasses are allowed to escape from cement factories. Up to the present, the imposition of sanctions prevents the repair of these industrial filters. Untreated heavy water from industrial centers are the media for growth of microbes, mainly typhoid, malta fever, and other pathogenic bacteria.

Ammash also reports fourteen crop diseases—including covered smut, sazamia moth, yellow crust, spickulated drought disease, gladosporium disease, and epical bent—which were never before recorded in Iraq's history. These are now infecting date trees and citrus trees. "Nothing, nothing is immune to these toxins."

Now let's return to those wheat fields.

When I arrived back in Baghdad, I followed up my research in Mosul with discussions with agriculture officials and with visits to small, local farms engaged in mixed agriculture. I spoke with experts at the Food and Agricultural Organization (FAO), a UN agency in Baghdad since before the Gulf War. Their mandate is to assist any nation to increase its food production and they are trying to help Iraq in this area.

Now, more than ever, with food unobtainable from abroad, Iraq is obliged to reverse its rather neglected agricultural policy with active food production schemes. Since the imposition of the embargo, Iraq has been trying to do so, bringing more land under grain production and improving irrigation.

Iraq Could Be Self-Sufficient

FAO officials were unequivocal about prospects. "Iraq could be self-sufficient in grain," said director Amir Khalil. "It has the water; it has the land; it has the expertise." Yet, despite efforts and the growing food crisis, production was declining. Why?

For agriculture experts and farmers alike, the explanation is simple: "No herbicides, no pesticides, no fertilizer, no improved seed." The animal husbandry and poultry situation is as severe as the grain crisis. Without vaccines and other medicines, all of which Iraq cannot furnish itself, animals—like people and plants—cannot survive.

According to an FAO report, since 1990, dairy herds were down forty percent. Before the war, dairy cows numbered 1,512,000; by 1995, their number fell to only one million. Water buffaloes suffered an even worse fate, and goat herds have declined from 1.3 million to fewer than a quarter of a million. Iraq's poultry system with 106 million hatching hens was virtually wiped out overnight by the bombing when electrically run poultry sheds across the country—8,400 units—shut down. Without vaccines and specialized, treated food, moreover, hens cannot survive long.

Why this devastation? Largely because agricultural imports, all essential in food production in any modern state today, are unavailable.

Like plant diseases, animal diseases too are almost completely uncontrollable. All of this is documented in the 1995 FAO Survey, itself commissioned by the UN. This is the same organization—the UN—whose Sanctions Committee either outright refuses to allow those imports (requested by the FAO), or simply (somehow) cannot manage to facilitate approval at the critical time.

If we are to believe FAO's own reports, it seems that another weapon in this cowardly secret war is the denial of agricultural essentials—a kind of sabotage—to ensure Iraq cannot become food self-sufficient.

Meanwhile unchecked infestations are spreading beyond Iraq's boundaries. Those wind-borne diseases are expected to infect every part of the region—crossing to the neighboring nations that border Iraq.

Iraqi officials hope that Turkey, Jordan, Iran and others will become sufficiently alarmed to call for international action. But thus far, Ammash and others say, "We do not know of any efforts outside Iraq to control these developments." This Iraqi biologist does not know what related research is being carried out in Jordan. "We are totally disconnected," Ammash says with distress. "We have no means of communication with others."

It is ominous that it was also during my research in the farming community that I found the first shocking evidence of a plague little discussed in the human population.

I went to small family farms around Baghdad to observe crop production there. I found myself annoyed to see fields again overrun with weeds. Even orchards were untended. This time I stopped myself asking foolish questions. I could see the tractors were broken. I knew the shortage of fertilizer had reduced yields of apples and grain as well as vegetables to half of what they were. I could see the plant spraying machine was idle; it was broken, explained the farmer. Anyway, even if it worked, where was he to get chemical sprays?

In the course of our long conversation in the farmhouse after my inspection of the fields, we spoke about social life. One farmer remarked that marriages were fewer now. "Why?" I asked. The answer was straightforward. "Young people fear the birth of malformed fetuses and still births." How was this?

"We look around our village," they said. "Everyone knows couples in the village who had deformed babies in the last four years."

With the help of several farmers and the local schoolteacher, I took an ad hoc survey. They had 160 houses here, and among these, they counted twenty where malformed babies had been born. My hosts noted that most of the fathers of these still born and abnormal births in their village are men who served in the army during the Gulf War. They noted many spontaneous abortions, but we did not include these. I had heard in Baghdad that more spontaneous abortions are reported across the country now than were before 1990.

The Iraqi Ministry of Health could not provide me with any statistics about this development. But my inquiries at five hospitals (in Mosul, Baghdad and Kerbala) revealed that the number of abnormal births recorded in hospitals had dramatically increased. Recalling their personal experience, all doctors with whom I spoke estimate they see ten times more such births today than five years ago. One doctor in Mosul said she saw two cases a year before 1991; she now sees four or five cases a month. The symptoms? "Babies born without ears, without eyes, without limbs or with foreshortened limbs, without formed genitalia, with cleft palate, club foot, enlarged heads." One doctor reported her first knowledge of a case of congenital leukemia.

'How can I have any plans?'

A professor of poultry science had accompanied us to the fields in Mosul. From seeing how he walked and stood, I already suspected he himself was unwell. Nevertheless, I inquired about his plans for further research. I still remember the bewildered look on his face when I asked him this. "Plans? Madam," he said softly, "I am trying to feed my family; I am looking for a medicine for my ill father. How can I have plans?"

I asked Dr. Ammash the same question. "It is difficult for anyone to have a plan," she quietly explained. "You have a plan when you have a settled situation—known circumstances. We don't have that anywhere in Iraq. My immediate plan is to provide tomorrow's means for life for my children, to help my students into another successful day. After that, I don't know."

As for her research, the professor says one major study is complete. She wants to enlarge the study concentrating on electro-magnetic fields. But that research requires instruments and expertise from outside; because of sanctions, this cannot proceed. She calls on other scientists from outside Iraq to join Iraqis in demanding that those powers imposing sanctions allow this research to be undertaken and experts in neighboring countries to begin collaborative work with her.

22 | Depleted Uranium Shells Make the Desert Glow

The Pentagon insists that depleted uranium is "very, very mildly radioactive" and that the shells are not radioactive enough to be classified as a "radiological weapon."

ERIC HOSKINS

The Gulf War lives on, as this week's air strikes against Iraq have proved (January 21, 1993). But the conflict goes beyond Iraqi missile batteries in forbidden places. It extends, frighteningly, to radioactive artillery shells used by coalition forces in early 1991. The spent rounds may be the cause of fatal illnesses, including cancer and mysterious new stomach ailments, showing up in Iraqi children. Because of sanctions and war, the death rate of children under five has tripled. In the first eight months of 1991 alone, fifty thousand children died.

Known as depleted uranium penetrators, the shells were developed by the Pentagon in the late 1970s as anti-tank, armor-piercing projectiles. DU, which makes up the shell's core, is a radioactive byproduct of the enrichment process used to make atomic bombs and nuclear fuel rods. The material is extremely hard and abundant, and provided free to weapons manufacturers by the nuclear industry.

When fired, the core bursts into a searing flame that helps it pierce the armor of tanks and other military targets. Diesel vapors inside the tank are ignited, and the crew is burned alive.

In the six-week air and land war against Iraq, U.S. and allied coalition tanks, artillery and attack planes fired at least ten thousand of the six-inch, six-to-eight pound shells. A confidential report by the United Kingdom Atomic Energy Authority, written in April 1991 and leaked to *The Independent* newspaper of London in November of that year, estimates that at least forty tons of depleted uranium were dispersed in Iraq and Kuwait during the war.

Among other things, the depleted uranium rounds forced the Pentagon to concede additional friendly-fire casualties when traces of radioactivity were found on destroyed coalition military vehicles. Iraqi forces did not have uranium penetrators.

While it's too early to prove a link, many health experts suspect that the postwar increase in childhood cancer and mysterious swollen abdomens is at least in part due to the radioactive shells. UN personnel and aid workers have seen children playing with empty shells, abandoned weapons and destroyed tanks. In Basra, a foreign doctor saw a child using depleted uranium shells as hand puppets.

The Pentagon insists that depleted uranium is "very, very mildly radioactive" and that the shells are not radioactive enough to be classified as a "radiological weapon." It has claimed that allied tank crews firing the rounds received little radiation, the equivalent of a chest X-ray each day.

Most doctors and scientists agree that even mild radiation is dangerous and increases the risk of cancer. The health risk becomes much greater once the projectile has been fired. After they have been fired, the broken shells release uranium particles. The airborne particles enter the body easily. The uranium then deposits itself in bones, organs and cells. Children are especially vulnerable because their cells divide rapidly as they grow. In pregnant women, absorbed uranium can cross the placenta into the bloodstream of the fetus.

In addition to its radioactive dangers, uranium is chemically toxic, like lead, and can damage the kidneys or lungs. Perhaps the fatal epidemic of swollen abdomens among Iraqi children is caused by kidney failure resulting from uranium poisoning. Whatever the effect of the DU shells, it is made worse by malnutrition and poor health conditions.

The British report called the presence of DU in Iraq and Kuwait a "significant problem," concluding that there is enough uranium there to cause "tens of thousands of potential deaths." Fortunately, there have been no reports of uranium-related illnesses in Kuwait. That may be because fewer uranium shells were used there—most of the heavy ground fighting took place in southern Iraq—and because the country was cleaned up after the war.

The danger posed by the uranium shells is widely recognized. In July, German authorities arrested Siegwart Guenther, director of the Albert Schweitzer Institute, when he arrived in Berlin carrying a spent round retrieved from Iraq. He was charged with illegally "releasing ionizing radiation."

The shell, its radioactivity confirmed by two laboratories, was sealed in a lead-lined box. Needless to say, there are not many lead-lined boxes in Iraq.

It's likely that the depleted uranium may have already contaminated soil and drinking water in Iraq. If this is the case, Iraqis could be exposed to the radioactive and toxic effects of uranium for generations to come.

Certainly such fears are not without foundation. In New Mexico, where uranium rounds are test-fired by the military, questions have been raised concerning ground water poisoning. In 1986, James Parker, then associate director of the Bureau of Land Management, told Congress that land used to test these weapons could be permanently contaminated.

Despite the risks associated with DU, there has been virtually no debate about its effects in postwar Iraq and Kuwait. The UN Environment Program, which has investigated ecological damage of the Gulf War, has been remarkably silent. To date, no effort has been made to assess the extent of radioactive contamination caused by DU rounds in Iraq or to locate and remove the shells. Similarly, although Congress has ordered the military to monitor the health of soldiers exposed to smoke from Kuwaiti oil fires, there has been no such directive concerning exposure to DU.

What should be done? Once current tensions in the Gulf have subsided, qualified research groups, like the 1991 Harvard Study Team, should go to Iraq to analyze the soil and water for evidence of uranium contamination. Epidemiologists should explore the connection between the uranium shells and cancer. The UN must take a more active role in investigating the danger posed by the shells, and begin clean-up efforts of all radioactive shells remaining in Iraq and Kuwait.

It should also consider recommending that DU penetrators be banned in accordance with international treaties on chemical and radioactive weapons.

[This article was the first article about DU's impact on Iraq to break into the mainstream media in the United States. Since it was published on the Op-Ed Page of The New York Times *on January 21, 1993, much new information has come out.]*

23 | How DU Shell Residues Poison Iraq, Kuwait and Saudi Arabia

A spent depleted-uranium shell I found in Iraq was confiscated by a large police detachment in Germany, carried away under enormous safety precautions and stored in a specially shielded deposit. My efforts to have it examined got me into serious trouble.

PROF. DR. SIEGWART-HORST GUENTHER

Depleted-uranium projectiles were used for the first time by the allied troops during the Gulf War in 1991, with devastating effects and consequences.

At the beginning of March 1991, I detected projectiles in an Iraqi combat area that had the form and size of a cigar and were extraordinarily heavy.

At a later point in time, I saw children play with projectiles of this kind; one of them died from leukemia.

As early as at the end of 1991 I diagnosed a hitherto unknown disease among the Iraqi population which is caused by renal and hepatic dysfunctions.

My efforts to have one of these hitherto unknown projectiles examined brought me into serious trouble in Germany: the material was highly toxic and radioactive. The projectile was confiscated by a large police detachment, carried away under enormous safety precautions and stored in a specially shielded deposit.

During the last five years I have been able to carry out extensive studies in Iraq. Their results produced ample evidence to show that contact with DU ammunition has the following consequences, especially for children:

- A considerable increase in infectious diseases caused by most severe immunodeficiencies in a great part of the population;
- Frequent occurrence of massive herpes and zoster afflictions, also in children;
- AIDS-like syndromes;
- A hitherto unknown syndrome caused by renal and hepatic dysfunctions;
- Leukemia, aplastic anemia and malignant neoplasms;
- Congenital deformities caused by genetic defects, which are also to be found in animals.

The results of my studies show similarities to a clinical picture described recently by the term of the so-called Gulf War Syndrome in American and British soldiers and their children. The congenital deformities caused by genetic defects in American and Iraqi children are identical.

According to U.S. statements, vaccinations against anthrax and botulism, malaria prophylaxis, benzenes used for delousing, pyridostigmine bromide taken as a prophylaxis against the nerve gas soman, the insecticides DEET or permethrin as well as the DU ammunition used are held responsible for the development of this syndrome. The Allied troops were not informed about the danger to health caused by the DU projectiles until nine days after the end of the war.

Uranium Is Toxic

Like all heavy metals, such as lead or cadmium, uranium is highly toxic. The human body must not get into contact with them. Newspapers recorded that many U.S. Gulf War soldiers felt uncertain and fear that they may have been used as "guinea pigs" in a radiation experiment. In the opinion of the American nuclear scientist, Leonard Dietz, the arms technology of the uranium projectiles is as revolutionizing as the machine gun was during the First World War. The Gulf War was, however, as he said, also the most toxic war in history.

According to statements by the U.S. Army, about fourteen thousand high-caliber shells alone were fired during the Gulf War. According to estimations by the British Atomic Energy Authority, about forty tons of this type of ammunition are supposed to be scattered in the frontier area between Iraq and Kuwait. Other experts assume there are as much as three hundred tons of it left in the area.

Not more than ten percent of these projectiles have been detected. The greatest part of them have been blown over and covered with sand or are lying deep in the ground. As rains fall even in these desert regions, the toxic substances permeate the ground water and thus enter the food chain. This is a source of danger in the long run in areas of Saudi Arabia, Kuwait and Iraq. A British company has rejected the order to remove this uranium ammunition because the health risk to its staff is too great.

Bedouins from Kuwait battlefields, which U.S. soldiers used as training grounds, reported that hundreds of camels, sheep and birds had died in the desert. Examinations made by an American veterinary—a specialist in infectious diseases—showed that the animals had died neither from bullets nor from diseases. Some carcasses were covered with insects, but the insects were also dead.

Saudi Arabia had demanded that all tanks, vehicles and instruments of war that had been destroyed by uranium ammunition on their territory be collected by the U.S. Army. This material was carried away and transported to the USA. Before that step it had been buried in the desert.

The National Gulf War Resources Center has busied itself with studying the so-called "Gulf War Syndrome." Symptoms include damage to organs, genetic manifestations, chronic fatigue, loss of endurance, frequent infections, sore throat, coughing, skin rashes, night sweats, nausea and vomiting, diarrhea, dizziness, headaches, memory loss, confusion, vision problems, muscle spasms and cramps, joint pain and loss of mobility, aching muscles, swollen glands, dental problems and malformations of newborns.

According to the center's estimations, fifty to eighty thousand U.S. Gulf War veterans are concerned and thirty-nine thousand have been dismissed from active service. Some twenty-four hundred to five thousand have died up to now. Contamination through DU ammunition could have engendered cancers. Soldiers reported that upon their return and going through airport controls, in several cases the detector had "become crazy." In Great Britain thirty-five hundred soldiers are suffering today from Gulf War Syndrome. Australian, Canadian and French soldiers are suffering too.

Similar symptoms have moreover occurred in Kuwait and are spreading. It is believed that in Iraq 250,000 men, women and children may have been affected; the death rate is high. A study carried out in 1993 by three American scientists is said to have shown that about fifty thousand Iraqi children had already died during the first eight months after the Gulf War from detrimental effects of the DU projectiles.

In March 1994, reports on some 251 families of veterans of the Gulf War living in the state of Mississippi were published in the United States. Sixty-seven percent of the children of these families were born with congenital deformities: their eyes, ears or fingers are missing or they are suffering from severe blood diseases and respiratory problems.

In the meantime, others studying the facts have adopted my view that a parallel can be drawn to the situation that developed after the accident in 1986 in the nuclear reactor in Chernobyl. Since then, there has been a sharp increase in cancer, especially among children. Their mortality rate is very high, as is the rate of malformations at birth.

One cannot fail to point out the disturbing situation that developed in Germany in 1988 after a U.S. Army A-10 aircraft crashed in Remscheid. A similar situation developed in the Netherlands in 1992 after an Israeli El Al transport plane crashed in Amsterdam. It is suspected that both planes were carrying radioactive material on board. In both cases in the regions around the crash there has been an increase of skin diseases, dysfunction of the kidneys, leukemia among children and malformations at birth.

In November 1996 it was reported that in ex-Yugoslavia about one thousand children are suffering from an unknown disease: headaches, aching muscles, abdominal pain, dizziness, respiratory problems and others. Similar symptoms were described in the so-called Gulf War Syndrome. In the meantime about six hundred of these children are getting hospital treatment. U.S. combat aircraft carrying DU ammunition were also used in ex-Yugoslavia.

About ten years ago, while working in a German spa, where the water was characterized by its large spectrum of minerals doubled with radioactivity, I had been struck with the fact that many of the treated patients were developing a number of side effects, especially infections and zoster development. This pointed to the breakdown of their immune system.

In my position as physician and scientist I call on those responsible—as well as on the public—to prohibit the use of DU ammunition, which is already at the disposal of several nations. This applies especially to recently developed laser weapons, the use of which leads to irreparable blindness in the victims.

Teams of Iraqi specialists proved that the coalition states had used radioactive weapons against the Iraqi armed forces, particularly their armored and mechanized units.

Some facts concerning the use of radioactive weapons by the coalition forces and their effects on the environment and the population in Iraq.

It is now common knowledge that, in their attack on Iraq following the events that took place in Kuwait in August 1990, the coalition forces used internationally prohibited weapons of mass destruction. Accordingly, in this paper we do not intend to elaborate on those forces' violations of the established principles of international humanitarian law, particularly the right to life, in spite of the serious nature of this issue in so far as it constitutes a flagrant violation of human rights; nor do we intend to speak of the intensive and unjustified bombardment of all areas of Iraq, including towns and villages situated at a great distance from the battlefields, which proved highly detrimental to the economic, social and cultural rights of the Iraqi people. Iraq has already provided details of those violations during previous sessions of the Commission on Human Rights.

Dangers from Depleted Uranium
However, almost five years after the aggression which was launched against Iraq, alarming facts are coming to light concerning the extremely dangerous effects of the use of radioactive weapons on the environment and the population. This applies in particular to projectiles made from depleted uranium, these being weapons that are internationally prohibited under the terms of the 1980 Convention on Prohibitions or Restrictions on the Use of Certain Conventional Weapons Which May Be Deemed to Be Excessively Injurious or to Have Indiscriminate Effects.

In fact, weapons and munitions of this type cause unjustifiable pain and suffering to both the civilian population and the belligerents and are an expression of hatred and of a desire to engage in random destruction and slaughter bordering on genocide, which the international community regards as a prohibited act, the perpetrators of which must be punished. Their use also constitutes a flagrant and gross violation of human rights.

In a letter (DS/S/SS 0692/94m dated 6 December 1994) addressed to the British Member of Parliament Sir David Steel, Malcolm Rifkind, the British Minister of Defense, admitted that depleted uranium had been used by the British forces in order to improve their ability to confront Iraqi armored vehicles. In that letter, the minister of defense also stated that, in their armored units and A-10 aircraft, the United States forces had used much larger quantities of depleted uranium than the British forces.

In his letter, the British Minister of Defense acknowledged that DU shells could disperse small quantities of toxic radioactive substances when they impacted on a hard surface and those substances posed a health hazard if they were inhaled or ingested. However, he thought that it was improbable that persons other than those targeted by such shells would be exposed to sufficient quantities of those substances to endanger their health. In his letter, the British Minister of Defense claimed that those shells had been used in sparsely populated desert areas and that the direct and immediate danger, namely the dust produced by those shells, dissipated rapidly, although the hazards arising from the contact with destroyed vehicles remained. He claimed that the residual hazards in both Iraq and Kuwait were considered to be limited.

In this connection, in its edition published in April 1995, the newspaper *Le Monde Diplomatique* quoted William M. Arkin, president of the Washington-based Institute of Science and International Security, as saying that the number of 30mm rounds containing three hundred grams of depleted uranium fired by A-10 aircraft amounted to 940,000, which the number of 120mm shells containing 1 kg of depleted uranium fired by tanks amounted to 4,000, in the light of which the total amount of uranium dropped on Iraq and Kuwait could be estimated at about three hundred tons.

That same newspaper also quoted the confidential report submitted by the United Kingdom Atomic Energy Authority to the British government in November 1991, which stated that there will be specific areas in which many rounds would have been fired where localized contamination of vehicles and the soil may exceed permissible limits and these could be hazardous to the local population. According to that report, the real danger arose from the inhalation of airborne particles of uranium dust produced when DU shells hit and burned armored vehicles since, when the shell impacted, a large proportion of its metallic mass was pulverized and the resulting fine airborne particles, which were toxic to the kidneys and lungs, could easily be swallowed.

The same *Le Monde Diplomatique* article mentioned above indicated that a program broadcast by NBC in February 1994 had reviewed two cases of possible contamination by DU. The first case was that of Sergeant Daryll Clark, who recalled that his unit had been in the vicinity of Iraqi tanks when A-10 aircraft destroyed them with 30mm shells. His young daughter had been born after the war with a tumor of the gall bladder and without a thyroid gland. The second case was that of Carol Picou, whose medical unit had also been caught in the smoke billowing from those Iraqi tanks. According to Thomas Calender, the physician treating her, her case was very similar to that of persons who had ingested radioactive substances.

The newspaper article affirmed that the U.S. Army had admitted that DU could be dangerous. It was impossible for it to conceal from the public the fact that it had repatriated twenty-nine vehicles hit by rounds of that type in order to decontaminate them on U.S. territory, where thirty-five soldiers had thus been exposed to radiation.

In addition to the above-mentioned facts, research has also been conducted by three American specialists (Grace Bukowski, Damacio Lopez and Fielding McGehee from three American organizations: the Rural Alliance for Military Accountability, the Progressive Alliance for Community Empowerment and Citizen Alert) on the use of DU by the U.S. Department of Defense during the attack on Iraq by the thirty-member coalition. Their research confirmed that depleted uranium rounds had been used, for the first time in the history of modern warfare, during the Gulf War and countless Iraqi soldiers had been killed either directly by DU shells or as a result of exposure to their radiation. They estimated that fifty thousand Iraqi children had probably died during the first eight months of 1991 from various diseases, including cancer, kidney failure and previously unknown internal diseases, caused by the use of DU.

In this connection, the researchers noted that, according to the U.S. Department of Defense, an unspecified number of American soldiers had been wounded or burnt when they were struck by uranium-contaminated shrapnel and others had died as a result of inhaling uranium when their tanks were burnt. In this context, the researchers stated that the fission of a DU atom produced gamma rays that led to radiation exposure. They also indicated that the reluctance of governments, particularly the USA, to study and publicize the hazardous effects of the use of depleted uranium was attributable to their desire to avoid having to pay compensation to the victims of radiation exposure, since the use of that type of uranium led to a wide variety of health hazards and incurable diseases, ranging from cancer to kidney failure, respiratory disorders, congenital abnormalities, skin diseases and other obscure, unknown and fatal diseases.

When uranium oxide entered the lungs, it remained there for long periods of time and, consequently, reduced the capacity of the lungs by half and led to their functional paralysis and total collapse of the respiratory system within one year or more. The continued presence of uranium oxide particles in the lung tissue caused continuous swelling therein as long as the affected person remained alive. With the passage of time, affliction with lung cancer became highly probable, if not certain. Their research showed that a single tank carried fifty thousand pounds of uranium-contaminated rounds; that the quantities of ammunition used by the aircraft and tanks of the United States and its allies were large enough to insure that their hazards and damage were not confined to the battlefield but extended into areas a great distance therefrom; and that the largest quantity of uranium fallout could be found in Iraqi territory.

They added that the quantities of DU used and consumed by U.S. and British aircraft and tanks in their battle against Iraq had never been made public and remained classified as confidential information. They emphasized that, according to the report of the United Kingdom Atomic Energy Authority, the real danger arose from the uranium dust produced when depleted uranium hit and burned out Iraqi armored vehicles, dispersing a large number of very small particles of uranium oxide, which were carried by the winds over great distances and, on entering the respiratory system, caused lung cancer.

The researchers quoted a telegram from the Munitions and Chemical Command addressed to Colonel Landri, one of the field commanders in the war, which stated as follows:

Please take the following information into consideration:

1. Any appliance containing and firing depleted uranium should be considered to be contaminated.

2. Any appliance that is attacked with depleted uranium should be considered to be contaminated.

3. No one should enter contaminated appliances before ascertaining that they have been decontaminated.

4. Protective gloves should be worn when handling bodies that are suspected of being contaminated by depleted uranium.

Iraqi Specialists Conduct Study

Teams of Iraqi specialists were formed to conduct a specialized study comprising measurements of radioactivity in areas of military operations. They also carried out such measurements and surveys of destroyed armored and other motorized vehicles (including those that had been damaged and withdrawn to repair locations) and took soil samples to measure their level of contamination. The conclusive material evidence obtained by these teams proved that the coalition states had used radioactive weapons against the Iraqi armed forces, particularly their armored and mechanized units.

The spectroscopic analysis of the environmental sample taken from inside destroyed armored vehicles, as well as some other environmental samples from the northern areas of Rumaila, Artawi and the border and demilitarized zones, proved that the radioactive contamination resulted from the use of warheads made of DU since some of the samples taken from inside destroyed armored vehicles in those areas were found to be highly radioactive and the laboratory tests of the environmental samples taken from the areas studied showed very high concentrations of uranium 238.

The competent Iraqi authorities also formed specialized teams from medical and other scientific research institutions to conduct medical and scientific field and clinical research and surveys concerning the effects on human health of the use of radioactive weapons by the coalition forces in the war against Iraq. Unusual pathological cases have appeared in Iraq, as illustrated by the abnormal increase in the incidence of cancer of the blood, the lungs, the digestive system and the skin, and there has also been a notable increase in the incidence of congenital diseases and fetal deformities, such as the presence of additional abnormal organs, hydrocephaly, anencephaly, eye diseases, and even the total absence or deformity of eyes.

Cases of twin births with Down's syndrome have appeared, in addition to skeletal abnormalities, congenital syndromes and chromosomal trisomies, as well as unexplained cases of falling hair and rare skin diseases among persons affected by, or living in the vicinity of areas affected by, the bombardments. There has been an increase in the number of persons afflicted with attacks of epidemic vertigo and severe vertigo accompanied by nausea and loss of balance, and also in the numbers of patients afflicted with attacks of distorted vision and loss of sight in part of the eye, accompanied by severe migraine, in addition to unexplained cases of sterility among both sexes and an increase in the incidence of miscarriages and of still, premature and difficult births.

The large-scale use of these militarily unjustifiable weapons contradicts the affirmations of the coalition states to the effect that the weapons they used were conventional weapons and that the war was a clean war.

The use of these weapons resulted in the mass slaughter of individuals, due to the highly destructive nature of the rounds, and the contamination of persons outside the theater of military operations due to the toxicity of the radioactive substance used, as well as the strange and unprecedented pathological symptoms with which they were afflicted. Moreover, they resulted in widespread contamination of the environment in Iraq and human suffering to which not only the present generation but also the future generations will be subjected as a result of their use.

[Subheads added by editor]

25 | U.S. First to Target Nuclear Reactor

"Every target that we have attacked, be it nuclear, chemical or biological, we have very carefully selected the destruction means, okay, after a lot of advice from a lot of very, very prominent scientists."—Gen. Norman Schwarzkopf, January 1991.

SUZY T. KANE

One fact of the Persian Gulf War seems to have been recorded in invisible ink: the United States is the first nation in history to have intentionally bombed an operating nuclear reactor.

When asked the Defense Department's position on the issue of nuclear reactors as military targets, Admiral Eugene Carroll of the Center for Defense Information was not aware that the reactor at the Tuwaitha Nuclear Research Center in Iraq had been in operation at the time it was bombed. "It's a legitimate cause of concern," Carroll admitted. "Once a war starts, the value system changes and anything you can do to hurt the adversary and cause him problems, you find justification for doing."

The military advantage is obvious in the quip Carroll recalled hearing: " 'You don't have to take the bang to the enemy; the bang is already there when you take out his nuclear plants.' " [1]

The reactor the U.S. destroyed at the Tuwaitha Nuclear Research Center in Iraq, just ten kilometers southeast of Baghdad, was a small Russian-made research reactor typical of the kind found at Western universities (Berkeley, the University of Chicago, New York University have them). Vulnerable now as military targets are the world's other three hundred research reactors in addition to almost five hundred larger nuclear power reactors for generating electricity that could become deliberate Chernobyls. [2]

"We knew that Tuwaitha had been severely hit in the course of numerous air raids," Maurizio Zifferero recalls, "the first of which occurred the night of 17 January [1991] resulting in the destruction of the Russian reactor."

An Italian national and former Deputy Director General of the International Atomic Energy Agency (IAEA), Zifferero helped establish the permanent Nuclear Monitoring Group in Iraq after the Gulf War. As leader of the United Nations Special Commission's 687 Action Team (687 refers to UN Resolution 687 that spells out the destruction of Iraq's weapons of mass destruction), Zifferero has directed thirty IAEA inspections in Iraq over the past five years. [3]

Zifferero describes Tuwaitha, situated on the left bank of the

Tigris River, as being "equipped with three nuclear research reactors, French supplied Tammuz 1 and Tammuz 2 and the Russian supplied IRT-5000. "Of these," he said, "only the Russian was in operation at the onset of the Gulf War, the French ones having been destroyed (without release of radioactivity) in an Israeli air raid in June 1981 while they were still in the cold commissioning phase.

"In addition to a large inventory of radioactive fission products contained in the Russian reactor core and in the spent fuel stored in the reactor pond, Tuwaitha had a number of other radiation sources, a steady production of radioisotopes for medical uses, gram quantities of plutonium in addition to a stock of depleted, natural and enriched uranium (these last under IAEA safeguards)."

Disagreeing that the responsibility of the first intentional bombing of an operating nuclear reactor falls uniquely on the United States, Zifferero believes responsibility is shared by member countries of the coalition. But the front page of *The New York Times* dated that same January 17 reports President George Bush emphasizing that "American planes struck at Iraqi nuclear and chemical-weapons production sites."

When questioned about the destruction of Iraqi nuclear facilities in a briefing on January 31, 1991, U.S. General H. Norman Schwarzkopf, commander of allied forces in the Persian Gulf, answered: "Every target that we have attacked, be it nuclear, chemical or biological, we have very carefully selected the destruction means, okay, after a lot of advice from a lot of very, very prominent scientists. So we selected the destruction means in such a way that we absolutely almost to a 99.9 percent assurance have no contamination."[4]

There was little contamination at Tuwaitha, however, only because the bombs missed the reactor core. "Looking back," Zifferero thinks, "it is almost a miracle that the Russian reactor core escaped destruction. Having seen the devastation produced at Tuwaitha by the coalition bombs, I am skeptical about the story of precision targeting there. It was, I am convinced, sheer chance. Or how would one explain bomb craters scattered around Tuwaitha in free areas between buildings?"

Iraq had not diverted the nuclear reactor fuel as some nuclear-proliferation experts like Leonard Spector, senior associate at the Carnegie Endowment for International Peace, suspected Iraq might do to hide its production of enriched uranium for use in a nuclear bomb.[5]

If the core of Iraq's Russian reactor had been hit, radioactive contamination would have been spread in the area surrounding the reactor building. "Health hazards caused by a high radiation level," Zifferero believes, "would have been limited to the Tuwaitha center with minimal consequences to the surrounding farm area."

"Tuwaitha is now a relatively clean place from the radiation level point of view," Zifferero avers. "Under IAEA's supervision the most dangerous material—the spent Russian reactor fuel—has been safely removed from Iraq in the course of 1993 and 1994 and sent back to Russia. All of it has been accounted for and none is missing."

Reporting that Russia did not initially want Iraq's nuclear waste back, the Arms Control Research Center (ARC) notes that the Russian Mayak Combine at Kyshtym in the Urals finally agreed to accept it. Because of accidents and wanton dumping, ARC says that Kyshtym is described as "the world's most radioactive site."[6]

While Zifferero would describe the release of radioactive material at Tuwaitha as "negligible," a recently declassified Pentagon document reports that the damage to a "production unit" that "processed spent nuclear fuel" and "contained two hot cells for this purpose," caused enough nuclear contamination to warrant closing Tuwaitha for two days after the bombing.

Radioactive contamination would have also depended on the plume of the explosion and wind and weather conditions, observes Bennett Ramberg, research director for The Committee to Bridge the Gap, a nuclear safety watchdog group.[7]

When asked if the subject of banning attacks on reactors had come up at the last Nonproliferation of Nuclear Weapons Treaty (NPT) review, Admiral Carroll replied that there "aren't any negotiations [on the subject of nuclear power plants as military targets in war] because it isn't an issue that has been introduced in the arms weapons discussion."

Bennett Ramberg, however, recalls that the issue of bombing nuclear reactors did come up at the NPT's Third Review Conference over ten years ago. "The Iraqis and Iranians raised the issue," Ramberg remembers, "and almost scuttled the conference. The [U. S.] Department of Defense doesn't want any limitation on their abilities to strike anywhere they wish." Ramberg was an early whistle-blower in 1980 with the first printing of his book *Nuclear Power Plants as Weapons for the Enemy: An Unrecognized Military Peril.* He believes the U.S. has set a dangerous precedent.

When radiation from the Chernobyl explosion in the Ukraine fell nine days later in contaminated rain on Spokane, Washington, we learned that there is no "over there."[8]

Or as William Sloane Coffin put it in referring to all human beings on our tiny planet as passengers in the same boat, "When you shoot a hole in the other side of the boat, we all sink."

[This article first appeared in the January/February 1997 issue of Fellowship, *the magazine of the Fellowship of Reconciliation, Nyack, New York.]*

References

1. Admiral Eugene Carroll, Telephone Interview, July 9, 1996.

2. Ruth Leger Sivard, *World Military and Social Expenditures* 1993, 15th Edition (Washington, DC: World Priorities, Inc., 1993), 13.

3. Dr. Maurizio Zifferero, fax interviews from Vienna, June 21 and July 8, 1996.

4. "Excerpts From Report by Schwarzkopf on the Fighting in the Persian Gulf," *The New York Times*, January 31, 1991, A12.

5. Leonard S. Spector, "Two Cautionary Thoughts as the U.S. Plunges into the Persian Gulf War," *The New York Times*, January 17, 1991, A23.

6. *Hidden Casualties: Environmental, Health and Political Consequences of the Persian Gulf War*, Edited by Saul Bloom, John M. Miller, James Warner and Philippa Winkler (Berkeley, California: North Atlantic Books and San Francisco, California: ARC/Arms Control Research Center, 1994), 253.

7. Dr. Bennett Ramberg, Telephone Interview, July 10, 1996. See also *Ramberg's Nuclear Power Plants as Weapons for the Enemy: An Unrecognized Military Peril* (University of California Press, 1984) and "Nuclear Plants—Military Hostages?" *Bulletin of the Atomic Scientists*, March 1986, 17-21.

8. Jay M. Gould and Benjamin A. Goldman, *Deadly Deceit, Low-Level Radiation, High-Level Cover-up* (New York: Four Walls Eight Windows, 1991), 15.

Section VII:

Can a Legal Battle
Be Waged to
Ban DU?

26 | The Role of Physicians in the Abolition of Nuclear Weapons

I believe those groups concerned with abolition of nuclear weapons should broaden their agendas to include abolition of depleted uranium weapons and other weapons, such as anti-personnel land mines, that are indiscriminate and inhumane.

VICTOR W. SIDEL, MD

The Work of PSR and IPPNW

In 1961 a group of Boston physicians, led by the renowned cardiologist Dr. Bernard Lown, analyzed in detail the potential medical consequences of use of the then newly-developed thermonuclear bombs.

While the physicians in the group had for years been individually concerned about the medical consequences of the nuclear bombing of Hiroshima and Nagasaki and the implications of the use of these weapons for the future, this concern was intensified by the development during the 1950s of much more powerful nuclear weapons. These new weapons, using nuclear fusion rather than nuclear fission and called hydrogen bombs or thermonuclear bombs, could produce an explosive force over one-thousand-fold greater than the bombs used in 1945.

When the energy distribution of these new weapons was published in the open literature in the late 1950s, the group in Boston, of which I was privileged to be a member, analyzed the potential medical consequences if these weapons were to be detonated over cities in the United States. This analysis, published in the *New England Journal of Medicine* in 1962,[1] concluded that the use of thermonuclear weapons would be so destructive to human health, to the environment, and to medical personnel and facilities that attempts at response by health professionals after the bombs had fallen would be almost entirely futile.

The report argued that physicians, because of their special knowledge of the medical effects of these weapons and because of their special responsibility to protect the health of their patients and their communities, had a special responsibility to help prevent the use of nuclear weapons. The report gained worldwide attention and contributed to the rapid growth of a group formed by the authors and other health professionals, Physicians for Social Responsibility, which has worked for over one-third of a century for the prevention of the use of nuclear weapons.[2]

The report documented both the short-term and the long-term health effects caused by the enormous blast energy, heat flux and ionizing radiation produced by nuclear weapons. The blast wave would cause severe trauma by collapse of buildings, flying debris and the throwing about of humans. The immediate radiation of enormous heat and the ignition of conflagrations and fires would cause severe burns and lung damage. The neutron and gamma ray flux from the initial detonation and alpha, beta and gamma radiation from short-range and long-range fallout of the radionuclides produced by the detonation would cause damage to tissues and organs. There would also be severe psychological damage to the survivors, both in the short-term and the long-term.

We pointed out that the use of nuclear weapons is likely to cause greatest injury to those most vulnerable—infants, the elderly and the infirm—a direct violation of one of the fundamental principles of international law. We also noted that the radioactive fallout, carried by the prevailing winds, would inevitably cross national boundaries and cause radiation injury among the population of neutral nations, another direct violation of a fundamental principle of international law.

In 1980 Dr. Lown, together with Dr. Yevgueni Chazov, a Soviet cardiologist, founded the International Physicians for the Prevention of Nuclear War (IPPNW), which now consists of affiliated physician organizations in eighty nations with some two hundred thousand supporters; PSR is the U.S. affiliate of IPPNW. The work of IPPNW and its affiliates was recognized by the Nobel Peace Prize in 1985. The Nobel citation in part read:

> (IPPNW) has performed a considerable service to mankind [sic] by spreading authoritative information and by creating an awareness of the catastrophic consequences of atomic war-fare. ...This in turn contributes to an increase in the pressure of public opposition to the proliferation of nuclear weapons and to a redefining of priorities, with greater attention being paid to health and other humanitarian issues. Such an awakening of public opinion...can give the present arms limitation negotiations new perspectives and a new seriousness.[3]

The nuclear stockpiles of the world's nations contain over twenty thousand weapons with an explosive force equivalent to eleven billion tons of TNT, two tons of TNT for every human being on the planet. Detonation of even a small fraction could cause catastrophic environmental damage, including the short-term damage that massive fires and short-lived radionuclides produced by the nuclear detonation would cause to the ecosystem and the long-term damage caused by long-lived radionuclides such as plutonium, which has a radioactive half-life of twenty-four thousand years.

There is a potential for a so-called "nuclear winter," a precipitous drop in surface temperatures on a hemispheric or global scale as a result of millions of metric tons of soot injected by mass fires into the upper atmosphere, blocking sunlight and absorbing heat. Even the modest temperature drop predicted by more recent calculations (which some have called "nuclear autumn") would be sufficient to cause serious disruptions of agriculture, posing a threat of malnutrition or famine among the survivors.

There is also potential damage from widespread ionizing radiation to human immune systems leading to epidemics of uncontrollable infectious disease and the potential damage to the human gene pool and its consequences for generations yet unborn. In addition to this damage to human beings and to human gene pools, the incremental international efforts of the past two decades to protect biodiversity and non-human gene pools could be dashed in just a few days. These worldwide environmental and ecological consequences, harming people and the environment in non-belligerent as well as belligerent nations, we have noted, would be violations of a fundamental principle of international law.

Even if use of nuclear weapons is limited to military targets, such as command bunkers and missile silos, weapons of large yield are likely to be detonated at ground level. Such use would produce even greater radioactive fallout than would be the result of airbursts over cities; the fallout would cause damage to humans hundreds and even thousands of miles from the site of the attack. Such consequences, even if "collateral" to attacks on military targets, would affect the people of neutral nations and therefore are contrary to international law.

The damage that the use of nuclear weapons would cause to medical personnel and medical facilities is a violation of the Geneva Conventions of 1949 and therefore also a violation of international law. The 1987 World Health Organization (WHO) report, "Effects of

Nuclear War on Health and Health Services," stated that the use of even a single nuclear weapon would overwhelm any health service, inflict indiscriminate and inhumane suffering on innocent civilians, and cause widespread and long-term environmental destruction that will affect many future generations.

The 1987 WHO report went on to state that, since no health service in the world could adequately cope with the casualties resulting from the use of even a single nuclear weapon, "the only possible solution is primary prevention; that is, the prevention of nuclear war." Since the WHO Constitution states that "the attainment of the highest possible level of health is a fundamental human right," the indiscriminate destruction of medical personnel and facilities and the massive increase in injury, disease, disability and death caused by the use of nuclear weapons would therefore represent a violation of rights specified by the WHO Constitution.

The Campaign to Abolish Nuclear Weapons
In sum, IPPNW and PSR have argued that the use of nuclear weapons would constitute a public health and environmental disaster. Representatives of IPPNW and of other groups—including the International Association of Lawyers Against Nuclear Arms and the International Peace Bureau—therefore worked with delegates to the World Health Assembly, the governing body of WHO, to support the introduction by the delegates of a resolution that would have instructed the Director-General of WHO, as a specialized agency of the United Nations, to request the following advisory opinion from the International Court of Justice (the "World Court") in the Hague:

> In view of the health and environmental effects, would the use of nuclear weapons by a State in war or other armed conflict be a breach of its obligations under international law including the WHO constitution?

On May 14, 1993, the 46th World Health Assembly adopted this wording for their historic resolution (WHA46.40, "Health and Environmental Effects of Nuclear Weapons"). WHO officially submitted the question to the World Court on August 27, 1993, and on September 13 the World Court requested written statements on the issue from WHO member nations. With the exception of those from the nuclear powers and their allies, the statements urged the Court to respond positively to the request.

Later, the nations affiliated with the Non-Aligned Movement initiated a resolution, adopted by the United Nations General Assembly, asking the Court to declare illegal both the use and the **threat of use** of nuclear weapons. Over one hundred million people around the world, including forty-three million people in Japan alone, signed declarations of conscience on this question; I personally had the privilege, as co-president of IPPNW, of participating in the presentation of the signatures to the World Court at the Peace Palace in the Hague.

In July 1996 the World Court declared that threat of use or use of nuclear weapons would be "contrary to the rules of international law applicable in armed conflict, and in particular the principles and rules of humanitarian law." The only exception to this sweeping declaration of illegality was the Court's holding that "the Court cannot conclude definitively whether the threat or use of nuclear weapons would be lawful or unlawful in an extreme circumstance of self-defense, in which the very survival of a State would be at stake." The Court also unanimously ruled that nations have "an obligation to pursue in good faith and to bring to a conclusion negotiations leading to nuclear disarmament in all its aspects."

The year 1996 brought additional extraordinary evidence of the success of the work of IPPNW and PSR over the years:

- In August the Canberra Commission on the Elimination of Nuclear Weapons, created by the Australian Government, issued a report that called for swift progress toward the elimination of nuclear weapons.
- In September the United Nations General Assembly approved by a vote of 158 to 3 the draft of the Comprehensive Nuclear Test Ban Treaty that had been negotiated in Geneva and opened it to the nations of the world for signature and ratification.
- In December, in an unprecedented act, an extraordinarily high-level group list of retired generals and admirals from around the world called on the world's nations to abolish nuclear weapons.

Much additional work is needed if we are to approach the ultimate goal of IPPNW and PSR since their founding, the abolition of nuclear weapons. In attempting to achieve this goal, IPPNW has a number of intermediate objectives. These objectives are important themselves and in addition further the effort to achieve abolition. They include:

- Cessation of fissile material production, including plutonium and highly enriched uranium, international control of all stockpiles, and prompt disposal of these materials as highly-radioactive waste.
- Strengthened international safeguards against export of fissile materials and nuclear weapons, built into both international and national law.
- Completion of the destruction of nuclear weapons called for under START I and II, with inclusion of UK, France and China in START III.
- And finally, agreement by the world's nations by the year 2000 on a timetable for negotiation of a convention on the illegality of nuclear weapons, similar to the 1993 Chemical Weapons Convention, banning development, production, testing, possession, transfer and use of nuclear weapons.

IPPNW and PSR are, in short, urging the nations of the world that possess nuclear weapons to destroy their stockpiles as rapidly as possible and to pledge that these weapons will never again be used under any circumstances. IPPNW and PSR also urge the nations of the world that do not possess nuclear weapons to refrain from acquiring them and to insist that all nations declare by solemn agreement that nuclear weapons will be abolished by a defined deadline in the near future.[4]

Abolition of nuclear weapons—like the abolition of human slavery over a century ago—is within our grasp. A top U.S. military officer—Air Force General Charles A. Horner, who as head of the U.S. North American Aerospace Defense Command is responsible for defending the United States and Canada against nuclear weapons—has publicly called for the abolition of nuclear weapons. He said, "The nuclear weapon is obsolete; I want to get rid of them all." "Think of the high moral ground we secure by having none," he continued. "It's kind of hard for us to say to North Korea, 'You are terrible people, you're developing a nuclear weapon' when the United States has thousands of them." This is the first time to our knowledge that a high-ranking U.S. military officer on active duty has made such an explicit statement calling for abolition.

In its Nobel-Prize-honored work IPPNW follows in a great tradition. The physician and humanist, and Nobel Peace laureate, Albert

Schweitzer wrote that "nuclear weapons are against international law and they have to be abolished," but he also warned that "all negotiations regarding the abolition of atomic weapons remain without success because no international public opinion exists which demands this abolition." His friend Albert Einstein, a Nobel laureate in Physics, whose name honors the medical school at which I work, warned us that "the explosive force of nuclear fission has changed everything except our modes of thinking and thus we drift toward unparalleled catastrophe. We shall require an entirely new pattern of thinking," he said, "if mankind is to survive."

To this warning Dr. Bernard Lown, IPPNW founding co-president, who together with Dr. Yevgueni Chazov accepted the Nobel Prize on behalf of IPPNW, has added, "The new way of thinking must be an awakening—to our common origins, to our shared problems, as well as to our common fate. If we are to prevail, we must never delegate in the presence of challenge and never whisper in the presence of wrong."[5]

In this volume on depleted uranium, it must be made clear that the term "nuclear weapons," as conventionally used and as used in this article, does **not** include weapons such as depleted uranium weapons used by the United States during the Gulf War and being sold by the United States to other countries. Weapons that include depleted uranium are extremely hazardous to health, as other articles in this volume point out, because of their radioactivity and their toxic chemical potential.

Careful investigation must be carried out of the health consequences of the depleted uranium weapons that have been used and the use of such weapons must be outlawed. But because depleted uranium weapons do not involve a nuclear explosion based on fission or fusion, they are not considered "nuclear weapons" as the term is usually used. Nonetheless, I believe those groups concerned with abolition of nuclear weapons should broaden their agendas to include abolition of depleted uranium weapons and other weapons, such as anti-personnel land mines, that are indiscriminate and inhumane.[6,7]

References

1. Special Study Section, Physicians for Social Responsibility. The Medical Consequences of Thermonuclear War. *New England Journal of Medicine* 266 (1962): 1126-1155.
2. Sidel, Victor W., H. Jack Geiger, and Bernard Lown. The Physicians' Role in the Post-Attack Period. *New England Journal of Medicine* 266 (1962): 1137-1145.
3. *Nobel Peace Prize* (Cambridge, Mass: International Physicians for the Prevention of Nuclear War, 1986).
4. Sidel, Victor W., The Role of Physicians in the Prevention of Nuclear War. In: *Genocide, War, and Human Survival*. Charles B. Strozier and Michael Flynn, editors. (Lanham, Maryland: Rowman and Littlefield Publishers, 1996), pp. 193-205.
5. Lown, Bernard, *Never Whisper in the Presence of Wrong: Selections from Speeches on Nuclear War and Global Survival* (Cambridge, Mass: International Physicians for the Prevention of Nuclear War, 1993).
6. Sidel, Victor W. The International Arms Trade and Its Impact on Health. *British Medical Journal* 311 (1995): 1677-1680.
7. Levy, Barry S., Victor W. Sidel, eds. *War and Public Health*. (New York: Oxford Unversity Press, 1997).

27 | UN Sub-Commission on Human Rights Votes Ban of DU

It is the U.S. government's contention that acts of war, even illegal acts of war, are not subject to victims' suits. If that were true, no person or government would ever be on trial for war crimes.

PHILIPPA WINKLER

A resolution calling for the ban of depleted uranium and certain other weapons was passed at the United Nations Sub-Commission on Prevention of Discrimination and Protection of Minorities in August 1996, (15 yes, 1 no, 8 abstentions). The resolution was introduced by Claire Palley, attorney appointed by the UK, as a result of a combined effort: attorney Karen Parker's statement under the agenda item human rights and disability at the Sub-Commission session; Dr. Beatrice Boctor's written report on the genetic effects of DU on the population in the Gulf region; and intensive lobbying by Parker and Boctor, and Fabio Marcelli of Bridges to Baghdad, Italy. The issues of DU and sanctions were raised for the first time at the UN Commission on Human Rights in April 1996 by the delegation led by Margarita Papandreou of Women for Mutual Security, Greece.

Text of the Sub-Commission Resolution 1996/16
Title: "International Peace and Security as an Essential Condition for the Enjoyment of Human Rights, above all the Right to Life."
    The Sub-Commission, guided by the principles of the Charter of the United Nations, the Universal Declaration of Human Rights, the international covenants on human rights, and the Geneva Conventions of 12th August 1949 and the additional protocols thereto, recalling General Assembly resolutions 42/99 of 7 December 1987 and 43/111 of 8 December 1988, affirming that all people have an inherent right of life, concerned at the alleged use of weapons of mass and indiscrimate destruction against both members of the armed forces and against civilian population resulting in death, misery and disability, concerned also at repeated reports of long term consequences of the use of such weapons upon human life, health and the environment, concerned further that the physical effects on the environment, the debris from the use of such weapons either alone or in combination, and abandoned contaminated equipment constituting serious danger to life, convinced that the production, sale and use of such weapons are incompatible with the provisions of the convention

against torture and other cruel inhumane and degrading treatment or punishment, believing that continued efforts must be undertaken to sensitize public opinion to the inhumane and indiscriminate effects of such weapons and for the need of their complete elimination,

1. urges all states to be guided in their international policies by the need to curb the production and spread of weapons of mass destruction and indiscriminate effect, in particular, nuclear weapons, chemical weapons, fuel air bombs, napalm, cluster bombs, biological weaponry and weaponry containing depleted uranium;

2. requests the Secretary General

   a. to collect information from governments, other UN bodies, and nongovernmental organizations on the use of nuclear weapons, chemical weapons, fuel air bombs, napalm, cluster bombs, biological weaponry, and weaponry containing depleted uranium, on their consequential and cumulative effects, and on the danger they represent to life, physical security and other human rights;

   b. to submit a report on the information gathered to the Sub-Commission on its 49th session together with any recommendations and views which he had received on effective ways and means of eliminating such weapons;

3. decides to give further consideration of this matter at its 49th session on the basis of any additional information which may be contained in reports of the Secretary General to the Sub-Commission or to other UN bodies or which may be submitted to the Sub-Commission by governments or nongovernmental organizations.

UN Sub-Commission Resolution 1996/16, introduced 19 August 1996 and adopted 29 August 1996, [15 yes, 1 no (the U.S.), and 8 abstentions.]

Co-sponsors were Sub-Commission members from India, Chile, Greece, Romania, Nigeria, UK, Morocco, Ethiopia. (Note wide co-sponsorship from Eastern bloc, Latin countries, Asia, Africa, Europe and that abstentions were mostly by Europeans.)

Significance of Resolution

Karen Parker comments: "Sub-Commission members are nominated by nations. David Weissbrodt, the U.S. nominated member of the Sub-Commission, tried to block the resolution then tried to delete depleted uranium from the text and to eliminate reference to the Geneva Conventions and torture and other cruel and inhumane punishment. He was insistent and insulting, and accused Claire Palley, the U.K. nominated member who introduced the resolution, of being 'unprofessional,' the typical message that men use on women, to make them be viewed as incompetent, irrational, not astute and academic enough.

"I reminded Claire Palley that even in the U.S. it is clearly established that torture is a *jus cogens* norm. There have already been some successful suits in U.S. courts invoking torture in other countries, so it's a particularly useful reference because of possible human rights actions or claims, including the possibility of insurance claims. It is the U.S. government's contention that acts of war, even illegal acts of war, are not subject to victims' suits. If that were true, no person or government would ever be on trial for war crimes."

The Sub-Commission can vote to send the resolution to the Commission on Human Rights, which in turn can send it to the United Nations General Assembly. This is an opportunity to change international law on the subject. SC 1996/16 can also be cited in all publicity material, letters to the editor, etc., concerning DU.

All Interested Parties Urged to Submit Reports on Depleted Uranium to UN Secretary General

Sub-Commission Resolution 1996/16 asks nongovernmental organizations (NGOs) to submit data on DU, its health effects, and ways of eliminating it. The UN Secretariat will submit a report based on this and other information submitted by other UN agencies and governments.

The report will be written by a staff member at the UN Center of Human Rights in Geneva, with considerable opportunities for NGO assistance.

DEADLINE: Although the official deadline for submission of data is May 8, prior to the Sub-Commission's 1997 session next August, the deadline for NGOs should be March 1997 when the UN Commission on Human Rights meets.

DU networking groups are urged to submit reports and any other documentation to Mr. Alexandre Ovsiak, Human Rights Officer, Room D404, UN Office at Geneva, CH-1211, Geneva 10, Switzerland. Phone: 22-917-3417; Fax: 22-917-0212. Cite the title and number of the resolution in the cover letter. Duplicates of data should be sent to: Mme. Fatma Zohra Ksentini, Special Rapporteur of the Commission on Human Rights on Toxics, UN Office at Geneva, CH-1211, Geneva 10, Switzerland. Phone: 22-917-3358; Fax: 22-917-0092. There is no e-mail address.

28 | Depleted-Uranium Weapons and International Law

The real objective must be the abolition of war. ...In the meantime it is possible to achieve prohibitions on certain practices or weapons which routinely violate the laws of war, including DU weapons.

ALYN WARE

"When the king fights with his foes in battle, let him not strike with weapons concealed in wood, nor with such as are barbed, poisoned, or the points of which are blazing with fire." (Seventh book of the legendary Hindu lawyer, Manu.)

For most of history there has been a battle between those who would justify the use of war as a necessary political tool, and those who would classify war as a crime of mass murder which must be abolished. Up until the twentieth century, war may have been opposed by the masses, but was seen by powerful rulers as politics by other means. However the devastation of the European wars and the two world wars moved even those in power to see the inhumanity of war and consider the possibility of prohibiting it.

The Hague Peace Conferences of 1899 and 1907 and the formation of the League of Nations and the United Nations had the abolition of war in mind, but failed to deliver due to the vested interests in continuing to use force and to the strongly held notion that force may be necessary in self-defense. What they could agree to, however, was that certain acts of war are "inhumane" and not necessary for the purpose of defeating the enemy. They therefore agreed to prohibit such acts. Other initiatives, such as the work of the International Committee of the Red Cross, have added to the list of proscribed actions.

What has emerged, therefore, is the development of a body of international law termed the humanitarian laws of warfare, which prohibit certain "inhumane" acts during wartime while not prohibiting the inhumane act of war itself. Such law was seriously debated during the recent International Court of Justice advisory opinion on the legality of the threat or use of nuclear weapons. The ICJ concluded that "the threat or use of nuclear weapons would generally be contrary to the rules of international law applicable in armed conflict, and in particular the principles and rules of humanitarian law."[1]

The question that arises, therefore, is whether the use of depleted uranium (DU) in weapons systems violates this body of law, and if so whether the law can be used to effectively constrain or prohibit such use.

Humanitarian Laws of Warfare

A general principle of humanitarianism in warfighting has been accepted, even if not universally adhered to, by many cultures and nations throughout the world, including some of the most warlike. Hugo Grotius, sometimes called the "father" of the laws of warfare, notes that prohibitions against inhumane methods of fighting existed in both the ancient Roman and Greek armies.[2] Similar prohibitions are found in the Koran.[3] The Lateran Council of 1139 prohibited the use of crossbows calling such use "hateful to God and unfit for Christians."[4]

The codification[5] of such principles into legal instruments began in the United States with the promulgation by U.S. President Abraham Lincoln in 1863 of "Instructions for the Government of Armies of the United States in the Field," written by Francis Lieber and commonly known as the "Lieber Code."[6] The first codification of such principles into an international agreement occurred in 1868 with the Declaration of St. Petersburg. This legal instrument intended to "reconcile the necessities of war with the laws of humanity."

Subsequent agreements, including the Hague Conventions of 1899 and 1907, the Geneva Conventions of 1925 and 1949, the Nuremberg Charter of 1945, and the Tribunal for the former Yugoslavia,[7] have affirmed that the following acts are prohibited under international law:

i.   use of weapons or tactics which cause unnecessary or aggravated devastation or suffering;

ii. use of weapons or tactics which cause indiscriminate harm, i.e., to noncombatants;

iii. use of weapons or tactics which violate the neutral jurisdiction of nonparticipating states;

iv. use of asphyxiating, poisonous or other gas, and all analogous substances including bacteriological methods of war;

v.   use of weapons or tactics which cause widespread, long-term and severe damage to the environment.

These principles are accepted by most states, including the U.S., the major user of DU weapons. The U.S., for example, has affirmed these principles in the U.S. Army Manual, "The Law of Land Warfare" (1956). More recently the U.S., UK, France and Russia affirmed their acceptance of these principles in their statements to the International Court of Justice in the advisory opinion on the legality of the threat or use of nuclear weapons.[8]

Application of Laws of Warfare to
Specific Weapons—the Nuclear Example
A number of States, including the U.S., hold the view that whatever is not specifically prohibited in international law is permitted. Specific prohibitions include conventions or customary law accepted by States. Thus, the U.S. accepts that the use of chemical and biological weapons are now prohibited according to the biological weapons convention[9] and the Geneva Gas Protocol (1925). However, the U.S. says that nuclear weapons, which have arguably even greater destructive effects than biological and chemical weapons, are not prohibited. "The use of explosive 'atomic weapons,' whether by air, sea or land forces, cannot as such be regarded as violative of international law in the absence of any customary rule of international law or international convention restricting their employment."[10]

The majority of States, however, believe that the application of the laws of war to specific weapons could indeed prohibit any use even if there is no specific prohibition of that weapon by convention. The most obvious example is that of nuclear weapons. A United Nations resolution adopted repeatedly since 1961 states that any use of nuclear weapons "would exceed even the scope of war and cause indiscriminate suffering and destruction to mankind and civilization and, as such, is contrary to the rules of international law and to the laws of humanity."[11]

The Hague Conventions of 1899 and 1907, which codified much of the customary laws of warfare and specifically prohibited expanding ("dum-dum") bullets and asphyxiating gases, also included a provision which stated that "[I]n cases not included in the Regulations adopted by them, the inhabitants and the belligerents remain under the protection and the rule of the principles of the law of nations, as they result from the usages established among civilized peoples, from the laws of humanity, and the dictates of the public conscience."

This provision, known as the Martens Clause, is an integral part of the body of international law. It was most recently reaffirmed in the Geneva Convention Additional Protocol of 1977. The Martens Clause confirms that the laws of war apply to weapons and methods of warfare not specifically mentioned, and therefore could prohibit the use of certain weapons even if there is no specific convention prohibiting such weapons. The drafters of the Hague Conventions apparently understood that the advance of technology could easily lead to the development of weapons which would be at least as inhumane as expanding bullets or as non-discriminatory as poison. The International Court of Justice referred to the Martens Clause in reaching its conclusion that the threat or use of nuclear weapons is generally contrary to humanitarian laws, even in the absence of a specific convention prohibiting their use.

The Court's conclusion makes clear that the prohibition of certain weapons under humanitarian law rests on the effects these weapons would have and the humanitarian principles which their use would violate. Thus, if a new weapon causes indiscriminate or unnecessary suffering, its use is illegal even if there is no specific mention of it in existing conventions such as the Geneva or Hague Conventions, or if it had not been invented at the time these conventions were adopted.

The laws of war therefore have direct applicability for DU weapons and may provide a basis for their prohibition.

Would DU Weapons Violate International Law?
The use of DU weapons creates aggravated suffering. DU particles, when ingested by military personnel, are known to create health problems which can persist over long periods of the individuals' lives, if not for the remainder of their lives.[12] However, the difficulty with this argument is that the users of the DU weapons may insist that there are situations when there is no alternative to DU use in order to achieve the military objective, and that such suffering is therefore necessary. The fact that there is no militarily useable metal as hard as uranium could support the user's argument.

The prohibition against indiscriminate harm is perhaps more applicable as it cannot be derogated by military necessity. DU shells spread DU over vast areas with the DU remaining potentially lethal for thousands of years. Whilst the initial impact of the DU weapon may be contained within the targeted area, the spread of DU after impact cannot be so contained.

"Upon impact a high velocity projectile of uranium metal partially burns up and generates huge numbers of micrometer-size particles of uranium oxide. Like dust, they can be carried great distances by the wind."[13]

Protected civilians, even if some distance from the target, are thus threatened.

In addition the offspring of military personnel who ingest DU from weapons can also be affected.[14] Offspring are noncombatants, and the indiscriminate harm that DU would cause them would thus be contrary to humanitarian principles.

One problem with the indiscriminate harm argument is that any States accept that some damage to civilians may occur as part of "collateral damage" when military facilities and personnel are targeted. In order for the indiscriminate harm argument to be shown to prohibit DU weapons, disproportionate damage to civilians in relation to the military purpose would need to be proven.

The fact that the spread of DU through wind and water systems would not be able to be contained could violate the laws protecting neutral states. DU users would no doubt argue that such spread of DU to neutral states is unintentional and therefore not prohibited.

The principal international treaty regarding neutrality, the 1907 Hague Convention V Respecting the Rights and Duties of Neutral Powers and Persons in Case of War on Land, does not discuss unintentional violations of neutrality, but neither does it specifically say that violations of neutrality must be intentional.

Christopher Weeramantry, a judge on the International Court of Justice, says that if the consequences of an action are known beforehand, one cannot claim unintentionality for these consequences, nor avoid responsibility for them. "It is not to the point that such results are not directly intended, but are 'by-products' or 'collateral damage.'... The author of the act causing these consequences cannot in any coherent legal system avoid legal responsibility for causing them any more than a man careering in a motor vehicle at a hundred and fifty kilometers per hour through a crowded market street can avoid responsibility for the resulting deaths on the grounds that he did not intend to kill the particular persons who died."[15]

The International Court of Justice addressed this issue in its advisory opinion on the legality of the threat or use of nuclear weapons by affirming the statement of Nauru: "It is clear, however, that the principle of neutrality applies with equal force to transborder incursions of armed forces and to the transborder damage caused to a neutral State by the use of a weapon in a belligerent State."[16] Even so, the ICJ did not determine that the probability of transborder damage to neutral States by the use nuclear weapons would be sufficient in every circumstance to affirm the illegality of every use of nuclear weapons on this basis. Thus, while some uses of DU weapons may be deemed illegal due to transborder damage, it is not clear that this would be true in all cases. Basing a general prohibition of DU weapons on the threat of transborder damage would therefore be difficult.

The law against use of poison or "poisoned weapons" in war would appear at first glance to provide a clearer prohibition against DU weapons. DU is clearly a poisoned weapon, the effects of which could easily be more devastating to human health than other poisons prohibited in war. Unfortunately, this prohibition received a setback when the International Court of Justice (ICJ) interpreted it to cover "weapons whose prime, or even exclusive, effect is to poison or asphyxiate."[17]

DU weapons' prime purpose is not to poison but to penetrate hard armor. The Court's interpretation on this matter was soundly opposed in dissenting opinions by judges Weeramantry and Koroma, who maintained that the poisonous effects of nuclear weapons in almost all cases would be more devastating than poisons expressly prohibited. Weeramantry notes that "It [radiation] poisons, indeed in a more insidious way than poison gas, for its effects include the transmission of genetic disorders for generations."[18]

Even if the Court's excessively restrictive interpretation provides a temporary setback, it is quite possible that the more consistent interpretations of Koroma and Weeramantry will eventually become the norm.

It could be argued that the use of DU weapons could cause widespread, long-term and severe damage to the environment. On the down side, the ICJ determined that the prohibition against environmental damage must be considered with respect to military necessity and proportionality (i.e., whether the military action is proportional to the precedent provocation). The ICJ stated therefore that it could not on environmental protection grounds condemn every use of nuclear weapons outright. It would be difficult to claim that the use of DU weapons has a greater environmental effect than any use of nuclear weapons.

On the positive side however, environmental law is one of the fastest growing areas of international law, with the development of provisions such as the precautionary principle and intergenerational equity which could apply to DU weapons. The precautionary principle, which is making its way into international environmental law, provides that when there is reason to believe a particular practice could generate transborder environmental damage, the onus is on the practicing party to prove its safety.

Intergenerational equity holds that subsequent generations should not be threatened by current practices. Use of DU weapons threatens particularly the latter of these principles, in that the radiation released affects subsequent generations both in terms of genetic damage to offspring, and the extremely long periods over which the uranium is radioactive.

Public conscience has been a vital component in determining the illegality of certain weapons. Citizens, mindful of the Martens Clause in the Hague Conventions, gathered 4 million "Declarations of Public Conscience" in support of the International Court of Justice case against nuclear weapons. This, along with the sixty-million strong Hiroshima and Nagasaki Appeal, the millions who marched against nuclear weapons in New York, London, Bonn and other major cities in the 1980s, the thousands of nuclear weapon free cities and the thousands of anti-nuclear groups which were established worldwide, demonstrated to the ICJ judges that there really was a strength of public sentiment against such weapons. A similar public condemnation against DU weapons would help considerably in establishing their illegality.

In conclusion it would seem that there are grounds for claiming that the use of DU weapons violates existing international law. While those grounds may not yet be strong enough in the current international climate to have such illegality affirmed through international bodies such as the United Nations General Assembly or the International Court of Justice, such law could be strengthened particularly through increasing public condemnation of DU weapons.

This is not to say however that legal action could not currently be taken against specific uses of DU weapons in order to get redress for health effects resulting from such use if such use was deemed to be negligent, nor that DU weapons could not be prohibited by means other than the existing laws of warfare.

Using the Law

The fact that DU weapons would violate the fundamental principles of international humanitarian law can be used as a motivating factor in the campaign to oppose such weapons. Citing violations of the law is another way to add to the moral outrage of citizens in order to motivate them into action. The laws of warfare are a way of opposing the erroneous belief that in war "anything goes," and that it is therefore impossible to oppose any weapons system.

Achieving International Prohibition

The real objective must be the abolition of war, the very practice of which is inhumane and should be affirmed as illegal. Such a prohibition is however likely to be some time off. In the meantime it is possible to achieve prohibitions on certain practices or weapons which routinely violate the laws of war, including DU weapons.

Unilateral proscriptions against DU use are unlikely to be adopted as very few countries will want to have armor and shells which are inferior to and can be beaten by DU weapons of opposing armies. Governments and militaries may, however, be persuaded to abandon DU if they can be assured that everyone else is also doing so. This would need an international agreement, most likely with verification and compliance measures. A proposal for such an agreement has not yet appeared on the international disarmament agenda of the United Nations or any of the DU-using states.

However, it may be possible for anti-DU campaigners to piggyback onto the anti-nuclear weapons campaign, by seeking to incorporate DU into the international nuclear weapons abolition treaty which is likely to be negotiated within the next ten years.

Abolition 2000, the international network of organizations which is campaigning for the conclusion of such a treaty by the year 2000, has drafted a model Nuclear Weapons Convention (NWC), which proposes to include radiological weapons and DU weapons in its list of weapons to be abolished. The verification and enforcement mechanisms set up by the NWC would be sufficient to also verify a prohibition on DU weapons, thus removing the problem of having to establish a separate, costly system.

Ultimately however it will be governments which decide whether or not to prohibit DU weapons whether as part of a NWC or according to a separate agreement. Anti-DU activists need to build up the same sort of global public pressure for such a ban as has been done for the anti-nuclear weapons campaign. Until then, the militaries which are using DU will continue to use what they see as one of the best materials to harden weapons.

References

1. Advisory Opinion of the International Court of Justice on the legality of the threat or use of nuclear weapons. ICJ General List No. 95, July 8, 1996, p. 36.
2. Hugo Grotius, De Jure Belli Ac Pacis (1625) as cited in Weiss, Weston, Falk and Mendlovitz "Draft Memorial in Support of the Application by the World Health Organization for an Advisory Opinion by the International Court of Justice on the Legality of the Use of Nuclear Weapons Under International Law, Including the W.H.O. Constitution," *Transnational Law and Contemporary Problems,* Vol. 4, Number 2, Fall 1994.
3. E. Meyrowitz, *Prohibition of Nuclear Weapons: The Relevance of International Law,* Transnational Publishers (1990), p. 209 n.2.
4. Weiss, Weston, Falk and Mendlovitz, *op. cit.,* p. 739.
5. Codification means writing such customary law into a treaty.
6. Wells, Donald, *The Laws of Warfare: A Guide to the U.S. Army Manuals,* Greenwood Press (1992) p. 1.
7. Statute of the International Tribunal for the Prosecution of Persons Responsible for Serious Violations of International Humanitarian Law Committed in the Territory of the Former Yugoslavia since 1991.
8. Statements made by France (November 1, 1996), Russia (November 10, 1996), U.S. (November 15, 1996) and UK (November 15, 1996) to the International Court of Justice.
9. Convention on the Prohibition of the Development, Production and Stockpiling of Bacteriological (Biological) and Toxin Weapons and on Their Destruction, 1975.
10. *Law of Land Warfare,* U.S. Army, 1956, paragraph 35.
11. "Declaration on the Prohibition of the Use of Nuclear and Thermonuclear Weapons," United Nations General Assembly Resolution 1653 (XVI), 24 November 1961.
12. Bukowski, G., D. Lopez, and F. McGehee, *Uranium Battlefields Home and Abroad,* Citizen Alert, March 1993, p. 43-54.
13. *Ibid.* at p. 11.
14. *Ibid.* at p. 48.
15. Advisory Opinion of the ICJ on the legality of the threat or use of nuclear weapons, *op. cit.* Dissenting Opinion of Judge Weeramantry, p. 43.
16. ICJ opinion, *op. cit.,* p. 31.
17. *Ibid.,* p. 21.
18. ICJ opinion. Dissenting opinion of Judge Weeramantry, *op. cit.,* p. 56.

Appendix I: Government Documents on DU

The following quotations from relevant U.S. government documents on depleted uranium were selected for inclusion in the book with the help of the Depleted Uranium Citizen's Network of the Military Toxics Project. The work of the DU Network resulted in the release of the previously suppressed Army Environmental Policy Report entitled, *Health and Environmental Consequences of Depleted Uranium Use in the US Army: Technical Report*, June 1995. Quotations from this and other reports reflect the duplicity of government statements concerning the risks of depleted-uranium weapons use and demonstrate the need for a complete independent investigation into the consequences, both medical and environmental, of DU contamination.

No available technology can significantly change the inherent chemical and radiological toxicity of DU. These are intrinsic properties of uranium. (Army Environmental Policy Institute (AEPI), *Health and Environmental Consequences of Depleted Uranium Use in the U.S. Army*, June 1995, p. xxii)

DU is a low-level radioactive waste and therefore, must be deposited in a licensed repository. (AEPI, p. 154)

The potential for internal and higher levels of external exposure exists if a vehicle's DU armor is damaged, if a vehicle is penetrated by a DU round, or if on-board ammunition ignites and burns. For example, when a DU penetrator cuts through armor and into the vehicle's crew compartment, it fractures, oxidizes, and burns, contaminating the vehicle with DU oxide dust. DU ammunition also oxidizes and contaminates the vehicle in the heat of a vehicle fire. Personnel who later work with the contaminated vehicles can be exposed to this DU oxide dust. (*Operation Desert Storm: Army Not Adequately Prepared to Deal With Depleted Uranium Contamination*, United States General Accounting Office (GAO/NSIAD-93-90), January 1993, p. 14)

When a kinetic energy round penetrates a vehicle, it contaminates the vehicle interior with dust and fragments. ... As much as 70 percent of a DU penetrator can be aerosolized when it strikes a tank (Fliszar et al., 1989). Aerosols containing DU oxides may contaminate the area downwind. DU fragments may also contaminate the soil around the struck vehicle (Fliszar et al., 1989). (AEPI, p. 78)

Equipment contaminated with DU oxides can become a source of contamination when the oxides are resuspended, blown, washed, or otherwise dislodged during transit. (AEPI, p. 80)

The Army does not know the full extent to which its personnel were exposed to DU contamination during the Gulf War. (GAO/NSIAD-93-90, p. 3)

Recovery and maintenance soldiers working in and around DU contaminated vehicles can inhale or ingest resuspended DU particles. (AEPI, p. 101)

Army and NRC (Nuclear Regulatory Commission) officials ... said the relationship between radiation dosage and health risks at low levels of exposure is not clearly understood and compliance with the NRC limits does not eliminate the risk of future health problems. (GAO/NSIAD-93-90, p. 4)

More than 50 current and former sites have been involved in the production, manufacture, development, testing and storage of DU for various DoD uses. (AEPI, p. 26)

DU is inherently toxic. This toxicity can be managed, but it cannot be changed. (AEPI, p. 113)

DU oxide dust, which is formed as a result of the DU being subjected to the intense heat that results from the round's penetration of the vehicle or from on-board vehicle fires, poses both a radioactive and a toxicity risk. Personnel working on or inside the contaminated vehicles can come into contact with the DU dust by either inhaling it or ingesting it. (GAO/NSIAD-93-90, p. 17)

Inhaled insoluble oxides stay in the lungs longer and pose a potential cancer risk due to radiation. Ingested DU dust can also pose both a radioactive and a toxicity risk. ... (GAO/NSIAD-93-90, pp. 17-18)

Personnel inside or near vehicles struck by DU penetrators could receive significant internal exposures. (AEPI, p. 119)

Replacing the DU in weapon systems with a non-toxic material would mitigate the health risks associated with DU. (AEPI, p. 114)

The Army has not assessed the risks to recovery and maintenance personnel working in and around vehicles contaminated with DU particles. Inhalation and ingestion present a potential pathway for internalization of DU by these personnel. (AEPI, p. 126)

The Department of Defense recognizes the hazards associated with depleted-uranium contamination caused by fires involving vehicles uploaded with depleted uranium munitions or by penetrations of vehicles by depleted uranium rounds. (DoD Response to GAO Draft Report–Dated November 25, 1992, GAO Code 393493, OSD Case 9266, Appendix III, GAO/NSIAD-93-90)

Health hazards occur primarily due to internal exposures. Soluble forms present chemical hazards primarily to the kidneys; while insoluble forms present hazards to the lungs from ionizing radiation, with particle size being an important factor. ... Short term effects of high doses can result in death, while long term effects of low doses have been implicated in cancer. (Science Applications International Corporation report, included as Appendix D of AMMCOM's *Kinetic Energy Penetrator Long Term Strategy Study*, Danesi, July 1990) (SAIC, p. 4-12).

As of February 1994, contractors had produced more than 1.6 million DU penetrators for tank ammunition and more than 55 million DU penetrators for small caliber (20, 25 and 30mm) applications. More than 99 percent of the U.S. production has been for the U.S. Air Force (30mm GAU-8). (AEPI, p.26)

Our conclusions regarding the health and environmental acceptability of DU penetrators assume both controlled use and the presence of excellent health physics management practices. Combat conditions will lead to the uncontrolled release of DU. ... We reiterate our recommendation that the studies of combat health and environmental impacts be performed. It is our initial hypothesis that impacts to civilian populations will not be significant from combat use, including post-combat impacts. However, aerosol DU exposures to soldiers on the battlefield could be significant with potential radiological and toxicological effects. These health impacts may be impossible to reliably quantify even with additional detailed studies. It is not our intention to overstate this issue given other combat risks, nor to imply that the health of soldiers will definitely be compromised. We are simply highlighting the potential for levels of exposure to military personnel during combat that would be unacceptable during peacetime conditions. (SAIC, 4-5) [This report was completed six months before Desert Storm.

Army officials believe that DU protective methods can be ignored during battle and other life-threatening situations because DU-related health risks are greatly outweighed by the risks of combat. (GAO/NSIAD-93-90, p.4)

It does not appear that Kuwait has addressed the long-term management of hazardous and radioactive materials in captured vehicles. (AEPI, p. 84)

No international law, treaty, regulation, or custom requires the United States to remediate Persian Gulf War battlefields. (AEPI, p. 154)

The number of DU patients on future battlefields probably will be significantly higher because other countries will use systems containing DU. (AEPI, p. 120)

Since DU weapons are openly available on the world arms market, DU weapons will be used in future conflicts. (AEPI, p. 119)

When DU (depleted uranium) is indicted as a causative agent for Desert Storm illness, the Army must have sufficient data to separate fiction from reality. Without forethought and data, the financial implications of long-term disability payments and health-care costs would be excessive. (AEPI, p. 4)

If DU enters the body, it has the potential to generate significant medical consequences. The risks associated with DU in the body are both chemical and radiological. (AEPI, p. 101)

There is no known way to reduce the chemical toxicity of DU in the body. Technology cannot significantly affect the solubility of uranium oxides formed in an uncontrolled environment such as the battlefield or in a fire. When munitions are fired or burned and when armor is pierced during battle, DU released to the environment will react with other nearby elements. These chemical reactions may produce compounds with various chemical toxicities ...[F]ires and high-energy penetrator impacts occurring in an uncontrolled environment result in uncontrolled dispersion of DU contamination. ... (AEPI, p. 114)

There are significant costs associated with implementing many of the programs suggested in the conclusion of this report. (AEPI, p. 3)

Despite all of the above quotations from U.S. government manuals, the Final Report of the Presidential Advisory Committee on Gulf War Veterans Illnesses report from December 1996 stated:

> The Committee concludes that it is unlikely that health effects reported by Gulf War veterans today are the result of exposure to depleted uranium during the Gulf War.

U.S. Government Books & Reports
To obtain a copy of the June 1995 AEPI report entitled, *Health and Environmental Consequences of Depleted Uranium Use in the U.S. Army*, or a copy of AEPI-PPR-1494, September 1994, *An Assessment of External Interest in Depleted Uranium Use by the U.S. Army* (not quoted in Appendix I), contact:

Army Environmental Policy Institute
Georgia Institute of Technology
430 Tenth St., N.W., Suite S-206 Atlanta, Georgia 30318-5768
Tel: (404) 892-3099

To obtain a copy of the GAO/NSIAD-93-90 report or other GAO reports, write or call:
U.S. General Accounting Office
P.O. Box 6015, Gaithersburg, MD 20884-6015
Tel: (202) 512-6000; fax: (301) 258-4066

Appendix II: Ordnance Containing DU

"The Army uses alloyed DU in the 25, 105, and 120-millimeter kinetic energy cartridges. The Bradley Fighting Vehicle will use the 25mm cartridge in its chain gun. The M1 and M60 series tanks use the 105mm cartridge; the Army also plans to use the 105mm in the main gun of the XM8 Armored Gun System. The M1A1 and M1A2 Abrams Tank main guns use the 120mm cartridge. ... DU is used as an armor component on the M1 series heavy armor (HA) tanks. Small amounts of DU are used as an epoxy catalyst for the M86 Pursuit Deterrent Munition (PDM) and the Area Denial Artillery Munition (ADAM)." The PDM and the ADAM are land mines. (AEPI, *Health and Environmental Consequences of Depleted Uranium Use in the U.S. Army: Technical Report*, June 1995, p. 26)

The following armor-piercing projectiles are among those in the U.S. military arsenal that use DU:

1. Gau-8: A U.S. Air Force 30mm round with approximately a 300-gram staballoy [DU tailing] penetrator core composed of 99.25% DU and 0.75% TI 9U-TI. (This alloy composition is also used in all the U.S. Army munitions discussed below. The U.S. Navy version (PGU-14 30mm) of this round has a penetrator consisting of 98% DU and 2% Molybdenum. Both versions incorporate metal propellant cases.) Fired at the rate of 4,200 projectiles per minute from Fairchild A-10A Thunderbolt II (Warthog).

2. M735A1: A U.S. Army 105mm round with approximately a 2.2-kg DU penetrator. This round was intended for use in tanks equipped with a M68 gun as an interim round prior to fielding the M774. These rounds are virtually identical to the M774 except for the staballoy penetrator in the projectile assembly of the round.

3. M774: A U.S. Army 105mm round with aproximately a 3.4-kg DU penetrator. Both the M735A1 and M774 have metal propellant cases.

4. M829 [M829E1& M829E2]: U.S. Army 120mm rounds with approximately 4.9-kg (10.7 pound) DU penetrator and combustible propellant cases. M829A1 and M829A2 120 mm APFSDS-T rounds are also produced containing approximately 4.9 kg (10.7 lbs.) of DU.

5. M833: A U.S. Army 105mm round with approximately a 3.7-kg DU penetrator and a metal propellant case. Cartridge used by the EX35 105mm Gun System.

6. XM 919: A U.S. Army 25mm round with approximately a 85-g DU penetrator and a metal propellant case. This round is used primarily in the Bradley Fighting Vehicle.

7. XM900E1: A U.S. Army 105mm round with approximately a 10.0-kg DU penetrator and a metal propellant case.

8. Land Mines: M86 Pursuit Deterrent Munition (PDM) and the Area Denial Artillery Munition (ADAM) contain approximately 0.1 gram of DU. The ADAM is fired as a submunition in the 155mm howitzer.

Chart of Army ammunition items containing DU include:

Cartridge	approximate DU weight
25MM XM919	85 g, 0.2 lb
30MM GAU-8	300 g, 0.66 lb
105MM 735A1	2.2 kg, 4.84 lb
105MM 774	3.4 kg, 7.48 lb
120MM M827	3.1 kg, 6.90 lb
120MM M829[E1 & E2]	4.0 kg, 8.69 lb
120MM M829A1	4.9 kg, 10.7 lb
120MM M829A2	4.9 kg, 10.7 lb
105MM M833	3.7 kg, 8.14 lb

List of ordnance printed with permission from *Uranium Battlefields Home & Abroad: Depleted Uranium Use by the U.S. Department of Defense*, March 1993 by Grace Bukowski and Damacio Lopez, and compiled from June 1995 AEPI report cited above.

Appendix III: Locations Involving DU Research, Testing and Storage

Research and Development and Test Sites Involving DU

SITE NAME & LOCATION:	ACTIVITY:
1. Army Research Laboratory; Aberdeen Proving Ground, MD	R&D of DU penetrators and armor.
2. Battelle Pacific Northwest Labs; Richland, WA	R&D DU metallurgical analyses, environmental, health hazard studies.
3. Energetic Materials Research and Technology Center, formerly known as TERA facility; Socorro, NM	Testing by Alliant Tech Systems, Olin Ordnance and Army.
4. Ethan Allen Firing Range (General Electric); Burlington, VT	Test 25mm DU munitions.
5. Jefferson Proving Ground; Madison, IN	Test DU munitions against soft targets.
6. Los Alamos National Laboratory; Los Alamos, NM	Interior ballistic studies and environmental, health hazard studies.
7. Manufacturing Sciences Corporation; Oak Ridge, TN	Research and Development of DU armor.
8. U.S. Army Ballistics Research Lab, Nevada Test Site; Mercury, NV	Army DU Research & Development.
9. Picatinny Arsenal; Dover, NJ	DU metallurgical studies R&D facility, former test range.
10. Sandia National Laboratories; Albuquerque, NM	Test DU armor and penetrators, weapons containers.
11. Tonopah Test Range; Tonopah, NV	Warhead simulation tests.
12. US Army Combat Systems Test Activity; Aberdeen Proving Ground, MD	Research, development, and testing of DU penetrators and armor.
13. Yuma Proving Ground; Yuma, AZ	Test DU R&D munitions against soft targets.

Fabrication and Assembly Sites Involving DU

SITE NAME & LOCATION:	ACTIVITY:
14. Aerojet Ordnance Company; Chino, CA	Assemble projectiles; Load, Assemble and Pack (LAP) 25mm DU rounds.
15. Aerojet Ordnance Tennessee; Jonesboro, TN	Fabricate 25mm and large caliber DU penetrators.
16. Detroit Army Tank Plant; Warren, MI	Assemble heavy armor turrets.
17. Lima Army Tank Plant; Lima, OH	Assemble heavy armor turrets.
18. Martin Marietta Energy Systems-Milan Army Ammunition Plant; Milan, TN	LAP large caliber ammunition.
19. Mason and Hanger at Iowa Army Ammunition Plant; Middletown, IA	LAP and demilitarize.
20. National Manufacturing Corporation; St. Louis, MO	Assemble projectiles.
21. Nuclear Metals, Inc.; Concord, MA	Fabricate DU penetrators.
22. Olin Ordnance Corporation; Red Lion, PA	Assemble Projectiles.
23. Specific Manufacturing Capability Facility Idaho National Engineering Laboratory; Idaho Falls, ID	Fabricate DU armor.
24. Tank Automotive Command; Warren, MI	Licensee for DU armor.
25. Twin Cities Army Ammunition Plant, Alliant Tech Systems; New Brighton, MN	Machine, LAP 25mm DU penetrators, manufacture molding compound for mines.
26. White Sands Missile Range; Green River, UT	Missile warhead ballast contamination.
27. White Sands Missile Range; White Sands, NM	Missile warhead ballast contamination.

Storage and Storage/Demilitarization Sites Involving DU-Containing Materials

SITE NAME & LOCATION:	ACTIVITY:
28. Defense Consolidation Facility; Snelling, SC	DU waste reduction, decontamination.
29. Hawthorne Army Ammunition Plant; Hawthorne, NV	Store ammunition.
30. Hunter Army Airfield; Savannah, GA	Store 120mm DU ammunition.
31. Letterkenny Army Depot; Chambersburg, PA	Store ammunition.
32. McAlester Army Ammunition Plant; McAlester, OK	Store DU ammunition, contaminated production equipment.
33. Savanna Army Depot; Savanna, IL	Store, demilitarize, maintain ammunition.
34. Seneca Army Depot Activity; Romulus, NY	Store, demilitarize ammunition.
35. Sierra Army Depot; Herlong, CA	Store, maintain, demilitarize ammunition.
36. Tooele Army Depot; Tooele, UT	Store, maintain, demilitarize ammunition.
37. U.S. Army Armament Munitions and Chemical Command; Rock Island, IL	Licensee responsible for bulk storage.
38. Watervliet Arsenal; Albany, NY	DU munitions applications research, currently stores DU contaminated saw, press, shotblast.

DU Processing Sites

SITE NAME & LOCATION:	ACTIVITY:
39. Carolina Metals; Barnwell, SC	Reduction, casting into DU derby.
40. Sequoyah Fuels Corp.; Gore, OK	Convert (UF6 to UF4 for AOT).

Waste Disposal Sites Involving DU

SITE NAME & LOCATION:	ACTIVITY:
41. Chem-Nuclear Systems Waste Management Facility; Barnwell, SC	Waste disposal.
42. Envirocare of Utah; Clive, UT	DU contaminated soil disposal.
43. US Ecology; Hanford, WA	Waste disposal.

Former DU Use or Storage Sites, and Sites Being Decommissioned

SITE NAME & LOCATION:	ACTIVITY:
44. Alliant Tech Systems, Inc.; Elk River, MN	Penetrator testing. Closed, decommissioned, NRC cleared in 1993.
45. Army Research Laboratory; Watertown, MA	Former R&D lab (being decommissioned).
46. Camp Roberts Military Reservation; Bradley, CA	Test firing of 120mm DU rounds for the Army (being decommissioned).
47. Chamberlain Manufacturing; Waterloo, IA	Projectile assembly (since closed).
48. China Lake Naval Weapons Center Alliant Tech Systems; Ridgecrest, CA	Test firing of 120mm DU rounds for the Army (being decommissioned).
49. Ford Aerospace and Communications Corp.; San Juan Capistrano, CA	Developed and tested 25mm DU ammunition.
50. Fort Hood; Killeen, TX	Stored 105mm DU rounds 1989-1990.
51. Fort Riley; Junction City, KS	Stored 105mm DU rounds 1989-1990. Facility improperly destroyed after damaged.
52. Lake City Army Ammunition Plant; Independence, MO	Former LAP, test range of 20mm, 25mm DU ammunition (decontamination planned).
53. National Lead Industries; Colonie, NY[1]	Produced R&D quantities of DU penetrators in 1978-1979. Closed 1980.

Other sites Involving DU Research, Testing, and/or Storage:

54. Aerojet General Corporation; Lockwood, Nevada
55. Armtec Defense Products; Coachella, California
56. Bulova Systems; Valley Stream, NY
57. Chamberlain Manufacturing; New Bedford, Massachusetts
58. Day and Zimmerman; Texarkana, Texas
59. Eglin Air Force Base's Munitions Test Facility; Valpariso, Florida
60. Feed Materials Plant, U.S. Department of Energy; Fernald, Ohio
61. General Defense; Red Lion, PA
62. General Dynamics; Detroit, Michigan
63. Hercules,; Redford, Virginia
64. Honeywell Corporation; Hopkins, Minnesota
65. Honeywell Corporation; Minnetonka, Minnesota
66. Hughes Heliocopter; Los Angeles, California
67. Hughes Heliocopter; Idaho Falls, Idaho
68. Kirtland Air Force Base; Albuquerque, New Mexico
69. Kisco; St. Louis, Missouri
70. NI Industries; Los Angeles, California
71. Remington Arms Company; Blue Springs, Missouri
72. Remington Arms Company; Lake City Army
73. Remington Arms Company Ammunition Plant; Independence, Missouri
74. Stresau Labs; Spooner, Wisconsin
75. Target Research, Inc.; Dover, New Jersey
76. U.S. Ecology, Department of Energy; Beatty, Nevada
77. U.S. Army Aberdeen Proving Ground; Aberdeen, Maryland
78. U.S. Army Camp Grayling; Grayling, Michigan
79. U.S. Naval Surface Weapons Center; Dahlgren, Virginia[2]

1. Source for sites 1-53 listed in the preceeding tables is the Army Environmental Policy Institute report of June 1995, *Health and Environmental Consequences of Depleted Uranium Use in the U.S. Army: Technical Report.*

2. Source for sites listed 54-79 is the book entitled, *Uranium Battlefields Home and Abroad: Depleted Uranium Use by the Department of Defense,* by Grace Bukowski and Damacio Lopez.

Appendix IV: Report from Laka Foundation, Netherlands

Laka Foundation was founded in 1982 as a documentation center on nuclear energy. The documentation center consists of more than 125,000 newspaper clippings, 5,000 books and several periodicals, TV documentaries, etc. Laka gives information on request to scholars, students, journalists, international groups, etc. Laka also does its own research and publishes regularly in magazines and newspapers.

After a visit to Iraq, Laka paid closer attention to the use of depleted uranium. Laka Foundation collects news on DU, writes articles and has several contacts in other countries. Special attention is given to the civilian use of DU. After a literature research, Laka made public the presence of DU counterweights in the 1992 crashed El-Al Boeing 747. Documents on this crash, the risks and the use in civilian airplanes are included in Laka's documentation center.

[The following are excerpts from the Laka article about the 1992 crash, received in time to be included in the appendices.]

Uranium Pollution from the Amsterdam 1992 Plane Crash

HENK VAN DER KEUR

A year after an El Al cargo jet crashed in Amsterdam on October 4, 1992, killing forty-three people, the Laka documentation and research center on nuclear energy in Amsterdam announced that the plane contained counterweights made of depleted uranium (DU).[1] This news considerably upset residents of the Bijlmer suburb (Amsterdam Southeast) who were suddenly confronted with information that the authorities would rather have kept silent about.

Even today, many details of the cause and effects of the disaster remain unclear. It is known that the destroyed Boeing aircraft had on board seventy-five tons of kerosene and ten tons of chemicals, as well as flammable liquids, gases, and caustic substances. We know now that half of these materials and probably some depleted uranium went up in a sea of flames.

The presence of DU on board the plane is based on a

publication by Paul Loewenstein,[2] then technical director and vice-president of the American company Nuclear Metals Inc., the supplier of the DU to Boeing. Loewenstein says in this document that each Boeing 747 contains 1,500 kilograms of DU in the form of counterweights. Other publications explain that these internal parts for flight control are also found in the tail rudder and the wings.[3]

Health Risks

In a press statement, Laka Foundation pointed out emphatically that bystanders and Bijlmer residents ran potential health risks as a result of airborne uranium from the burning wreck. Loewenstein says in his article that "large pieces of uranium will oxidize rapidly and will sustain slow combustion when heated in air to temperatures about 500 degrees Celsius." The great danger from this chemical reaction is that the escaping cloud of dust with thousands of microparticles of uranium oxide can be inhaled or swallowed by bystanders.

The American physicist Robert L. Parker wrote in *Nature*[3], in a worst-case scenario involving the crash of a Boeing 747, that about 250,000 people would run health risks (or near-poisoning) as a result of inhalation or swallowing of uranium oxide particles. Parker's conclusion assumed the presence of 450 kilos of DU in a Boeing 747. He says: "Extended tests by the American Navy and NASA showed that the temperature of the fireball in a plane crash can reach 1200 degrees C. Such temperatures are high enough to cause very rapid oxidation of depleted uranium."

Proof

Loewenstein says: "Counterweights are used in the aerodynamic controls of planes, rockets, and helicopters to maintain the aircraft's center of gravity. Heavy density is important in keeping the counterweight small in comparison with airfoil steering surfaces. DU is very appropriate for this kind of application, and uranium counterweights are used in many civil and military aircraft."[2] The report mentions as an example the Boeing 747, a plane which, according to its supplier, contains 1,500 kg of DU as a standard amount at that time. Directly after the announcement of DU in the accident, Boeing, ... stated that there was only

380 kg in the tail of the plane.

Laka called together the Bijlmer residents and the Dutch Greens for a long-term in-depth epidemiological search for the presence of uranium in the bodies of the service personnel and residents and for further research to examine the presence of DU in the soil and the ground water. Since the publication of the final report from the City Council, which strongly played down the health and environmental effects of DU, Laka obtained additional documents which strongly emphasized the chemical and radiological toxicity of DU.

The most interesting one in this particular case is probably the report "Health risks during exposure of uranium" by radiation expert Leonard A. Hennen from the Dutch Ministry of Defense. By accident, this report was published just a week after the final report on DU from the city council of Zuidoost. The author thoroughly documents the radiotoxic effects of DU in the human body. The findings of Hennen strongly contradicts the findings in the final DU report of Zuidoost. He said that people at the DU crash site are running risks. In his report (chapter 5, p. 9) he proposes taking urine samples and *in vivo* measurements when there is suspicion of internal contamination of the DU. This is exactly what we insist upon, but it has not yet happened.

References

1. "Crashed El-Al Boeing contained Depleted Uranium," Laka Foundation press release, October 12, 1993.

2. Loewenstein, P., "Industrial Uses of Depleted Uranium," American Society for Metals. Photocopy in *Uranium Battlefields Home & Abroad: Depleted Uranium Use by the U.S. Department of Defense*, Bukowski, G. and Lopez, D.A., March, 1993, pp. 135-141.

3. Parker, Robert L., "Fear of Flying," *Nature*, Vol. 336, 22/29 December 1988. Also, *Uranium Battlefields Home and Abroad*, and "RLD searches for uranium on the crash place," Trouw, December 3, 1993.

4. Bukowski, G. and D.A Lopez, *Uranium Battlefields Home and Abroad: Depleted Uranium Use by the U.S. Department of Defense*, p. 136.

Appendix V: DU Around the World

Radioactive pollution spread by DU weapons has aroused growing opposition around the world. We include several recent examples here.

Japan

Rising anger at the continuing U.S. military occupation of Okinawa reached new levels with the belated admission by the U.S. government that 1,520 rounds of DU ammunition had been fired by U.S. Marine Corps AV-8B Harrier jets in late 1995. The U.S. government did not notify the Japanese government for over a year. The news first broke in the February 10, 1997, *Washington Times*. The U.S. government then promised to clean up the DU, but assured Okinawan officials that DU weapons are not dangerous. Press reports made no mention of U.S. government reports that confirm the radioactive dangers of DU.

The Netherlands

In the Netherlands, the January 24, 1996, edition of the Dutch newspaper *Volkskrant* reported on the use of DU munitions in Bosnia. In reaction to this article the Dutch soldiers' pressure group, ACOM, asked the Dutch Minister of Defense Gmelich Meijling whether Dutch soldiers were at risk. Meijling confirmed the possible radiological and chemical risks of DU particles and the presence of U.S. tanks containing DU in the Netherlands. In December 1996 the Dutch soldiers' group published an article in their magazine, entitled, "The Radioactive Bullet from the Pentagon," which generated Dutch media attention and discussion in Parliament.

Bosnia

There is growing awareness that U.S. and British NATO forces in Bosnia use weapons containing DU. There were over 4,000 aerial sorties by NATO forces against Bosnian Serb positions in the summer and fall of 1995. Many of the sorties were carried out by A-10 aircraft deployed on board U.S. aircraft carriers stationed in the Adriatic Sea. The A-10 Warthog fires 4,200 30mm rounds a minute. Each 30mm round contains a 300-gram DU core.

The armor and the ammunition of U.S./NATO tank units stationed throughout Bosnia also contain DU, as do the land mines that have been extensively planted around NATO bases. This will have a devastating impact on the civilian population of all the nationalities in the Balkans for generations to come.

Appendix VI: International Action Center

The IAC was initiated in 1991 by former U.S. Attorney General Ramsey Clark and other anti-war activists who had rallied hundreds of thousands of people in the United States to oppose the U.S./UN war against Iraq. It incorporates the demand to end racism, sexism, homophobia and poverty in the United States with opposition to U.S. militarism and domination around the world.

The IAC was the main organization in the U.S. to expose the damages of U.S. bombing of innocent Iraqi civilians and the massive destruction of the Iraqi infrastructure. Its organizers compiled and distributed this evidence in videos, international forums and the book, *War Crimes*.

The IAC coordinated an International War Crimes Tribunal that held hearings in twenty countries and thirty U.S. cities probing the Pentagon's systematic destruction of Iraq. In 1992, the IAC published the ground-breaking book, *The Fire This Time*, which reports the evidence presented at the tribunal implicating the United States government for gross violations of international law. In it, Clark discusses the military use of depleted-uranium weapons during the Gulf War and its danger to both Iraqis and Gulf War veterans.

In 1993, when President Clinton proposed resuming nuclear testing, the IAC initiated a call titled "End Nuclear Testing Now/Never Another Nuclear Explosion." Over three hundred organizations and prominent individuals signed this call, which was published as an advertisement in the New York Times. One of the many groups that have shared office space with the IAC was the World Uranium Hearing, which held an international meeting in Salzburg in 1992 exposing the effects of uranium mining and testing on peoples throughout the world, with special emphasis on indigenous peoples.

For the last five years the IAC has been a leader of the movement to unconditionally end U.S./UN sanctions against Iraq. The 1996 publication of the book *The Children Are Dying* was the latest step in that effort. The IAC has also mobilized opposition to the U.S. blockade of Cuba, delivered numerous medical shipments to both Cuba and Iraq and actively opposed U.S. military involvement throughout in Haiti, Somalia, Panama and Bosnia. A major part of the IAC's work is to expose the intricate web of lies woven before, during and after each U.S.

military intervention. It shows instead that U.S. intervention is dictated by the drive for profits and that as military funding expands, the money available for education, healthcare and needed social programs contracts.

Depleted Uranium Education Project
In mid-1996 the IAC initiated the Depleted Uranium Education Project to fight against radioactive waste, contamination and nuclear testing. This led to the September 12, 1996 meeting of Non-Governmental Organizations at the United Nations Church Center to expose the health and environmental consequences of DU weapons and eventually to this book, *Metal of Dishonor.*

The International Action Center is a volunteer activist organization. In its campaigns opposing U.S. intervention, the center relies totally on the donations and assistance of supporters around the country. To be part of a growing network, or to make a donation, request a speaker, or volunteer your support, contact the IAC.

International Action Center
39 West 14th Street, Room 206, New York, NY 10011, USA
Tel: 212-633-6646; fax 212-633-2889
email: iacenter@iacenter.org
Web Page: http://www.iacenter.org/

2489 Mission St., Room 28, San Francisco, CA, 94110, USA
Tel: 415-821-6545; fax 415-821-5782; email: npcsf@igc.org

Visit the IAC Web Site

The IAC maintains a web site dedicated to keeping its visitors informed about the latest IAC activities. In the Depleted Uranium Section, visitors can find: reprinted articles from *Metal of Dishonor*; updates on information contained in that book; other articles, lectures and speeches on depleted uranium and related issues.

Other sections of the web site cover issues such as economic sanctions against Iraq and other countries; the Balkans—No to NATO Expansion; The Cuban Blockade; Haiti;   Mumia Abu-Jamal and other political prisoners; Organizing Workfare Workers in the group Workfairness; and Labor Solidarity.

Visitors can also learn about upcoming meetings and other political events and activities, order books and videos, link to online videos, volunteer on-line, obtain information about how to support the crucial projects sponsored by the IAC, and link to other relevant sites.

Web Page: http://www.iacenter.org/

Appendix VII:
Organizations Concerned with
DU Weapons and Uranium Waste

United States

Aberdeen Proving Ground Citizens Superfund Coalition
1443 Gorsuch Avenue, Baltimore, MD 21218
Tel: 410-243-2077; fax: 410-235-5325

Alliance of Atomic Veterans (AAV)
Anthony Guarisco
PO Box 32, Topock, AZ 86436
Tel: 520-768-6623
email:aav1@ctaz.com

Black Veterans for Social Justice, Inc.
686 Fulton St., Brooklyn, N.Y. 11217
Tel: 718-935-1116; fax: 718-935-1629

Center for Defense Information
1500 Massachusetts Ave., NW, Washington, DC 20005
Tel: 202-862-0700; fax: 202-862-0708

Citizen Soldier/Tod Ensign
175 Fifth Avenue, #2135, New York, NY 10010
Tel: 212-679-2250; fax: 212-679-2252
works with veterans and active duty GIs

Citizens Research & Environmental Watch
Judy Scotnicki
52 Prairie St., Concord, MA 01742
Tel: 508-369-7146, 508-369-8480

Citizens for Safe Water Around Badger
Laura Olah
E12629 Weigands Bay, South Merrimac, WI 53561
Tel & fax: 608-643-3124

Coalition for Nuclear Disarmament
40 Witherspoon St., Princeton, NJ 08542
Tel: 609-924-5022; fax: 609-924-3052

Columbia River Education and Economic Development
Wilbur Slockish, Jr.
PO Box 184, The Dalles, OR 97058
Tel: 509-748-2077

Leonard Dietz
DU Citizens' Network, Technical Advisor
1124 Mohegan Road, Niskayuna, NY 12309-1315
Tel: 518-377-8202

Global Resource Action Center for the Environment
15 East 26th St., #915, New York, NY 10010
Tel: 212-726-9158

Healing Global Wounds
PO Box 5058, Gallup, NM 87301
Tel: 408-338-0147; fax: 202-544-1187

Indigenous Environmental Network
PO Box 485, Bemidji, MN 56601
Tel: 218-751-4967; fax: 218-751-0561

International Action Center
39 West 14th Street, Room 206, New York, NY 10011
Tel: 212-633-6646; fax: 212-633-2889
email: iacenter@iacenter.org
http://www.iacenter.org/

International Action Center
2489 Mission St., Room 28, San Francisco, CA 94110
Tel: 415-821-6545; fax: 415-821-5782
email: npcsf@igc.org

International Physicians for Prevention of Nuclear War
126 Roger St., Cambridge, MA 02142
Tel: 617-868-5050

Iraq Action Coalition, Rania Masri, Coordinator
7309 Haymarket Lane, Raleigh, NC 27615
Tel: 919-846-8264; fax: 919-846-7422
email: rmasri@ncsu.edu
http://www.lebnet.iac/

Lawyers' Committee on Nuclear Policy
Alyn Ware
666 Broadway #625, New York, NY 10012
Tel: 212-674-7790; fax: 212-674-6199

Livermore Conversion Project
1600 Clay St., San Francisco, CA 94109
Tel: 415-567-4337; fax: 415-512-8699

Damacio Lopez
PO Box 1688, Bernalillo, NM 87004
Tel: 505-867-0141
Pamphlet available: *Friendly Fire*

Military Toxics Project, Dolores Lymburner
471 Main Street, 2nd Floor, Lewiston, ME 04240
Tel: 207-783-5091; fax: 207-783-5096
email: mtp@igc.apc.org
http://www.gulfwar.org/resource_center/radioactive.html

MISSION Project
Carol Picou
PO Box 92574, Layfayette, LA 70509-2574
Tel: 318-234-1971

National Association of Radiation Survivors
Desert Storm Coordinator, Coy Overstreet
PO Box 2815, Weaverville, CA 96093-2815
Tel: 800-798-5102; fax: 916-623-2027
email: falling229@aol.com
email: nars1@tcoe.trinity.k12.ca.us

The National Gulf War Resource Center, Inc.
1224 M Street, NW, Washington , DC 20005
Tel: 202-628-2700 ext. 162; fax: 202-628-6997
email: charles@gulfwar.org
http://www.gulfwar.org/resource_center/

National Association of Atomic Veterans
Pat Broudy
35492 Periwinkle Dr., Monarch Beach, CA 92629
Tel: 714-661-0172

National Association of Black Veterans
Tom Wynn Jr.
PO Box 11432, Milwaukee, WI 53211
Tel: 800-842-4597; fax: 414-342-0840

Nolachuckey River Task Force
John Paul Hasko
PO Box 944, Jonesboro, TN 37659-0944
Tel: 423-753-9511

NGO Committee on Disarmament
Roger Smith
777 United Nations Plaza, Rm. 3B, New York, NY 10017
Tel: 212-687-5340; fax: 212-687-1643
email: disarmtimes@igc.apc.org

Nuclear Information Resources Services
1424 16th St., NW, #404, Washington, DC 20036
Tel: 202-328-0002; fax: 202-462-2183
email: nirsnet@igc.apc.org
http://www.nirs.org/

Patriots for Peace
Chris Larson
PO Box 1092, Shalimar, FL 32579
Tel: 904-651-0392

Peoples Video Network
39 West 14th Street, Room 206, New York, NY 10011
Tel: 212-633-6646; fax: 212-633-2889
email: pvnnyc@peoplesvideo.org
http://www.peoplesvideo.org/

Physicians for Social Responsibility
1101 14th Street, NW Suite 700, Washington, DC 20005
Tel: 202-898-0150; fax: 202-898-0172
email: psrnatl@igc.apc.org

Portsmouth/Piketon Residents for Environmental Safety &
Security
Vina K. Colley
3706 McDermott Pond Creek, McDermott, OH 45652-8932
Tel: 614-259-4688; fax: 614-259-3912

Rural Alliance for Military Accountability
Grace Bukowski
PO Box 60036, Reno, NV 89506
Tel & fax: 702-677-7001
email: rama@accutek.com
book: *Uranium Battlefields Home and Abroad: Depleted Uranium use
by the U.S. Department of Defense*, March 1993, $20

Save Ward Valley/Opposition to Radioactive Waste Dump
107 F St., Needles, CA 92363
Tel: 619-326-6267; fax: 619-326-6268
email: savewardvalley@bbs.rippers.com
Colorado River Tribes affiliated to Save Ward Valley:
Fort Mojave Indian Tribe, Steve Lopez, Tel: 619-326-2468
Cocopah Tribe, Pauline Allen, 520-627-2102
Chemehuevi Indian Tribe, Levi Esquerra, Tel: 619-858-4219
Quechan Indian Tribe, Michael Jackson, Tel: 619-572-0213
Colorado River Indian Tribes, David Harper, Tel: 520-669-1391

Seventh Generation Fund
Chris Peters/Tina Oras
PO Box 4569, Arcata, CA 95518
Tel: 707-825-7640; fax: 707-825-7639

Shundahai Network/Corbin Harney, Executive Director
5007 Elmhurst, Las Vegas, NV 89108
Tel: 702-647-3095, fax: 702-647-9385
email: shundahi@intermind.net
http://macronet.org/macronet/shunda
nuclear abolition organization founded by Newe (Western Shoshone)
spiritual leader Corbin Harney

Southwest Indigenous Uranium Forum
Anna Rondon
PO Box 5058, Gallup, NM 87301
Tel: 505-778-5834

Swords to Plowshares
Dan Fahey*
995 Market, 3rd Floor, San Francisco, CA 94103
Tel: 415-247-8777; fax: 415-227-0848
*also on Board of Directors, National Gulf War Resource Center,Inc.

The War & Peace Foundation
32 Union Square East, New York, NY 10003
Tel: 212-777-4210; fax: 212-777-2552
email: warpeace@interport.net
http://www.interport.net/~warpeace

WESPAC (Westchester Peace Action Coalition, Inc.)
255 Grove Street, Box 488, White Plains, NY 10607
Tel: 914-682-0488; fax: 914-682-9499

Women for Mutual Security
c/o Lenora Foerstel
5110 West Penfield Rd., Columbia, MD 21045
Tel: 410-730-7483; fax: 410-964-9248

Women Strike for Peace
Edith Villastrigo
110 Maryland Ave., NE, Washington, DC 20002
Tel: 202-543-2660; fax: 202-544-1187

International Organizations

Canadian Pugwash Group
Maj.-Gen. (Ret.) Leonard V. Johnson, Chairperson
RR 2 Westport, ON K0G 1X0 Canada
Tel: 613-273-3000; fax: 613-273-4269
email: general@rideau.net

Coalition to Oppose the Arms Trade (COAT)
489 Metcalfe Street, Ottawa ON K1S 3N7 Canada
Tel: 613-231-3076; fax: 613-231-2614
email: ad207@freenet.carleton.ca

International Bureau for Children's Rights
Jean-Guy Desgagne, Secretary General
85, de Martigny Ouest St., Jerome QC J7Y 3R8 Canada

LAKA Foundation
Kotelhulsplein 43, 1054 RD, Amsterdam, Netherlands
Tel: +31-20-6168-294; fax: +31-20-6892-179
email: laka@laka.antenna.nl

Nuclear Free Future Award, c/o Petra Kelly Foundation
Claus Bigert
Ismaninger Str. 17, 81675 Munich, Germany
Tel: 011-49-84-41900490; 011-49-84-41900491

Ontario Public Interest Research Group (OPIRG)
1 Trent Lane, University of Guelph, Guelph ON N1G 2W1
Canada
Tel: 519-824-2091, 519-824-4120 ext. 2129; fax: 519-824-8990
email: opirg@uoguelph.ca

Probe International
225 Brunswick Avenue, Toronto ON M5S 2M6 Canada
Tel: 416-964-9223; fax: 416-964-8239
email: eprobe@web.net

Radio for Peace International
P.O. Box 88, Santa Ana, Costa Rica, Central America
Tel: +516-249-1821; fax: O+506-249-1095
email: rfpicr@sol.racsa.co.cr
http://www.rfpi.org
U.S. address: RFPI, P.O. Box 20728, Portland, OR 97294
Tel: 503-252-3639; fax: 503-255-5216

Saskatchewan Eco-Network Energy Working Group
c/o P.O. Box 7724, Saskatoon, SK S7K4R4, Canada
Tel: 306-934-3030
email: icuc@web.net

Science for Peace University College
University of Toronto, Toronto, ON M5S 1A1 Canada
Tel: 416-978-3606
email: peter.shepherd@utoronto.ca

Voice of Women
736 Bathurst Street, Toronto, ON M5S 2R4 Canada
Tel: 416-537-9343 fax: 416-531-6214

World Information Service on Energy Uranium Project
PO Box 59636, 1040 LC Amsterdam, Netherlands
Tel: +31-20-612-6368-; fax: +31-20-689-2179
email: wiseamster@antenna.nl
http://antenna.nl/~wise/address.html

Yellow Cross–Austria
Prof. Dr. Siegwart-Horst Guenther
AHRIMAN-Verlag GmbH
Stuebeweg 60, D79108 Freiburg, Germany
Book: *Uranium Projectiles: Severely Maimed Soldiers,
Deformed Babies, Dying Children*, 1996

*[This list represents the groups focusing on depleted-uranium weapons,
uranium waste or nuclear weapons we were in touch with as this project
developed. It shows the diversity of the environmental, peace and justice, anti-
nuclear, and veterans organizations who have addressed this issue. Others who
wish to be included on our web site and in future reprints should contact the
Depleted Uranium Education Project of the IAC.]*

INDEX

Books and Videos from the International Action Center

BOOKS

NATO IN THE BALKANS
Voices of Dissent
Selections from Ramsey Clark, Sean Gervasi, Sara Flounders, Nadja Tesich, Thomas Deichmann and others
The truth about what NATO is doing in the Balkans is simply not being told in the mass media. Those who have the facts and the courage to voice them have been all but excluded. For an understanding of the secret deals behind the U.S.-imposed Dayton Accords and the implications of a U.S.-controlled War Crimes Tribunal, *NATO in the Balkans* fills in the missing pieces of the picture.
International Action Center, 236 pp., indexed, $15.95.

THE CHILDREN ARE DYING
The Impact of Sanctions on Iraq
Report of the UN Food and Agriculture Organization, supporting documents and articles by Ramsey Clark, Ahmed Ben Bella, Tony Benn, Margarita Papandreou and other prominent international human rights figures.
The human face of those targeted by the new weapon of sanctions. The UN FAO report shows with facts and statistics that over 500,000 Iraqi children under the age of five have died as a result of US/UN imposed sanctions. The accompanying photos and chapters define the social implications.
International Action Center, 1998 (Revised edition), 170 pp., photos, resource lists. Soft Cover $10.00.

CHALLENGE TO GENOCIDE: LET IRAQ LIVE
Essays and detailed reports on the devastating effects of economic sanctions on Iraq since the Gulf War. Features "Fire and Ice," a chapter in the history of the U.S. war against Iraq by former U.S. Attorney General Ramsey Clark. Also included are personal memoirs from many who defied the sanctions and U.S. law by taking medicines to Baghdad as part of the May 1998 Iraq Sanctions Challenge.
International Action Center, 1998, 264 pp., photos, index, resource lists. Soft Cover $12.95.

VIDEOS

Eyewitness Sudan

Depicts the findings of the investigative team that went to
Khartoum, Sudan in August 1998 after U.S. missiles struck a
pharmaceutical plant that produced half of the medicines used
in that impoverished African country.
VHS, 1999, 28 minutes, $20 individuals, $50 institutions.

Blockade: The Silent War Against Iraq

The human suffering caused by the US/UN imposed sanctions
has taken the lives of over half a million children. Moving
footage taken from hospitals, marketplaces, factories, and
Moslem, Jewish and Christian places of worship. Concrete
facts on infant mortality, skyrocketing inflation and disease are
skillfully incorporated.
VHS, 1994, 25 minutes, $20 individuals, $50 institutions

The Children Are Dying

A companion video to the book, *The Children Are Dying.* A
trip by a human rights delegation to Iraq in 1996 includes a
view of the hospitals, schools and neighborhoods. The impact
of the sanctions from destroyed water purification plants to
empty pharmacy shelves takes on a visual form that
supplements the statistics and charts of the UN Food and
Agricultural team studies.
VHS, 1996, 28 minutes, $20 individuals, $50 institutions
*(Videos are excellent for libraries, schools and community groups or for
cable access television programs.)*

*All mail orders must be pre-paid. Send check or money order
including $4. shipping and handling on first item, (book or video)
add $1. for each additional item per order. Send to International Action
Center, 39 West 14 St., #206, New York, NY 10011*

You can help

END THE COVER-UP

The most crucial task of this book, **Metal of Dishonor**, is to help ban the use of DU. Help us get this information into libraries, schools, community organizations, religious institutions and veterans groups. Political figures, media commentators, veterans and community leaders should see this book. We can send a book or video in your name to individuals or organizations who will benefit from its contents.
$12.95. (add $4 shipping/handling on first item,
$1 for each additional item)

BULK ORDERS

The book, **Metal Of Dishonor,** is also available at discounted bulk rates for organizing, educational, or fundraising use by community organizations. **Bulk orders of 20 or more copies are available at 50% off the cover price**.

Companion Video: METAL OF DISHONOR

Interviews with noted scientists, doctors and community activists explaining the dangers of radioactive DU weapons. Explores the consequences of DU from mining to production, testing and combat use. An excellent resource for schools, libraries and community meetings. *45 minutes, VHS,*

$20 individuals, $40 institutions.
($4 shipping and handling
on first item, $1 additional items)

All mail orders must be pre-paid. Send check or money order to: International Action Center, Depleted Uranium Education Project
39 West 14th St., #206, New York, NY, 10011
Tel: 212-633-6646, Fax: 212-633-2889
e-mail: iacenter@iacenter.org

To place CREDIT CARD orders (VISA & MC)
call **800-247-6553** (toll-free, 24-hour service, 7 days a week)
or Fax: **419-281-6883**
Price: $12.95 each (add $4 s&h first book,
$1 each additional book)

For bookstore and university invoice orders and discounts call: 800-247-6553